™

References for the Rest of Us!®

BESTSELLING BOOK SERIES

Do you find that traditional reference books are overloaded with technical details and advice you'll never use? Do you postpone important life decisions because you just don't want to deal with them? Then our *For Dummies*® business and general reference book series is for you.

For Dummies business and general reference books are written for those frustrated and hard-working souls who know they aren't dumb, but find that the myriad of personal and business issues and the accompanying horror stories make them feel helpless. *For Dummies* books use a lighthearted approach, a down-to-earth style, and even cartoons and humorous icons to dispel fears and build confidence. Lighthearted but not lightweight, these books are perfect survival guides to solve your everyday personal and business problems.

> **"More than a publishing phenomenon, 'Dummies' is a sign of the times."**
>
> — *The New York Times*

> **"A world of detailed and authoritative information is packed into them…"**
>
> — *U.S. News and World Report*

> **"…you won't go wrong buying them."**
>
> — *Walter Mossberg, Wall Street Journal, on For Dummies books*

Already, millions of satisfied readers agree. They have made For Dummies the #1 introductory level computer book series and a best-selling business book series. They have written asking for more. So, if you're looking for the best and easiest way to learn about business and other general reference topics, look to For Dummies to give you a helping hand.

Wiley Publishing, Inc.

5/09

Latin
FOR
DUMMIES®

by Clifford A. Hull, Steven R. Perkins,
and Tracy Barr

WILEY

Wiley Publishing, Inc.

Latin For Dummies®

Published by
Wiley Publishing, Inc.
111 River Street
Hoboken, NJ 07030
www.wiley.com

For general information on our other products and services or to obtain technical support, please contact our Customer Care Department within the U.S. at 877-762-2974, outside the U.S. at 317-572-3993, or fax 317-572-4002.

Wiley also publishes its books in a variety of electronic formats. Some content that appears in print may not be available in electronic books.

Library of Congress Cataloging-in-Publication Data:

Library of Congress Control Number: 2002103270

ISBN: 978-0-7645-5431-5

Printed in the United States of America

18 17 16

1B/RQ/QZ/QU/IN

About the Authors

Clifford A. Hull has been a Latin teacher for more than 23 years. He received a bachelor of arts degree, BA (Honours)(Latin) degree, and an HED (Higher Education Diploma) from the University of Stellenbosch (South Africa). He taught Latin and Classical Culture in South Africa at the high school and university levels for ten years. He came to the United States of America where he received an MA in Classical Studies, an MA in Classical Archaeology, and an MLS in Library and Information Science from Indiana University. Over the past 13 years he has taught Latin, Greek, Medical Terms, and Classical Mythology at both the high school and college levels. At the present time, he teaches Latin and Classical Greek at Park Tudor School in Indianapolis, Indiana, and Classical Mythology at Indiana University-Purdue University Indianapolis. His main interests are Latin grammar, epigraphy, Roman architecture, especially Roman houses and buildings, archaeology, and Morris Minor cars.

Steven R. Perkins is an award-winning Classics instructor who has published numerous articles on Latin pedagogy. A member of Phi Beta Kappa and a former Texas Latin Teacher of the Year, he has taught Latin from the middle school through university levels. (To be honest, I hate this self-praise business, though I know it is helpful to add credibility for the book. Just to back up a bit of what I just said, I was awarded for excellence in Classics from Indiana University, was recognized for outstanding Classics instruction at the University of Texas, was twice recognized by the Austin Texas school board, was twice listed in *Who's Who Among America's High School Teachers,* and was awarded the silver chalice from Classics Technology on the Web for an article based on a conference presentation.)

Tracy Barr has been a part of the *Dummies* phenomenon for almost a decade. In that time, she has served as editor, editorial manager, writer, and consultant to the folks who write and edit *For Dummies* books. Most recently, she helped write *World War II For Dummies* with Keith D. Dickson and *Vocabulary For Dummies* with Laurie Rozakis. She lives and works in Indianapolis.

Authors' Acknowledgments

Clifford A. Hull: Many thanks to all the people at Wiley for making this book possible, especially to Tracy Barr, whose help was invaluable. Thanks also to Esmeralda St. Clair for her help and input. Thanks to my co-author, Steve Perkins, and to his wife, Melissa. I would like to give special recognition and much appreciation to my wife, Lynn Thomsen, and my son, Clifford P. Hull, for all the time, help, patience, encouragement, love, and support they gave me. I could not have done this without them. Lastly, I would like to dedicate this book to the memory of my father, Stanley Clifford Hull. I love you, Dad.

Steven R. Perkins: I would like to thank my wife and Latin colleague, Melissa, for her loving support and critique throughout this project. "Ad exemplum tu mihi semper ades." Thank you, too, Austin, for helping Daddy type his manuscript.

Tracy Barr: I would like to thank the following people: Steve Perkins and Clifford Hull, who made the writing a joy; Roxane Cerda, who made my participation in the project possible, and Tim Gallan and Esmeralda St. Clair, who made the editing (relatively) painless. I would also like to thank Larry, Adam, Sarah, Mary, and Alex for sundry reasons that have absolutely nothing to do with writing or Latin.

Publisher's Acknowledgments

We're proud of this book; please send us your comments through our online registration form located at www.dummies.com/register.

Some of the people who helped bring this book to market include the following:

Acquisitions, Editorial, and Media Development

Senior Project Editor: Tim Gallan

Acquisitions Editor: Roxane Cerda

Copy Editor: Esmeralda St. Clair

Technical Editor: William Nethercut, PhD

Editorial Manager: Christine Meloy Beck

Editorial Assistant: Melissa Bennett

Illustrator: Liz Kurtzman

Composition

Project Coordinator: Jennifer Bingham

Layout and Graphics: Barry Offringa, Laurie Petrone, Jacque Schneider, Betty Schulte, Rashell Smith, Jeremey Unger, Erin Zeltner

Proofreader: Steven Krebs, PhD, Andy Hollandbeck, Susan Moritz, Carl Pierce, Linda Quigley

Indexer: Maro Riofrancos

Special Help
Rev. Dennis M. Duvelius, FSSP

Publishing and Editorial for Consumer Dummies
Diane Graves Steele, Vice President and Publisher, Consumer Dummies
Joyce Pepple, Acquisitions Director, Consumer Dummies
Kristin A. Cocks, Product Development Director, Consumer Dummies
Michael Spring, Vice President and Publisher, Travel
Brice Gosnell, Associate Publisher, Travel
Suzanne Jannetta, Editorial Director, Travel

Publishing for Technology Dummies
Richard Swadley, Vice President and Executive Group Publisher
Andy Cummings, Vice President and Publisher

Composition Services
Gerry Fahey, Vice President of Production Services
Debbie Stailey, Director of Composition Services

Contents at a Glance

Cartoons at a Glance

By Rich Tennant

page 7

"Stuart — would you like to come up and rap some Vergil for us?"

page 63

"Sorry, but I don't understand your 'Ecclesiastical Latin.' Could you repeat that using 'Classical' pronunciation?"

page 293

"One of my students just told me he wanted to study Latin because he was going to Latin America this summer and wanted to be able to speak the language."

page 195

page 311

Cartoon Information:
Fax: 978-546-7747
E-Mail: richtennant@the5thwave.com
World Wide Web: www.the5thwave.com

Table of Contents

Introduction

· ·

*P*eople fall into two camps: those who took (or are taking) Latin in school and those who didn't (or aren't). Which camp you fall into depends on how great your tolerance for pain is and how much delayed gratification motivates you. Why? Because Latin has a reputation of being hard to learn, boring as all get out, and not good for much once you know it, unless, heaven forbid, you want to become a Latin teacher.

But Latin has been given a bad rap. First, it's not really hard to learn. Sure, you have to know a few rules and master a few tricks, but after you do, Latin is actually pretty easy to figure out. Second, it's not boring. Latin was the language of the Romans, the movers and shakers of the ancient world. These are the folks who built a republic and then an empire that stood for hundreds of years; who created (and destroyed) Caesars; who produced the Colosseum, the Pantheon, and Hadrian's Wall; and who can take credit for one of the most lasting man-made concoctions of all time: concrete.

Finally, knowing Latin is useful in many ways. True, you're probably not going to speak it; after all, no one learns Latin as a native language any more. But Latin continues to influence the world through the many languages, such as French, Italian, and Spanish, that come from it. And Latin has had much influence on English, too, given that more than half of all English words are derived from Latin words. (In fact, you use Latin words without even knowing it.) One of the best-kept secrets about learning Latin is that not only does studying Latin help you understand Latin, but it also helps you understand English, too.

Not too shabby for a dead language.

About This Book

What's great about this book? *You* decide where to start and what to read. It's a no-holds reference that you can jump into and out of at will. Just go to the table of contents or the index to find the information that you need.

Each chapter is divided into sections, and each section contains information about some part of understanding Latin, like

- How to decline Latin nouns and adjectives and conjugate Latin verbs
- How to translate a sentence so that it makes sense in English

✔ How Latin continues to influence English

✔ All sorts of interesting tidbits about Roman culture

Conventions Used in This Book

To make this book easy for you to navigate, we've set up a few conventions:

✔ Latin terms are set in **boldface** to make them stand out.

✔ Pronunciations and translations are set in parentheses and follow the Latin terms. Within the pronunciation key, words of more than one syllable are separated by a hyphen. An italicized syllable tells you to stress that syllable. For example, **exercere** (ehks-ehr-*kay*-reh; to train or exercise).

✔ Latin has two pronunciations: Classical (used in Latin literature and manuscripts) and Ecclesiastical (used in church): Except where noted, this book shows the Classical pronunciation.

✔ Verb conjugations (lists that show you the forms of a verb) appear in two-column tables. The first column contains the singular forms in this order: the "I" form, the "you" (singular) form, and the "he/she/it" form. The second column lists the plural forms: "we" form, the "you" (plural) form, and the "they" form. Here's an example, using the verb **amo, amare, amavi, amatus** (to love):

Singular	*Plural*
amo	amamus
amas	amatis
amat	amant

Language learning is a peculiar beast, so this book includes a few elements that other *For Dummies* books don't include:

✔ **Talkin' the Talk dialogues:** One of the best (and most fun) ways to learn a language is to see it in action. Although you probably won't be speaking Latin to many folks, you can still see how the language works. The dialogues under the heading "Talkin' the Talk" show you the Latin words, their pronunciation, and then the English translation.

✔ **Words to Know lists:** Memorizing key words and phrases is important in learning a language, so we collected the important words within the chapters (or sections) and placed them in these lists. Some things to keep in mind about these lists are

- The function of Latin nouns depends on their declension and their gender, so the nouns in these lists include the first two dictionary forms (which tell you the noun's declension) and the gender. For more on gender, see Chapter 2.

  coquus, coqui, m (*koh*-kwus, *koh*-kwee; cook)

- Because Latin adjectives have to match the nouns that they modify in case and gender, adjective entries show the masculine, feminine, and neuter forms.

  frigidus, frigida, frigidum (*free*-gih-dus, *free*-gih-duh, *free*-gih-dum; cold)

- The translation of a verb depends on its conjugation, so the Words to Know lists include the four dictionary forms of the verb.

  paro, parare, paravi, paratus (*puh*-ro, puh-*rah*-reh, puh-*rah*-wee, puh-*rah*-tus; to prepare)

✔ **Fun & Games activities:** Chances are, you won't have actual Latin speakers to practice your new language skills on. So we provide fun activities to reinforce what you learn. These word games are fun ways to gauge your progress.

Foolish Assumptions

In writing this book, we made a few assumptions about you:

✔ You know no Latin — or if you took Latin in high school, you don't remember a word of it.

✔ You're not looking for a book that makes you fluent in Latin; you just want to know some words, phrases, and sentence constructions so that you can understand basic Latin when you see it (or recognize it when you hear it).

✔ You don't want to have to memorize long lists of vocabulary words or a bunch of boring grammar rules.

✔ You want to have fun and learn a little bit of Latin at the same time.

How This Book Is Organized

To help you find the information that you want more easily, this book is organized into five parts, each covering a particular topic. Each part contains several chapters relating to that part.

Part 1: Getting Started

This part gives you the basics that you need to know to understand Latin — how to pronounce words, how to deal with an inflected language (which Latin is), and what the basic Latin grammar rules are. To boost your confidence, we also introduce you to some Latin that you probably already know.

Part 11: Latin in Action

The Roman world was a fascinating one. In this part, we give you all sorts of info about Roman life and the language the Romans used relating to those areas. In Part II, you can find information on the Roman family, the mighty Roman army, Roman entertainment, and more.

Part 111: Latin in the Modern World

Although it's not a spoken language anymore, Latin is still used today in many professions. The obvious ones are the legal and medical professions, but Latin is used in the Church, too, and in the sciences, such as botany and zoology. Because you run into (or up against) Latin in so many places, this part gives you the terms that you're most likely to hear. With all these words at your disposal, you'll be able to translate Latin, so this part also gives you the low-down on how to make sense of what you read or hear.

Part 1V: The Part of Tens

Perfect for the person who wants useful info in digestible chunks, the Part of Tens gives you lists that you'll find helpful. In this part, you can find ten Latin words that give people the most trouble, ten common Latin abbreviations, Latin prefixes and suffixes, and more.

Part V: Appendixes

This part of the book includes important information that you can use for reference. We include noun tables, verb tables, and a Mini-Dictionary so that you can easily look up words that you just can't seem to remember. For those of you who want to grade yourself on the Fun & Games activities, we give you the answer keys, too.

Icons Used in This Book

To help you find information you're interested in or to highlight information that's particularly helpful, we've used the following icons:

This icon points out advice, suggestions, and pointers that you'll find helpful as you learn Latin.

You find this icon next to important information that you'll want to remember.

This icon appears beside information that you may find interesting but can skip without impairing your understanding of the topic. This is a standard Dummies icon.

Latin is full of quirks that can trip you up, exceptions that you need to know to translate the language accurately, or fuller discussions about grammar rules that can help you understand why Latin is the way that it is. This icon draws your attention to these grammatical quirks.

This icon highlights cultural tidbits and information relating to Latin and the Romans. Search this icon out if you want to know more about the culture that led to the Latin language.

Where to Go from Here

This book is organized so that you can jump in any where you want. You don't need to start at the beginning and work your way through to the end. But if you wouldn't know Latin if a tablet hit you in the head, then you should probably start in Part I, where you can find out the basic grammar and pronunciation rules of Latin. Beyond that, go wherever you want to go. Thumb through the book, flip through the index, or head to the table of contents. You're bound to find a topic that interests you and information that increases your knowledge of Latin.

Part I
Getting Started

In this part . . .

Many people find Latin intimidating because they consider it so foreign. After all, how familiar could an ancient, dead language be to modern English speakers? We have a hard enough time figuring out medieval English (Shakespeare's language), let alone old English.

The truth is that Latin isn't as foreign as you may think. More than half of the words of the English language come from Latin. Many of the words we use *are* Latin words — that is, they have the same meaning, the same spelling, and the same use. Even some grammar rules (like not splitting infinitives or not ending sentences with prepositions) have their origins in Latin sentence structure. Still, Latin *is* different from English, and to be able to read or speak Latin competently, you have to understand these differences.

This part is a good starting place if you don't know (or remember) any Latin. It helps you see how much Latin you already know and explains basic Latin grammar.

Chapter 1

You Already Know a Little Latin

*T*ake one look at Latin, and you might say, "That's Greek to me!" You hear stories of demanding schoolmasters, and images of endless hours of memorization dance through your head. After all, Latin is not the language of intellectual lightweights. It's the language of Julius Caesar, Marc Antony, Vergil, Ovid, and St. Augustine. Intellectuals, such as Thomas Jefferson and W.E.B. Du Bois, founder of the NAACP, used it, and Leonardo da Vinci used it as code by writing it backwards so that ordinary folks couldn't read his notes. And in the movie *Tombstone,* Doc Holliday recognizes that his rival is an educated man just because he quotes the language of the Caesars.

Noli timere! (*no*-lee tih-*may*-reh), the Romans would say. "Have no fear!" What do you think the slaves, gladiators, and working-class folks were speaking in those days? They used Latin, too, and so can you. In fact, you probably already know some Latin. This chapter takes a look at these familiar words and phrases. So sit back and enjoy this little jaunt back to the golden age of Rome.

Latin: Not as Dead as You May Have Hoped

An old rhyme about Latin goes like this: "Latin is a dead, dead language, as dead as it can be. It killed the ancient Romans, and now it's killin' me!" Well, Latin may have seemed deadly to the student who first penned those lines, but the rumors of Latin's demise have been greatly exaggerated.

Latin was originally the language of a small group of people living in central Italy around the eighth century B.C. Eventually those people, the citizens of a town called Rome, spread their culture and influence across the Mediterranean world, making Latin the common language for many nations in antiquity.

Wars, intrigue, and general decline led to the fall of the mighty Roman Empire in A.D. 476, but Latin did not die with the last Roman emperor. People continued to write, read, and speak Latin for years. Although its use eventually began to dwindle, university scholars still used it until just about 300 years ago. Latin is dead today only in the sense that no group of people has it as their native language. In other words, no one learns Latin as a first language. Latin continues to influence the world, however, through the many languages derived from it, as well as through the wealth of culture, art, and literature rooted in, as Edgar Allan Poe put it, "the grandeur that was Rome."

Familiarity Breeds Comfort: Latin You Already Know

Have you ever sent someone a *memento*? Have you watched a *video*? Listened to an *audio* cassette? If you understand the italicized words in the preceding sentence, then you're already using Latin. **Memento** is the Latin word for "remember," **video** is the Latin word for "see," and **audio** is the word for "hear." Are you a *homo sapiens*? Not only are you a member of the human race, but the Latin says that you're a wise person as well. Do you watch sporting events in a *coliseum*? Then you're tipping the hat to ancient Rome's most famous gladiatorial arena.

Some Latin expressions are so much a part of the English-speaking world that you know what they mean, even when changed. "Veni! Vidi! Veggie!" for example, has become a popular slogan that even non-Latinists recognize as "I came! I saw! I had a salad!"

English uses many Latin words without any change in spelling or any significant change in meaning. You can read more about these words in Chapter 17, but here are a few to get you started:

- **senator** (seh-*nah*-tohr; senator)
- **gladiator** (gluh-dih-*ah*-tohr; gladiator)
- **consul** (*kon*-sul; consul)

Many other Latin words involve the change of only a few letters:

- ✔ **copiosus** (ko-pee-*o*-sus; copious)
- ✔ **defendo** (day-*fehn*-do; defend)
- ✔ **signum** (*sihng*-num; sign)

This section takes a look at some Latin derivatives and loanwords, proving why Latin is anything but a dead language.

English in a toga: Latin derivatives

Do you recognize this famous quotation?

> I **pledge allegiance** to the flag of the **United States** of **America,** and to the **republic** for which it **stands, one nation,** under God, **indivisible,** with **liberty** and **justice** for all.

That, of course, is the U.S. Pledge of Allegiance.

Or how about this?

> Four score and **seven** years ago our **fathers** brought forth on this **continent** a new **nation, conceived** in **Liberty,** and **dedicated** to the **proposition** that all men are **created equal.**

Many of you know that as the opening of President Lincoln's *Gettysburg Address.* Guess what? If you can read these sentences, then in a way you have been reading Latin. All the highlighted words are Latin *derivatives,* that is, English words that look like Latin words and have similar meanings.

Many people study Latin because of the influence of Latin on the English vocabulary. With more than half of English derived from Latin, it makes sense. Table 1-1 lists just a few Latin words and the cornucopia (that's **cornu,** *kohr*-noo — "horn" and **copia,** *ko*-pih-uh — "supply") of English words they provide.

Table 1-1	Latin Words and Their Derivatives		
Latin	*Pronunciation*	*Definition*	*Derivatives*
aequus	*igh*-kwuhs	level, fair	equinox, equal, equivocate, iniquity
augere	ow-*gay*-reh	to increase	augment, auction, author

(continued)

Table 1-1 *(continued)*

Latin	Pronunciation	Definition	Derivatives
bene	*beh*-neh	well	beneficiary, benediction, benign, benevolent
capere	*kah*-peh-reh	to seize	precept, capture, captious
dicere	*dee*-keh-reh	to say	diction, indict, edict, dictate
ducere	*doo*-keh-reh	to lead	ductile, induction, reduce, education
magnus	*muhng*-nus	large	magnify, magnitude, magnate, magnanimous
pater	*puh*-tehr	father	patrimony, patristics, patronize, patrician
rogare	roh-*gah*-reh	to ask	interrogate, arrogance, prerogative, surrogate
scribere	*scree*-beh-reh	to write	inscribe, prescription, nondescript
tenere	teh-*nay*-reh	to hold	tentative, tentacle, attention
videre	wih-*day*-reh	to see	visual, vision, visor, provide, advise, envy

Many derivatives come from various parts of Latin words.

One word worthy of note is the verb meaning "to bear" or "to carry." The full dictionary entry for this word is **fero, ferre, tuli, latus** (*feh*-ro, *fehr*-reh, *tu*-lee, *lah*-tus). From this word, English gets both "fertile" and "collateral."

This also accounts for some of the changes in spelling among related words. The full dictionary entry of the verb meaning "stick" or "cling" is **haereo, haerere, haesi, haesus** (*high*-reh-o, high-*ray*-reh, *high*-see, *high*-sus). From the parts with *r* come words such as *adhere* and *cohere,* but from the parts with *s* you find *adhesion* and *cohesion.* You can see more about verbs and their dictionary forms in Chapter 2.

You can also find certain patterns in how a word changes from Latin to English. Many Latin words for intangible virtues or qualities end in **–as.** These words appear as English words that end in **–ty:**

Latin Word	Pronunciation	English Word
gravitas	*gruh*-wih-tahs	gravity
humilitas	hu-*mih*-lih-tahs	humility
pietas	*pih*-eh-tahs	piety
dignitas	*dihng*-nih-tahs	dignity
paupertas	pow-*pehr*-tahs	poverty

The Romans made a distinction in types of poverty. They referred to simple lack of wealth or meager resources as **paupertas,** but used **egestas** (eh-*geh*-stahs) for absolute destitution. Here's another interesting tidbit regarding how Latin elements continue to appear: Many Roman army camps, or **castra** (*kuhs*-truh), eventually turned into towns. Their military origin is preserved in such town names as Lancaster, Manchester, Worcester, and Chester.

In the debit column: Latin loanwords

Derivatives retain their Latin origins in subtle, altered forms. Loanwords wear a gleaming toga and let everyone know that they're Latin words and won't change for anyone. Many areas of study, such as law, medicine, the church, and science, have specialized vocabularies made up of a large percentage of loanwords from Latin. You can explore these areas in more detail in Chapters 11 through 14.

Loanwords are Latin words that have entered the English language with no change in spelling, although sometimes there may be a slight difference in the words' meaning. Table 1-2 lists several common loanwords, together with their original Latin pronunciation and meanings, and the current English definitions.

A guessing game

Cover up the last column and see if you can guess the meaning of the Latin verbs that the following English words are derived from:

Derivative	Latin Verb	Pronunciation	Latin Definition
amateur	amare	uh-*mah*-reh	to love
sedentary	sedere	seh-*day*-reh	to sit
navigate	navigare	nah-wi-*gah*-reh	to sail
vivacious	vivere	*whi*-weh-reh	to live
exclaim	clamare	klah-*mah*-reh	to shout

Table 1-2		Latin Loanwords	
Latin	*Pronunciation*	*Latin Meaning*	*English Meaning*
agenda	uh-*gehn*-duh	things to be done	list of things to be done
agent	*uh*-gehnt	he will do	person/thing that does something
data	*duh*-tuh	things given	information used to make a decision
genius	*geh*-nih-us	creative spirit	person of above-average ability
habitat	*huh*-bih-tuht	he lives	place where a plant or animal typically lives
interim	*ihn*-teh-rihm	meanwhile	intervening period of time
memento	meh-*mehn*-to	remember!	gift of remembrance
propaganda	proh-pah-*guhn*-duh	things to be spread	spread of ideas to help or harm
scribe	*skree*-beh	write!	person who writes for others
tenet	*teh*-neht	he holds	belief held by a particular group
video	*wih*-deh-o	I see	a visual recording
virile	wih-*ree*-leh	masculine	having the nature of a male

When a Roman ran for office, he wore a special toga that had been whitened to reflect the sun. Called a **toga candida** (*toh*-guh *kuhn*-dih-duh), this garment let everyone know who the candidates were. In the days before paid political commercials and televised debates, you had to do something to get yourself noticed!

From A to Z: The Latin Alphabet

One feature that makes Latin easy is the alphabet. Latin has no strange characters and no funny accent marks. If you know the English alphabet, then you already know the Latin and then some. Present-day readers can also remember a couple of tricks to help them decipher Latin:

> ✔ **Latin uses the same letters as English with a few exceptions:**
>
> - The letter *W* was never used
>
> - Few Latin words use *K;* they use *C* instead.
>
> - Latin used *I* and *V* as both consonants and vowels until much later when someone had the bright idea to bend the *I* into a *J* and round the *V* into a *U*.
>
> ✔ **Everything ran together.** That's right. No spaces, no punctuation.

INTHEEARLYSTAGESOFTHELANGUAGEYOUCANSEETHATLATINWASWRIT
TENONLYINMAJUSCULEORCAPITALLETTERSANDWITHOUTANYPUNCTUA
TIONTHEREWASNOMORESPACEBETWEENWORDSTHANTHEREWASBETWEEN
LETTERSAPPARENTLYTHEROMANSHADNODIFFICULTYWITHTHISSYSTEMBE
CAUSETHEYCARRIEDLATINTOTHEENDSOFTHEIRWORLD

Here it is again with spacing and punctuation:

In the early stages of the language, you can see that Latin was written only in majuscule or uppercase letters and without any punctuation. There was no more space between words than there was between letters. Apparently, the Romans had no difficulty with this system because they carried Latin to the ends of their world.

Fortunately, most Latin texts today include modern conventions, such as punctuation and capitalization. Most texts also make a distinction between *V* and *U*, but many still keep *I* as both consonant and vowel.

Can I have a transcriber *and* a translator, please?

The earliest editions of a Roman manuscript were often made centuries after the original. These copies, handwritten mostly by monks, not only preserved the texts but also contributed to their legibility because the monks added features, such as punctuation and lowercase letters. Not all the changes in calligraphy, however, made the Latin text easier to read. In the thirteenth through fifteenth centuries, the monks used a script in which the quill strokes were the same width as the space between letters. Too many similar letters next to each other often produced a "picket fence" look, like this:

Miniumiumnibiumminiminiumniumminium
bininumiminumminmuinibibiminimumbolunt

Translated, this sentence says, "The tiny mimes of the snow spirits in no way wish, while they are alive, the tremendous task of [serving] the wine of the defenses to be diminished."

Well, I guess that one, even translated, isn't that much easier to understand. But you get the point.

Soundin' Like a Roman: Pronunciation

You may hear that Latin is not a spoken language, and it's true that no one learns Latin as a native language anymore. In its heyday, however, everyone in the civilized world — that is, the part of the world the Romans considered civilized because they'd conquered it — spoke Latin. In fact, more people spoke Latin than read or wrote it because most folks were illiterate. An education was available only to families who could afford it.

Fortunately, later Latin grammarians who taught the increasing number of **barbari** (*buhr*-buh-ree; foreigners) how to speak the language of the new world power left some pronunciation clues. Latin literature itself also offers hints about pronunciation. In one of his poems, for example, the poet Catullus (84–54 B.C.) pokes fun at someone for the way he pronounces certain words. Arrius, the object of the poet's wit, over-aspirates some of his words. That is to say, he puts the "h" sound in front of vowels, perhaps to sound more Greek and, therefore, more refined. Understanding that Catullus is making fun of Arrius, you can reason backward to see that such pronunciation wasn't common — or at least not acceptable — among Romans of that time.

Combining these clues with knowledge of how languages form and change over the years (called *historical linguistics*), scholars have more or less established an agreed-upon pronunciation, which is often referred to as the *Classical pronunciation*. Another system for pronouncing Latin comes from a later period of the language and is sometimes called the *Ecclesiastical pronunciation* because of its use in the Latin Mass and church hymns.

If you deal mostly with secular texts before the second century A.D., then you need to focus on the Classical pronunciation. If your primary interest is in Latin related to the church or in secular writings from the second century onward, then you should know the Ecclesiastical pronunciation.

Classical pronunciation

The big advantage for those who want to learn how to pronounce Latin is that it doesn't have any silent letters. You hear every letter in a Latin word. Pronunciation becomes a simple matter of knowing the sounds of vowels (see Tables 1-3 and 1-4) and consonants (see Table 1-5).

Table 1-3	Vowel Sounds		
Long Vowel	*Pronunciation*	*Short Vowel*	*Pronunciation*
a	ah (father)	a	uh (idea)
e	ay (mate)	e	eh (bed)

Long Vowel	Pronunciation	Short Vowel	Pronunciation
i	ee (seed)	i	ih (pit)
o	o (note)	o	oh (pot)
u	oo (moon)	u	u (put)
y	uw/umlaut (German über)	y	uw/umlaut (German Hütte)

A few vowel combinations, called *diphthongs,* are so common that their sounds have merged into one. Table 1-4 shows how they sound.

Table 1-4	Diphthong Sounds in Classical Latin	
Diphthong	**Pronunciation**	**As In English**
ae	igh	fight
au	ow	how
ei	ey	they
eu	eyoo	they too
oe	oi	toil
ui	uey	chewy

Most Latin consonants have the same sounds as in English but with the exceptions listed in Table 1-5.

Table 1-5	Consonant Sounds in Classical Latin
Latin Consonant	**Pronunciation**
c	k (can; never as in "cereal")
g	g (good; never as in "genuine")
j	y (youth)
r	r (always trilled)
s	s (soft; never as in "fans")
v	w (woman)

(continued)

Table 1-5 *(continued)*

Latin Consonant	Pronunciation
x	ks (wa**x**; never as in "xenophobic")
z	dz (a**dz**e)
bs	ps (la**ps**e)
bt	pt (exce**pt**)
ch	kh (**ch**aos; never as in "cheer")
gn	ngn (ha**ngn**ail)
ph	p-h (to**p-h**eavy)
th	t (**t**ourist)
ti	ti (pa**ti**o; never as in "nation")

Talkin' the Talk

A Roman senator talks with his father.

Senator: **Pater, cur dignitatem in viris Romanis non video?**
puh-tehr kur dihg-nih-*tah*-tehm ihn *wi*-rees ro-*mah*-nees non-*wih*-deh-o?
Father, why do I not see dignity among the Roman men?

Pater: **Cur me rogas?**
kur may *ro*-gahs?
Why are you asking me?

Senator: **Quod magna de dignitate scribis et dicis.**
kwohd *muhg*-nuh day dihg-ni-*tah*-teh *scree*-bihs eht *dee*-kis.
Because you write and speak great things about dignity.

Pater: **Fama in magnis, dignitas autem in humilitate habitat.**
fah-muh ihn *muhg*-nees *dihng*-nih-tahs *ow*-tehm ihn hu-mih-lih-*tah*-te *hah*-bih-tuht.
Fame lives in great things, but dignity lives in humility.

Remember that in ancient times, the letter *I* was used as a consonant instead of the letter *J*. Many modern editions of Latin texts retain this spelling.

Ecclesiastical pronunciation

Later Latin pronunciation is similar to the Classical pronunciation. In fact, you pronounce the vowels the same way. (Refer to Table 1-3 for the Classical pronunciation of vowels.) The only differences occur in diphthongs and consonants. See Tables 1-6 and 1-7.

Table 1-6	Diphthong Sounds in Ecclesiastical Latin	
Diphthong	*Pronunciation*	
ae	ay	m**a**te
au	ow	h**ow**
ei	ey	th**ey**
eu	eyoo	th**ey too**
oe	ay	m**a**te
ui	uey	ch**ewy**

The sounds of consonants in Ecclesiastical pronunciation are mostly the same as in Classical pronunciation (refer to Table 1-5). A few sounds soften somewhat, though, in the later Latin pronunciation, and there is a different pronunciation for the consonant combinations *cc*, *gg*, and *sc*. See Table 1-7.

Table 1-7	Consonant Sounds in Ecclesiastical Latin
Latin Consonant	*Pronunciation*
c	ch (**ch**oose before *e*, *i*, *ae*, or *oe*; otherwise *k* as in **c**an)
g	g (**g**enuine before *e* or *i*; otherwise *g* as in "**g**ood")
j	y (**y**outh)
r	r (always trilled)
s	s (**s**oft; never as in fans)
v	v (**v**ine)
x	ks (wa**x**; in words beginning with **ex** and followed by a vowel, *h*, or *s*, then *gz* as in e**x**haust)

(continued)

Table 1-7 (continued)

Latin Consonant	Pronunciation
z	dz (a**dz**e)
bs	bs (o**bs**ess; if occurring as the last two letters, then as in o**bs**erve)
bt	bt (o**bt**ain)
cc	tch (ca**tch** before *e* or *i*; otherwise as *kk* in boo**kk**eeper)
ch	kh (**ch**aos; never as in cheer)
gg	dj (a**dj**ourn before *e* or *i*, otherwise *gg* as in le**g g**uard)
gn	ny (ca**ny**on)
ph	ph (tele**ph**one)
sc	sh (**sh**irt before *e* or *i*)
th	t (**t**ourist)
ti	tsee (as in tse**tse** fly)

Don't stress out: Accenting syllables

You need to know one more thing before launching out into the world of spoken Latin: accenting. Accenting, or placing the proper stress on a Latin word, is as simple as one, two, three . . . literally. The first syllable of a two-syllable word is accented. For words with at least three syllables, always try to put the accent on the third to the last syllable. If the second to the last syllable is long, however, put the accent there.

How do you know if the second to last syllable is long? Again, it's as easy as one, two, three. A syllable is long if

- ✔ **The vowel is long.** For example, **videre** (wih-*day*-reh; to see).
- ✔ **Two consonants follow the vowel.** For example, **perditum** (*pehr*-dih-tum; ruined).
- ✔ **The vowel sound is a diphthong.** For example, **inaures** (ihn-*ow*-rays; earrings).

Ultimately confusing? Not really

In Latin, the last three syllables have names that you may hear or see in other Latin books: *antepenultimate, penultimate,* and *ultimate.* They sound a little confusing, but you can look at this as an opportunity to practice your understanding of derivatives.

If **ante** (*ahn*-teh) means "before," **paene** (*pigh*-neh) means "almost," and **ultimus** (*ul*-tih-mus) means "last," then you can pretty easily figure out what these words actually mean:

Antepenultimate means "almost before the last" or "third from last."

Penultimate means "before the last."

Ultimate means "last."

In modern English, you say "last," "next to last," and "the syllable next to the next to last syllable, which I don't know why I have to identify anyway."

Fun & Games

Here is the U.S. Pledge of Allegiance, translated into Latin. See if you can pronounce it, using both the Classical and Ecclesiastical pronunciations.

Fidem meam obligo
Vexillo civitatium Americae
Foederatarum et rei publicae
Pro qua stat.
Uni nationi, Deo ducente,
Non dividendae
Cum libertate
Iustitiaque omnibus.

See Appendix C for the answers.

Chapter 2

The Nitty Gritty: Basic Latin Grammar

In This Chapter

▶ Understanding word order and gender

▶ Using noun cases and conjunctions

▶ Recognizing first- and second-declension nouns

▶ Reading present, imperfect, and future verb tenses

The Monty Python comedy *The Life of Brian* has a scene that's famous among Latin enthusiasts everywhere. A Judean rebel paints graffiti on a wall, in Latin, telling the Romans to go home. Instead of apprehending the rebel, a grammatically nit-picking centurion approaches and reads the graffiti aloud, "Romanus eunt domus" (ro-*mah*-nus *ay*-unt *doh*-mus), and asks if the rebel really intended to paint, "Roman they go the house." The centurion makes the rebel repaint the grammatically correct version of the slogan a hundred times to make sure he gets it right.

Latin is more than just knowing some vocabulary, and believe it or not, grammar is your friend here. In fact, Latin is such an expressive language that you can convey an entire thought with one word. This chapter introduces you to the basics, nouns and verbs, plus a few other items along the way.

Bending the Rules: All about an Inflected Language

Consider the following English sentences:

Dog bites man.

Man bites dog.

This is the way the English language works: You know what is happening to whom because of the word order. Generally, in simple English sentences, the subject appears first, the verb next, and the direct object (whatever receives the action) last. That being the case, you know that in the first sentence the dog (the subject) is doing the biting and the man (the direct object) is the one being bitten. In the second sentence, it's the other way around: The man is biting the dog. What you may not know is that not all languages use a word's place in the sentence to convey meaning. Some languages, like Latin, use word endings to tell you how a word functions in the sentence. The words themselves can be in just about any order.

What if I say that adding an asterisk (*) to a word makes it the subject and adding a percent sign (%) makes it the direct object? Now consider these sentences:

> Dog* bites man%.

> Man% bites dog*.

Although the word order is different, these two sentences say the same thing. The suffix (the asterisk or percent sign) determines which word is the subject and which word is the direct object. Latin nouns, of course, don't use percent signs or asterisks. Instead, they use different letter combinations to indicate the different *cases* (noun functions in a sentence).

 English gets most of its meaning from the order of words in a sentence, but languages such as Latin get most of their meaning from the suffixes of words. Such languages are called *inflected languages,* because the basic words are changed to show such things as who is doing or who is receiving the action or even when the action takes place.

Latin Nouns (Or Why You Should Love Your English Teacher)

To understand Latin, you have to understand how Latin nouns work:

- ✔ Latin nouns have gender: That is, they're masculine, feminine, or neuter. Which one they are depends on the suffix attached to the word.

- ✔ Latin nouns have five basic cases that determine what function the noun serves in the sentence. Like gender, the word's suffix determines the noun's case.

- ✔ Latin has five declensions (noun groups that use the same suffix for each case). Like cases, declensions help you accurately translate Latin sentences. (For more on declension, see the "Declining a Latin noun" section, coming up later in this chapter.)

Now don't you wish you'd kissed your English teacher because the only thing *she* made you learn about nouns was that they're persons, places, or things?

Talking about the birds and the bees: Gender

A little boy once asked his father why people referred to ships with the pronoun *she.* The dad replied that it was because ships don't have to shave. When the boy pointed out that neither did he, the father was at a grammatical loss. Too bad he didn't have this book!

A distinction exists between biological and grammatical gender. Most people understand the biological sense (you're male or female), but grammatical sense is a little shaky. Simply put, grammatical gender further distinguishes Latin nouns as masculine, feminine, or neuter through the use of a suffix. You don't really need to know why this is so, you just need to understand how it works.

Words that have a biological gender have a corresponding grammatical gender. The Latin word for *girl* is grammatically feminine, and the word for *boy* is grammatically masculine. It's easy enough to get the right grammatical gender when who or what the word refers to has a biological gender. But some things, such as *table* or *house* or *truth,* don't have a biological gender; they still have a grammatical gender, though. The Latin word for *ship,* for example, is feminine; the Latin word for *food* is masculine; the word for *river* is neuter.

Checking a Latin dictionary is an easy way to verify a noun's gender. Noun entries give the abbreviations *m, f,* or *n* to tell you if a noun is masculine, feminine, or neuter. (This last gender, neuter, may look like an English word, but it's actually the Latin word **neuter** (*neyoo*-tehr), which means "neither." See Chapter 1 for a few other loanwords from Latin.)

Grammatical gender plays its most important role when talking about adjectives (words that describe nouns), because the gender of the adjective and the noun it goes with have to be the same; otherwise, the sentence won't make much sense. You can investigate adjectives in Chapter 4, but here's a quick example. The phrase "good girl" in Latin is **puella bona** (pu-*ehl*-luh *boh*-nuh). **Bona** is the feminine adjective form, which is appropriate to modify the Latin word for girl, which is grammatically feminine. If you use **bonus** (*boh*-nus), which is the masculine form, you get something that doesn't sound quite right. It would be like saying, "See that girl? He's a good person."

Some languages indicate gender through the use of articles. Latin, however, is not one of them. In fact, during the Classical period, Latin had no articles (words such as *a, an,* and *the,* for example). Whether a person referred to *a* dog (any dog, that is), for example, or *the* dog (a specific dog) was left entirely to interpretation and context clues. Eventually, forms of the demonstrative pronouns (see Chapter 7) came to fill the function of articles.

Casing a Latin noun

Nouns can perform as subjects, direct objects, indirect objects, and so on, within a sentence. Language students often use the word *case* to refer to the particular use of a noun in a sentence. English, for example, has three basic cases: subject, object, and possession. As explained in the earlier section "Bending the Rules: All about an Inflected Language," a word's placement within a sentence often determines an English noun's case.

Latin, on the other hand, has *five* basic noun cases. A noun can have a wider range of uses just by changing its suffix (or the letters attached to the end of the word). What follows are the most commonly used cases:

- ✔ **Nominative:** The subject. (The <u>cook</u> burned the cookies.)

  Latin doesn't really have articles (such as *a, an,* and *the*). When you translate a sentence from Latin to English, you'll have to add those yourself.

- ✔ **Genitive:** Indicates possession. (The survival <u>of the team</u> depends on working together.)

  When you come across a genitive noun, stick the words *of* in front of the noun. That'll help you as you translate.

- ✔ **Dative:** Indirect object. (The commissioner gave <u>the man</u> a medal for bravery.)

- ✔ **Accusative:** Direct object, purpose, or motion toward something. (Who let <u>the dogs</u> out?)

- ✔ **Ablative:** Expresses how, when, where, or why. (The general was informed <u>with a message</u>.)

  Basically, the ablative case is the way Latin shows adverbial phrases. These phrases aren't considered nouns in English, but they are in Latin because the case ending is attached to the noun.

Unlike English, where a noun's placement indicates its use, Latin nouns use suffixes instead. The following sections tell you more about suffixes and how they're used.

Declining a Latin noun

They say that old Latin teachers never die — they just decline. Whether this is true of teachers, declining and declension are facts of life that all Latin nouns must face. A *declension* is a group of nouns that form their cases the same way — that is, use the same suffixes. To *decline* a noun means to list all possible case forms for that noun.

Latin has five declensions, and this chapter looks at the first two. (See Chapters 4 and 7 for the other three declensions.)

First-declension nouns

The first noun group that uses the same suffixes to form case is, not surprisingly, called *first declension.* All the nouns in the first declension use the endings shown in Table 2-1 to indicate case in a sentence. These nouns are masculine or feminine because the first declension has no neuter nouns.

Table 2-1	First-Declension Case Endings	
Case	*Singular*	*Plural*
Nominative	−a	−ae
Genitive	−ae	−arum
Dative	−ae	−is
Accusative	−am	−as
Ablative	−a	−is

Table 2-2 shows the full declension of the noun **puella** (pu-*ehl*-luh), which means "girl."

Table 2-2	Declining a First-Declension Noun	
Case	*Singular*	*Plural*
Nominative	puella (pu-*ehl*-luh)	puellae (pu-*ehl*-ligh)
Genitive	puellae (pu-*ehl*-ligh)	puellarum (pu-ehl-*lah*-rum)
Dative	puellae (pu-*ehl*-ligh)	puellis (pu-*ehl*-lees)
Accusative	puellam (pu-*ehl*-luhm)	puellas (pu-*ehl*-lahs)
Ablative	puella (pu-*ehl*-lah)	puellis (pu-*ehl*-lees)

Here's an example with the words **terra** (*tehr*-ruh; land), **agricola** (uh-*grih*-koh-luh; farmer), and **puella** (pu-*ehl*-luh; girl):

> **Terram agricolarum puella amat.**
> *tehr*-ruhm uh-gri-ko-*luh*-rum pu-*ehl*-luh *uh*-muht.

Using the case endings to put the nouns in the right position, you can translate this sentence: "The girl loves the land of the farmers." Here's how:

- ✔ **Terra** (land) ends in **–am,** so its case is accusative. In other words, it's the direct object.

- ✔ **Agricola** (farmer) ends in **–arum,** the plural genitive, which shows possession. Because it's genitive, stick the words *of the* in front of the noun: *of the farmers*.

- ✔ **Puella** (girl) ends in **–a,** which is the singular nominative case. That makes **puella** the subject.

- ✔ **Amat** (love) is the verb. It means "she loves." (For verb conjugations, see the section "Lights! Camera! Action! — Introducing Verbs.")

Put it all together, and you have "Land of the farmers girl loves." Okay; that doesn't read like an English sentence. So put the words in the order they would be in an English sentence — subject, verb, and direct object — throw in a couple articles for good measure, and *now* you get "The girl loves the land of the farmers." Voila!

Second-declension nouns

Flamma fumo est proxima (*fluh*-muh *foo*-mo ehst *prohks*-ih-muh). According to the Roman playwright Plautus, "Flame is closest to smoke." In English, you say, "Where there's smoke, there must be fire." And where there's one noun declension, there must be more.

Second-declension nouns are a bit more expressive than first-declension nouns because they have two separate sets of endings for masculine and neuter genders. Second declension has few feminine nouns, and these have the same endings as masculine nouns.

Table 2-3   Second-Declension Masculine/Feminine Case Endings

Case	Singular	Plural
Nominative	–us (occasionally –r)	–i
Genitive	–i	–orum

Case	Singular	Plural
Dative	–o	–is
Accusative	–um	–os
Ablative	–o	–is

Note: Some second-declension nouns use **–r** for the nominative singular form. Two examples of second declension masculine nouns are **amicus** (uh-*mee*-kus), the word for "friend," and **ager** (*uh*-gehr), the word for "field."

Table 2-4 shows the full declension of the masculine nouns **amicus** and **ager.**

Table 2-4	**Declining a Second-Declension Masculine Noun**			
Case	*Singular*	*Plural*	*Singular*	*Plural*
Nominative	amicus (uh-*mee*-kus)	amici (uh-*mee*-kee)	ager (*uh*-gehr)	agri (*uh*-gree)
Genitive	amici (uh-*mee*-kee)	amicorum (uh-mee-*ko*-rum)	agri (*uh*-gree)	agrorum (uh-*gro*-rum)
Dative	amico (uh-*mee*-ko)	amicis (uh-*mee*-kees)	agro (*uh*-gro)	agris (*uh*-grees)
Accusative	amicum (uh-*mee*-koom)	amicos (uh-*mee*-kos)	agrum (*uh*-grum)	agros (*uh*-gros)
Ablative	amico (uh-*mee*-ko)	amicis (uh-*mee*-kees)	agro (*uh*-gro)	agris (*uh*-grees)

Ouch! That had to hurt

As a multicultural society, Rome imported many religious practices from other places. By the third century B.C., the cult of Cybele, a Phrygian mother-goddess, had come to Italy. Associated with the cult of the **Magna Mater** (*mung*-nuh *muh*-tehr), or "Great Mother," were castrated temple attendants, the first of whom was a man named Attis. In his *Carmen* 63, the poet Catullus details how Attis performed this surgery on himself. Interestingly, Catullus then uses feminine adjectives for Attis throughout the rest of the poem.

Second-declension neuter nouns have endings similar to those of the masculine/ feminine genders. In fact, because they're so much alike, they can be grouped together in this declension. Pay particular attention to where the suffixes are different (shown in boldface in Table 2-5).

Table 2-5	Second-Declension Neuter Case Endings	
Case	*Singular*	*Plural*
Nominative	**–um**	**–a**
Genitive	–i	–orum
Dative	–o	–is
Accusative	**–um**	**–a**
Ablative	–o	–is

Table 2-6 shows the decline of **saxum** (*suhk*-sum), a second-declension neuter noun that means "rock."

Table 2-6	Declining a Second-Declension Neuter Noun	
Case	*Singular*	*Plural*
Nominative	saxum (*suhk*-sum)	saxa (*suhk*-suh)
Genitive	saxi (*suhk*-see)	saxorum (suhk-*so*-rum)
Dative	saxo (*suhk*-so)	saxis (*suhk*-sees)
Accusative	saxum (*suhk*-sum)	saxa (*suhk*-suh)
Ablative	saxo (*suhk*-so)	saxis (*suhk*-sees)

You can see that the only place where neuter nouns are different is in the nominative singular and nominative and accusative plural forms, which have the endings **–um** and **–a**. This presents an interesting situation: The suffix **–a** can also be a singular ending in first declension. Look at the following sentence:

Portat saxa puella in aqua.
pohr-tuht *suhk*-suh pu-*ehl*-luh ihn *uh*-kwuh.

Portare means "to carry," a **saxum** is a "rock," **puella** means "girl," and **aqua** is "water." But if you know the definitions, you're only halfway to understanding the sentence. The preceding Latin sentence means one of the following translations, but which one?

> The girl in the water carries rocks.
>
> The girls in the water carry rocks.
>
> The girl in the water carries a rock.
>
> The girls in the water carry a rock.
>
> The girl on the rocks carries water.
>
> The girls on the rocks carry water.
>
> The girl on the rock carries water.
>
> The girls on the rock carry water.

Remember that word order in Latin plays less of a role in determining meaning than it does in English. The only way to know for certain is to know to what declension each of the nouns belongs, and checking a Latin dictionary can tell you this. Along with the definition and gender, each noun entry gives the nominative and genitive singular forms. You can spot a first-declension noun from a genitive singular ending in **–ae,** and a second-declension noun from a genitive singular ending in **–i.** The dictionary entries for the nouns in the preceding Latin sentence look like this:

> **saxum, saxi,** n (rock)
>
> **puella, puellae,** f (girl)
>
> **aqua, aquae,** f (water)

From this, you can see that **saxum** is a second-declension word, and both **puella** and **aqua** are first declension because of the genitive singular endings (**saxi, puellae,** and **aquae**). Knowing this, you can figure out that the correct translation of the sentence is actually "The girl in the water carries rocks."

Some second-declension masculine nouns have **–ius** for a nominative singular ending, and some neuter nouns have **–ium.** These nouns used a single **–i** for the genitive singular ending until the Age of Augustus, which began in the first century B.C. After that time, the genitive singular for these nouns became **–ii.** Most dictionaries retain the older spelling with a single **–i,** and that is the form you see in this book.

You can always determine the declension and gender of a noun just by checking its dictionary entry.

Talkin' the Talk

A **regina** (ray-*gee*-nuh; queen) and a **servus** (*sehr*-wus; slave) discuss dinner preparations.

Servus:	**Cibum et aquam ad triclinium portabo.** *kih*-bum eht *uh*-kwuhm uhd tree-*klee*-nih-um pohr-*tah* bo. I shall carry the food and water to the dining room.
Regina:	**Cultellos et mappas in mensa quoque pone.** kul-*tehl*-los eht *muhp*-pahs ihn *mayn*-sah *po*-neh. Put the knives and napkins on the table, too.
Servus:	**Cibus et aqua nunc sunt in triclinio.** *kih*-bus eht *uh*-kwuh nunk sunt ihn tree-*klee*-nih-o. The food and water are in the dining room.
Regina:	**Cur non cultelli et mappae sunt in mensa? Erat iussum meum.** kur non kul-*tehl*-lee eht *muhp*-pigh sunt ihn *mayn*-sah? *eh*-rut *yoos*-sum *meh*-um. Why are the knives and napkins not on the table? That was my order.
Servus:	**Defessus eram et non memini.** day-*fehs*-sus *eh*-rum eht non *meh*-mih-nee. I was tired, and I did not remember.
Regina:	**Tu es servus reginae, et regina iussa servo dat!** too ehs *sehr*-wus re-*gee*-nigh, eht ray-*gee*-nuh *yoos*-suh *sehr*-wo duht! You are the queen's slave, and the queen gives the slave orders!
Servus:	**Mox ero servus in Elysio.** mohks *eh*-ro *sehr*-wus ihn ay-*lih*-sih-o. Soon I shall be a slave in Elysium.

The ancient Romans didn't believe good people went up to heaven and bad people went down to hell after death. Instead, many believed that everyone went **apud inferos** (*uh*-pud *een*-feh-ros), that is, to the underworld. Once there, however, souls of the wicked received torturous punishments in a region called **Tartarus** (*tuhr*-tuh-rus), while good souls enjoyed eternal happiness in **Elysium.**

Words to Know

agricola, agricolae, m	uh-*grih*-koh-luh, uh-*grih*-koh-ligh	farmer
amicus, amici, m	uh-*mee*-kus, uh-*mee*-kee	friend
aqua, aquae, f	*uh*-kwuh, *uh*-kwigh	water
cibus, cibi, m	*kih*-bus, *kih*-bee	food
puella, puellae, f	pu-*ehl*-luh, pu-*ehl*-ligh	girl
regina, reginae, f	ray-*gee*-nuh, ray-*gee*-nigh	queen
saxum, saxi, n	suhk-sum, suhk-see	rock
servus, servi, m	*sehr*-wus, *sehr*-wee	slave
terra, terrae, f	*tehr*-ruh, *tehr*-righ	land
triclinium, triclini, n	tree-klee-*nih*-um, tree-klee-nee	dining room

Lights! Camera! Action! Introducing Verbs

Nouns may describe persons, places, things, or ideas, but without verbs, a sentence goes nowhere. A similarity exists between the organization of Latin nouns and verbs that helps to keep everything straight. For example, nouns are grouped into declensions, and verbs are grouped into conjugations. Nouns use case endings to show how they function in a sentence, and verbs use personal endings to show who is doing the action. From a noun suffix you can quickly tell whether a word is singular or plural, and you can get the same information, along with the tense, from a verb suffix. To paraphrase the poet Ovid, **Ille dies nefastus erit, per quem verba silentur** (*ihl*-leh *dih*-ays neh-*fah*-stus *eh*-riht pehr kwehm *wehr*-buh sih-*lehn*-tur) meaning "It will be an unfortunate day when the verbs are silent."

Joining the ranks of verb conjugation

The word *conjugation* is a derivative of the Latin **coniungere** (kohn-*yun*-geh-reh), which means "to join together." Just as a declension is a group of nouns that form their *cases* the same way, so a conjugation is a group of verbs that form their *tenses* the same way — by using certain endings. In this section, you find out how to spot the conjugation of any regular verb, as well as how to recognize who is doing the action and when.

The dictionary entry for a Latin verb has four principal parts, just as English verbs do. An English verb might look like this:

(to) sing	singing	sang	sung
infinitive	present participle	past tense	past participle

Latin verbs are presented much the same way. A typical verb might be:

amo (*uh*-mo)	**amare** (uh-*mah*-reh)	**amavi** (uh-*mah*-wee)	**amatus** (uh-*mah*-tus)
present tense	infinitive	past tense	past participle

Regular Latin verbs belong to one of four conjugations. The key to recognizing what conjugation a verb belongs to is to look at the verb's infinitive. Table 2-7 serves as a quick reference.

Table 2-7	The Infinitive Forms			
Infinitive Suffix	*Conjugation*	*Example*	*Pronunciation*	*Definition*
–are	first	amare	uh-*mah*-reh	to love
–ere	second	tenere	teh-*nay*-reh	to hold
–ere	third	ponere	*po*-neh-reh	to put
–ire	fourth	audire	ow-*dee*-reh	to hear

You may notice that second and third conjugations seem to have the same infinitive ending, **–ere.** But if you look carefully at the pronunciation of the examples, you see that the second conjugation involves a long **–e,** pronounced "ay," and the third conjugation uses a short **–e,** pronounced "eh."

As an extra help in identifying which is which, second-conjugation verbs end with **–eo** in their first principal part. So the full dictionary entry for a second-conjugation verb might look like

Teneo (*teh*-neh-o), **tenere** (teh-*nay*-reh), **tenui** (*teh*-nu-ee), **tentus** (*tehn*-tus) meaning "to hold."

For a third-conjugation verb, it would look like

Pono (*po*-no), **ponere** (*po*-neh-reh), **posui** (*poh*-su-ee), **positus** (*poh*-sih-tus) meaning "to put."

When you can recognize a verb's conjugation, you can handle the vast majority of Latin verbs. You can read about a few of the *irregular verbs,* that is, verbs that don't fit any of the regular conjugations, in Chapters 3 and 5.

A sort of hybrid conjugation, called *third–io,* is a cross between the third and fourth conjugations. Basically, it has the short **–ere** (eh-reh) ending on the infinitive but has an **–io** on the first principal part, as fourth-conjugation verbs do. See Table 2-9 to compare an example of this type of verb with the others.

Taking it personally — personal endings

A child on her way to school calls back over her shoulder to her parents, "Love you!" but what does she really mean? "We love you," making reference to the stuffed animal she has for show-n-tell? Perhaps she intends, "They love you," indicating the other children on the bus. Of course, she is most likely trying to say, "I love you," but in English, you can't know for certain without context clues or the addition of a pronoun. In short, English requires at least two words to express an action and who is performing it.

Latin is more compact. Recognizing a particular verb suffix, you can tell exactly who is doing the action in a sentence. In fact, you can have a complete sentence with just one word. Take a look:

> **Canto.**
>
> *kuhn*-to.
>
> I am singing.

Because these suffixes show who performs the action, they're called *personal endings,* and for the active voice (see active and passive voice in Chapter 9) in the majority of tenses, they look like this.

Table 2-8	Personal Endings		
Singular Ending	*Meaning*	*Plural Ending*	*Meaning*
–o (–m)	I	–mus	we
–s	you	–tis	you
–t	he, she, it	–nt	they

You can see that two first-person endings, **–o** and **–m,** are possible. Which one you use depends on the tense, and you can find out more about tenses later in this chapter. For now, notice that a simple suffix identifies the subject of the verb. Take a look at a nonsense sentence to see how simple understanding Latin verbs can be:

Cibum ****tis et aquam ****nt, sed vinum ****mus.

Even though the symbols in the above are not real verbs, you can still tell who is doing the action. For example, *you* are doing something to the **cibum** (*kih*-bum; food) because the suffix of the verb is **–tis.** *They* are doing the action to the **aquam** (*uh*-kwuhm; water) because of the **–nt** ending of the verb, and **–mus** says that *we* are performing some action on the **vinum** (*wee*-num; wine). Now look at the same basic sentence with actual verbs.

Cibum portatis et aquam gustant, sed vinum amamus.

kih-bum pohr-*tah*-tihs eht *uh*-kwuhm *gus*-tuhnt, sehd *wee*-num uh-*mah*-mus.

You carry the food and they taste the water, but we love the wine.

You'll see third-person verb forms more than any other. This makes sense when you consider that literature frequently tells the story of something or someone other than the speaker. To memorize the various components of grammar, the following little verse can help you keep these important third-person endings straight.

The Latin verbs that end in **–t** show action that is done by "he,"

But if that **–t** should follow **n,** it's "they" who do the action then.

The same rules for subject-verb agreement apply in English as in Latin. If the verb ends in **–t,** look for a nominative-singular noun for the subject. If the verb ends in **–nt,** then look for a nominative plural. Of course, if the subject is unexpressed, you still know that **–t** can indicate "he," "she," or "it," and **–nt** can indicate "they."

Relax! It's just the verbs that are tense

Latin verbs present plenty of information in just one word. Not only do they describe the action of a sentence and tell who's doing it, but they also show the time when that action occurs — all with a simple system of suffixes.

When learning Latin verb tenses, you can see that Latin is a specific language. Latin has six basic tenses, and you discover three of them in this chapter. For the remaining three, head to Chapter 4.

What kind of Mickey Mouse tip is this?

Latin students often become quite adept at making rhymes to memorize the various components of grammar. As it turns out, the personal verb endings fit the rhythm of the theme song to the old *Mickey Mouse Club* children's show. If you remember the tune, substitute **–o, –s, –t, –mus, –tis, –nt** for the letters M-I-C-K-E-Y, M-O-U-S-E. For the really ambitious, the song goes like this:

–o, –s, –t, –mus, –tis, –nt

Personal endings, personal endings;

They show who does the action of the verb.

Verb! Verb! Verb!

Hey there, hi there, ho there

It's as simple as can be.

–o, –s, –t, –mus, –tis, –nt.

Now, aren't you glad there isn't an audio CD with this book?

No time like the present

The personal endings shown in Table 2-8 combine with a thematic vowel in each conjugation to form the present tense. The thematic vowels are

- ✔ First conjugation — a
- ✔ Second conjugation — e
- ✔ Third, third–io, fourth conjugation — i

Table 2-9 shows how thematic vowels look on sample verbs from each of the five conjugations.

Table 2-9	Present-Tense Verb Forms	
First Conjugation	*Singular*	*Plural*
	amo (*uh*-mo)	amamus (uh-*mah*-mus)
	amas (*uh*-mahs)	amatis (uh-*mah*-tihs)
	amat (*uh*-muht)	amant (*uh*-muhnt)
Second Conjugation	*Singular*	*Plural*
	teneo (*teh*-neh-o)	tenemus (teh-*nay*-mus)
	tenes (*teh*-nays)	tenetis (teh-*nay*-tihs)
	tenet (*teh*-neht)	tenent (*teh*-nehnt)

(continued)

Table 2-9 *(continued)*

Third Conjugation	Singular	Plural
	pono (*po*-no)	ponimus (*po*-nih-mus)
	ponis (*po*-nihs)	ponitis (*po*-nih-tihs)
	ponit (*po*-niht)	ponunt (*po*-nunt)
Third-io Conjugation	**Singular**	**Plural**
	capio (*kuh*-pih-o)	capimus (*kuh*-pih-mus)
	capis (*kuh*-pihs)	capitis (*kuh*-pih-tihs)
	capit (*kuh*-piht)	capiunt (*kuh*-pih-unt)
Fourth Conjugation	**Singular**	**Plural**
	audio (*ow*-dih-o)	audimus (*ow*-dih-mus)
	audis (*ow*-dihs)	auditis (*ow*-dih-tihs)
	audit (*ow*-diht)	audiunt (*ow*-dih-unt)

You can understand the Latin present tense to have the same meaning as the English "am," "is," "are," "do," and simple present. This is one instance in which English is more obvious in its meaning than Latin. Consider the following sentence.

> **Cantas, sed laboro.**
> *kuhn*-tahs, sehd luh-*bo*-ro.

Here are some possible translations:

> You are singing, but I am working.
> You sing, but I work.
> You do sing, but I work.
> You sing, but I do work.

Clearly, each of these renderings has a different connotation, yet each is a grammatically correct translation. To determine the best rendering for a Latin present tense, you need to use other context clues in the surrounding text.

Verbs don't worry if they're imperfect

No, you haven't bought a defective book, nor have you come to the part that we just couldn't get right. The imperfect tense refers to past action that was continued for a period of time, was never completed, or was still happening at the time of the main verb in the sentence. A simple English sentence can help this make sense:

The bell was ringing when the teacher called my name.

This sentence describes two past actions, the ringing of a bell and the calling of a person's name. The name calling happened only once, but the bell rang for some length of time. There is no indication in this particular sentence that the bell stopped ringing, and the sound could still be heard by the time the main action, calling my name, took place.

As with the present tense, the same basic personal endings from Table 2-9 help form the imperfect. Instead of combining with one thematic vowel, however, they unite with the letters **ba** to form this instantly recognizable tense.

✔ First-conjugation verbs always have **a** before the **ba**.

✔ Second, third, third–io, and fourthconjugations all have **e** in front of the **ba**.

Table 2-10 shows only examples from first and second conjugations.

Table 2-10	Imperfect-Tense Verb Forms	
First Conjugation	**Singular**	**Plural**
	amabam (uh-*mah*-buhm)	Amabamus (uh-*mah*-bah-mus)
	amabas (uh-*mah*-bahs)	amabatis (uh-*mah*-bah-tihs)
	amabat (uh-*mah*-buht)	amabant (uh-*mah*-buhnt)
Second Conjugation	**Singular**	**Plural**
	tenebam (teh-*nay*-buhm)	tenebamus (teh-*nay*-bah-mus)
	tenebas (teh-*nay*-bahs)	tenebatis (teh-*nay*-bah-tihs)
	tenebat (the-*nay*-buht)	tenebant (teh-*nay*-buhnt)

Notice that the imperfect tense uses the **–m** suffix for first person singular, rather than the **–o** ending used in the present tense.

You can render the imperfect tense into English in a number of ways. Some of the more common are with the words *was, were, used to,* and *kept on.* Sometimes the simple English past is the only translation that sounds correct. See the following examples to start putting it all together:

Dicebas et audiebamus, sed nunc dicimus et discedis.

dee-*kay*-bahs eht ow-dih-*ay*-bah-mus, sehd nunk *dee*-kih-mus eht dihs-*kay*-dihs.

You were speaking and we were listening, but now we are speaking and you are leaving.

. . . et vario noctem sermone trahebat infelix Dido longumque bibebat amorem. (*Aeneid* I.748-749)

eht *wuh*-rih-o *nohk*-tehm sehr-*mo*-neh truh-*hay*-buhteen-*fay*-leeks *dee*-do lohn-*gum*-kweh bih-*bay*-buht uh-*mo*-rehm.

. . . unlucky Dido was dragging out the night in varied conversation and continually drank long draughts of love.

Telling the future

The last tense to explore in this chapter is the future tense. Simply put, the future tense describes action that has not yet happened but will sometime later.

For first- and second-conjugation verbs, the future tense is similar to the imperfect. Again, it uses the personal endings listed in Table 2-8, but in combination with the letters **b, bi,** or **bu.** See Table 2-11.

Table 2-11	Future-Tense Verb Forms: First and Second Conjugations	
First Conjugation	*Singular*	*Plural*
	amabo (uh-*mah*-bo)	amabimus (uh-*mah*-bih-mus)
	amabis (uh-*mah*-bihs)	amabitis (uh-*mah*-bih-tihs)
	amabit (uh-*mah*-bit)	amabunt (uh-*mah*-bunt)
Second Conjugation	*Singular*	*Plural*
	tenebo (teh-*nay*-bo)	tenebimus (teh-*nay*-bih-mus)
	tenebis (teh-*nay*-bihs)	tenebitis (teh-*nay*-bih-tihs)
	tenebit (teh-*nay*-biht)	tenebunt (teh-*nay*-bunt)

Third-, third–io-, and fourth-conjugation verbs work a little differently. You can recognize the future tense for these verbs because they use a different thematic vowel from the present tense. Using the same personal endings, the future tense for these conjugations uses the vowels *a* and *e,* as shown in Table 2-12.

Table 2-12	Future-Tense Verb Forms: Third, Third-io, and Fourth Conjugations	
First Conjugation	*Singular*	*Plural*
	ponam (*po*-nuhm)	ponemus (po-*nay*-mus)
	pones (*po*-nays)	ponetis (po-*nay*-tihs)
	ponet (*po*-neht)	ponent (*po*-nehnt)
Third–io Conjugation	*Singular*	*Plural*
	capiam (*kuh*-pih-uhm)	capiemus (kuh-pih-*ay*-mus)
	capies (*kuh*-pih-ays)	capietis (kuh-pih-*ay*-tihs)
	capiet (*kuh*-pih-eht)	capient (*kuh*-pih-ent)
Fourth Conjugation	*Singular*	*Plural*
	audiam (*ow*-dih-uhm)	audiemus (ow-dih-*ay*-mus)
	audies (*ow*-dih-ays)	audietis (ow-dih-*ay*-tihs)
	audiet (*ow*-dih-eht)	audient (*ow*-dih-ehnt)

You usually render the future tense with the words *shall* and *will*. The following example, taken from the *Vulgate,* the Latin translation of the Bible, shows several different forms of the future tense. Because this is a later Latin text, the pronunciation guide follows the Ecclesiastical pronunciation. For more on Latin pronunciation, see Chapter 1.

> **Et invocabitis me et ibitis et orabitis et exaudiam vos; quaeretis et invenietis me cum quaesieritis me in toto cordo vestro.** (Jeremiah 29:12-13)

eht ihn-woh-*kah*-bih-tihs may eht *ee*-bih-tihs eht o-*rah*-bih-tihs eht eg-*zow*-dih-uhm wos; kway-*ray*-tihs eht ihn-wehn-ih-*ay*-tihs may koom kway-see-*eh*-rih-tihs may ihn *to*-to *kohr*-deh *wehs*-tro.

And you will call on me and you will come to me and you will pray to me, and I shall hear you; and you will seek and will find me when you have searched for me in your whole heart.

Here's another little Latin student rhyme that can help you remember the future tense (and you thought great Latin poetry died with Vergil!):

bo, bi, bu for one and two (as in first and second conjugations)

a and **e** for four and three (as in the third and fourth conjugations)

The future tense is one place where you need to know how to recognize different verb conjugations. Remember that you can always determine a verb's conjugation from its infinitive — second principal part.

In this chapter, one Latin suffix appears twice with two completely different meanings. The ending **–am** can indicate an accusative-case noun in the first declension, or it can signal a first-person-singular-future-tense verb from the third, third–io, or fourth conjugations. The following sentence illustrates this peculiarity.

> **Puellam audiam.**
>
> pu-*ehl*-luhm *ow*-dih-uhm.
>
> I shall hear the girl.

Of course, most nouns and verbs are easy to distinguish from each other because of their meanings. When in doubt, check the dictionary.

Talkin' the Talk

Catullus and his friend Fabullus discuss their dinner plans. (Watch for different verb tenses in this dialogue.)

Catullus: **Fabulle, ad cenam apud me advenies?**
fuh-*buhl*-leh, uhd *kay*-nuhm *uh*-pud may uhd-*weh*-nih-ays?
Fabullus, will you come to my house for dinner?

Fabullus: **Cum Horatio cenare in animo habebam.**
koom hoh-*rah*-tih-o kay-*nah*-reh ihn *uh*-nih-mo huh-*bay*-buhm.
I was planning to dine with Horatius.

Catullus: **Sed coqui mei cibum optimum parabunt.**
sehd *koh*-kwee *meh*-ee *kih*-bum *ohp*-tih-mum puh-*rah*-buhnt.
But my cooks prepare the best food.

Fabullus: **Adveniam, et vinum feram.**
uhd-*weh*-nih-uhm eht *wee*-num *feh*-ruhm.
I shall come, and I shall bring the wine.

Catullus: **Bene! Cibum quoque feres?**
beh-neh *kih*-bum *kwoh*-kweh *feh*-rays?
Good! Will you bring the food, too?

Fabullus: **Cur? Me invitabas?**
kur? may ihn-wih-*tah*-bahs?
Why? You were inviting me?

Catullus: **Sed coqui non parant quod non habeo.**
sehd *koh*-kwee non *puh*-ruhnt kwohd non *huh*-beh-o.
But the cooks do not prepare what I do not have.

Words to Know

amo, amare, amavi, amatus	*uh*-mo, uh-*mah*-reh, uh-*mah*-wee, uh-*mah*-tus	to love
audio, audire, audivi, auditus	*ow*-dih-oh, ow-*dee*-reh, ow-*dee*-wee, ow-*dee*-tus	to hear
canto, cantare, cantavi, cantatus	*kuhn*-to, kuhn-*tah*-reh, kuhn-*tah*-wee, kuhn-*tah*-tus	to sing
capio, capere, cepi, captus	*kuh*-pih-o, kuh-*peh*-reh, kay-pee, kahp-tus	to take
dico, dicere, dixi, dictus	*dee*-ko, dee-*keh*-reh, deek-see, dihk-tus	to speak
habeo, habere, habui, habitus	*huh*-beh-o, huh-*bay*-reh, huh-bu-ee, huh-bih-tus	to have
invenio, invenire, inveni, inventus	ihn-*weh*-nih-o, ihn-weh-*nee*-reh, ihn-*way*-nee, ihn-*wehn*-tus	to find
oro, orare, oravi, oratus	*o*-ro, o-*rah*-reh, o-*rah*-wee, o-*rah*-tus	to pray
paro, parare, paravi, paratus	*puh*-ro, puh-*rah*-reh, puh-*rah*-wee, puh-*rah*-tus	to prepare
pono, ponere, posui, positus	*po*-no, po-*neh*-reh, poh-su-ee, poh-*sih*-tus	to put
teneo, tenere, tenui, tentus	*teh*-neh-o, teh-*nay*-reh, teh-nu-ee, tehn-tus	to hold
traho, trahere, traxi, tractus	*truh*-ho, truh-*heh*-reh, trahk-see, truhk-tus	to drag

Making Connections through Conjunctions

Conjunctions join things together. But unlike the word *conjunction* itself, which has an easily recognized Latin root, **coniungere**, actual Latin conjunctions have no recognizable English derivatives. These little words are important, but they just have to be memorized. Sorry, no rhymes for these! Some of the conjunctions that you're most likely to encounter are

- ✔ **et, atque, –que** (eht, *uht*-kweh, kweh; and): The suffix **–que** is used on the second of the two words being joined, as shown in the following sentence:

  Cornelia et Flavia aquam harenamque amat.
  kohrn-*nay*-lih-uh eht *flah*-wih-uh *uh*-kwuhm huh-ray-*nuhm*-kweh *uh*-muht.
  Cornelia and Flavia love the water and sand.

- ✔ **etiam, quoque** (*eh*-tih-uhm, *kwoh*-kweh; also)

  multa quoque et bello passus dum conderet urbem (Vergil, *Aeneid* I.5)
  muhl-tuh *kwoh*-kweh eht *behl*-lo *puhs*-sus dum *kohn*-deh-reht *ur*-behm
  and having endured many things also in war while he established his city

- ✔ **aut** (owt; or): When this word appears twice, it often means "either . . . or"

  Aut viam inveniam aut faciam.
  owt *wih*-uhm ihn-*weh*-nih-uhm owt *fuh*-kih-uhm.
  I shall either find a way or make one.

- ✔ **sed, autem, verum** (sehd, *ow*-tehm, *weh*-rum; but)

  sed non videmus manticae quod in tergo est. (Catullus, 22)
  sehd non wih-*day*-mus *muhn*-tih-kigh kwohd ihn *tehr*-go ehst.
  But we do not see the burden on our own back.

- ✔ **tamen** (*tah*-mehn; however)

  Discipuli tamen multa de Romanis discunt.
  dee-*skih*-pu-lee *tah*-mehn *mul*-tuh day ro-*mah*-nees *dee*-skunt.
  The students, however, are learning much about the Romans.

- ✔ **nam, enim** (nuhm, *eh*-nihm; for)

  Nam illa nimis antiqua praetereo. (Cicero, *In Catilinam* I)
  nuhm *ihl*-luh *nih*-mihs uhn-*tee*-kwuh prigh-*teh*-reh-o.
  For I pass over those things that are too old.

- ✔ **ergo, igitur, itaque** (*ehr*-go, *ih*-gih-tur, *ee*-tuh-kweh; therefore)

  Cogito ergo sum.
  ko-gih-to *ehr*-go sum.
  I think, therefore I am.

Fun & Games

Draw a line to match the case use with the correct form of the Latin noun.

1. saxa   possession, plural

2. regina   indirect object, singular

3. amicorum   direct object plural

4. servo   subject singular

Which English word would you use to translate each of these verbs?

5. audimus   a. is   d. were

6. habebant   b. are   e. will

7. parabitis   c. was   f. shall

8. capies

See if you can figure out what these sentences mean. (**Note:** All the words appear in some form in this chapter.)

9. **Agricolae saxa invenient.**
    uh-*grih*-ko-ligh *suhk*-suh ihn-*weh*-ni-ehnt.

10. **Servi et puellae reginam audiebant.**
    sehr-wee eht pu-*ehl*-ligh ray-*gee*-nuhm ow-dih-*ay*-buhnt.

11. **In triclinio cibum paramus.**
    ihn tree-*klee*-nih-o *kih*-bum puh-*rah*-mus.

See Appendix C for the answers.

Chapter 3

Salve! Hello! Greetings and Introductions

*E*very language has phrases to say hello, start a conversation, acknowledge someone's presence, and so on. Some greetings are more formal, some less formal. What greeting you use depends on the situation you're in. In American English, "How do you do?" is appropriate for some situations; "Whassup?" or "Hi!" is appropriate for others. The same is true for Latin. Although greeting the emperor may require that you simply stand in your toga and snap a salute, you need to know a bit more for day-to-day interactions. From gladiators in the arena to citizens on the street, ancient Romans greeted each other in different ways.

So what do you do after the introductions? You talk about anything you want: politics, philosophy, your nosy neighbor, the fresh fish in the market, or whatever. If you're new to the language, however, you may want to stick with the basics: being able to identify yourself, tell where you come from, and ask a few questions. To that end, this chapter explores some of the more common salutations, farewells, and ways to carry on simple conversations in the ancient Eternal City.

Hello, Goodbye: Roman Salutations and Farewells

The ancient Romans considered anyone who didn't speak their language a **barbarus** (*buhr*-buh-rus; barbarian), that is, someone who needed to learn Latin as soon as possible. One of the quickest ways to reveal yourself as a barbarus was to flub the Roman greetings. Fortunately, they're not hard to remember:

- ✔ **Salve!** (*suhl*-way): This literally means "be well," but the Romans used it to greet someone or to take leave of them.

- ✔ **Salvete!** (*suhl*-way-teh): This also means "be well," but you use this form when you're speaking to two or more people at the same time.

- ✔ **Civis** (*kee*-wihs; citizen): When you address a fellow Roman citizen whose name you don't know, you can use this word, calling him a citizen. Using **civis** is similar to addressing an American as "guy" or "buddy."

- ✔ **Nos morituri te salutamus!** (nos moh-rih-*too*-ree tay suh-loo-*ta*-mus): Don't use this greeting unless you're a gladiator about to fight and aware of your own mortality. Addressed to the emperor or sponsor of the games, it means "we who are about to die salute you."

The Roman goodbyes are similar to the hellos: The form you use depends on how many people you're addressing:

- ✔ **Vale!** (*wuh*-lay): Like **salve, vale** means, "Be well," but you use it only when you're parting company with someone.

- ✔ **Valete!** (*wuh*-lay-teh): Like **salvete,** you use this form only when you're bidding farewell to several people.

- ✔ **Pax tecum!** (pahks *tay*-koom): Said to one person, this means, "Peace be with you."

- ✔ **Pax vobiscum!** (pahks wo-*bee*-skoom): Use this phrase to wish peace to several people.

The boys 'n the 'hood: Addressing males

Freeborn-male citizens typically had three names:

- ✔ **praenomen** (prigh-*no*-mehn; first name)

- ✔ **nomen** (*no*-men; family name)

- ✔ **cognomen** (kohg-*no*-men) — an extra name that denotes such things as a distinguishing physical feature (the name Rufus, for example, means "red-haired"), place of origin, or occupation.

And you thought Ashley was a popular name.

Praenomina (prigh-*no*-mih-nuh; first names) for males were relatively few in number and usually abbreviated to a letter or two. Some of the more common names were

M. Marcus

T. Titus

P. Publius

Q. Quintus

C. Gaius (This abbreviation never changed from Caius, the older spelling of this name.)

Cn. Gnaeus (The older form of this name was Cnaeus.)

Take Julius Caesar, for example. His full name was Gaius Julius Caesar. His wife may have called him by his praenomen, **Gaius** (*gigh*-us), and his friends would have called him by his praenomen or his nomen, **Julius** (*yoo*-lih-us). Only in formal situations would people have addressed him with all three names, including his cognomen, **Caesar** (*kigh*-sahr), which means "hairy," by the way.

Slave names showed who owned them as well as something about their background. Slaves usually took the praenomen and nomen of their master and kept their original name or a title of origin as a cognomen. **Publius** (*poo*-blih-us) **Terentius** (teh-*rehn*-tih-us) **Afer** (*ah*-fehr), a slave from Africa, became a famous Roman playwright whose works were admired and imitated by the likes of Montaigne and Moliere.

When addressing a male with a name or title ending in **–us,** you need to use a special form of the name called the *vocative case*. Related to the verb **vocare** (wo-*kah*-reh; to call), the vocative case indicates who you're addressing.

✔ If the name ends in **–us,** use **–e** for the singular and **–i** for plural.

✔ If the name ends in **–ius,** use **–i** for both singular and plural.

Say, for example, that you're addressing Marcus. Following this rule, you'd call him **Marce** (*muhr*-keh). If you're addressing Antonius, you'd call him **Antoni** (uhn-*to*-nee). If you're addressing more than one **amicus** (uh-*mee*-kus; friend), you'd use **amici** (uh-*mee*-kee). In addressing more than one **filius** (*fee*-lih-us; son), you use **fili** (*fee*-lee).

Addressing females

Women didn't have to worry about as many names as men did. Instead, they took on a feminine form of their father's **nomen** (*no*-men; first name).

Caesar's wife **Calpurnia** (kuhl-*pur*-nih-uh), for example, was named after her father, **Calpurnius** (kuhl-*pur*-nih-us); Cicero's daughter was **Tullia** (*tul*-lih-uh) (the feminine form of **Tullius** (*tul*-lih-us), Cicero's **nomen**).

After the first daughter (who got the father's name), the girls that came later often had names that indicated their place in the family, such as **Secunda** (seh-*kun*-duh; second), **Tertia** (*tehr*-tih-uh; third), and so on.

This made addressing women a fairly simple matter. To address a woman more formally, you simply noted whose daughter she was. If some confusion resulted about which Tullia you meant, you just repeated that you were asking for **Tullia Marci filia** (*tul*-lih-uh *muhr*-kee *fee*-lih-uh), or Tullia, daughter of Marcus.

Being There: Esse (To Be)

You may bluff your way into a senator's house with a well-placed "**Salve!**" but that won't get you far beyond the **ianitor** (*yah*-nih-tohr; doorkeeper). To keep from being labeled a **barbarus** (*buhr*-buh-rus; barbarian), you need to say a little about yourself, and this requires using the verb **esse** (*ehs*-seh; to be).

Like the English verb "to be," **esse** is an irregular verb. What that means is that **esse** doesn't follow the tense pattern that most Latin verbs follow. (See Chapter 2 for Latin's regular verbs.) Therefore, the best way to remember the conjugation of **esse** is to memorize its basic forms.

Following is the present tense of the verb **esse**:

Singular	*Plural*
sum	sumus
es	estis
est	sunt

Here's the imperfect tense of **esse**:

Singular	*Plural*
eram	eramus
eras	eratis
erat	erant

Finally, here's the future tense of **esse**:

Singular	*Plural*
ero	erimus
eris	eritis
erit	erunt

Latin has three distinct past-tense forms. The imperfect tense shows ongoing action in the past and is distinct from the perfect tense, which shows completed action and is more akin to the simple past tense used in English. Chapter 4 introduces the other two past tenses (perfect and pluperfect).

Here are a few examples to help you put it all together:

✔ **Gallia est omnis divisa in partes tres.**

guhl-lih-uh ehst *ohm*-nihs dee-*wee*-suh in *puhr*-tays trays.

Gaul is on the whole divided into three parts. (Julius Caesar's *Commentary on the Gallic War* I.1)

✔ **Tantae molis erat Romanam condere gentem.**

tuhn-tigh *mo*-lihs *eh*-ruht ro-*mah*-num *kohn*-deh-reh *gehn*-tehm.

It was such a great task to found the Roman race. (*Aeneid* I.33)

✔ **et eritis mihi in populum et ego ero vobis in Deum**

eht *eh*-rih-tihs *mhi*-hih ihn *poh*-pu-lum eht *eh*-goh *vo*-bees ihn *deh*-um

and you will be my people and I will be your God (Jeremiah 11:4)

If you know **esse** and its various forms and you understand place names (see the "Saying Where You're From" section, coming up next), you can communicate who you are and where you're from.

Saying Where You're From

The Roman Empire was a multicultural society, as Table 3-1 shows. It spanned millions of square miles, going through Europe (including the British Isles), across Asia, and deep into Africa. At its peak, it claimed a population of more than 50 million people.

Table 3-1	A Few Cities and Countries in the Roman Empire	
Location	*Pronunciation*	*Modern Name*
Aegyptus	igh-*gihp*-tus	Egypt
Britannia	brih-*tuhn*-ni-uh	Britain
Carthago	kuhr-*tah*-go	Carthage
Corinthus	koh-*rihn*-thus	Corinth
Gades	*gah*-days	Cadiz
Germania	gehr-*mah*-nih-uh	Germany
Graecia	*grigh*-kih-uh	Greece
Massilia	muhs-*sih*-lih-uh	Marseille
Patavium	pu-*tuh*-wih-um	Padua
Roma	*ro*-muh	Rome

To indicate nationality, you'd say **Sum a Britannia** (sum ah brih-*tuhn*-ni-ah), which means "I am from Britain" or **Sum a Massilia** (sum ah muhs-*sih*-lih-ah) to say "I am from Marseille." You could also turn these place names into adjectives (to say "I am Roman," for example), as the following "Identifying Yourself" section shows.

Identifying Yourself

Perhaps the Emperor Augustus can tell from the way you wear your toga that you're not a native of Rome. Naturally, he wants to know if you're a friend or a foe, so he asks where you call home. If you know the verb of being (**esse;** to be) and you know your birthplace (refer to the preceding "Saying Where You're From" section), then you can communicate exactly who you are.

Actually, describing yourself involves your gender. You can read about grammatical gender in Chapter 2, but here we're talking about biology. If you go to the bathroom marked **VIRI** (*wih*-ree; men), then you need to use an adjective ending in **–us** or **–i** to indicate the male gender. If you use the one labeled **FEMINAE** (*fay*-mih-nae; women), you need adjectives that end in **–a** or **–ae** to indicate female gender.

In English, when you say, "I am Roman," you're not specifying gender; you're merely specifying nationality. In Latin, however, Roman men and women indicated their gender in the adjectives they used to describe themselves. Using certain suffixes in the adjective itself (see Table 3-2) indicated gender.

Table 3-2		Showing Gender in Adjectives	
Gender	*Number*	*Ending*	*Examples*
Masculine	Singular	–us	Romanus (ro-*mah*-nus; Roman) Graecus (*grigh*-kus; Greek) Aegyptus (igh-*gihp*-tus; Egyptian)
Masculine	Plural	–i	Romani (ro-*mah*-nee; Roman) Graeci (*grigh*-kee; Greek) Aegypti (igh-*gihp*-tee; Egyptian)
Feminine	Singular	–a	Romana (ro-*mah*-nuh; Roman) Graeca (*grigh*-kuh; Greek) Aegypta (igh-*gihp*-tuh; Egyptian)
Feminine	Plural	–ae	Romanae (ro-*mah*-nigh; Roman) Graecae (*grigh*-kigh; Greek) Aegyptae (igh-*gihp*-tigh; Egyptian)

Following are a few examples:

- A Roman man would say **Sum Romanus** (sum ro-*mah*-nus), which means "I am Roman." A Roman woman, however, would say **Sum Romana.**

- A group of men from Greece would say **Sumus Graeci** (*su*-mus *grigh*-kee); "we are Greek." Their wives or daughters would say **Sumus Graecae** (*su*-mus *grigh*-kigh).

- If you want to identify your sister-in-law as Egyptian, you'd say **Est Aegypta** (est igh-*gihp*-tuh); "She is Egyptian." To identify your brother's male friends as German, you'd say **Sunt Germani** (sunt gehr-*mah*-nee); They're German.

With few exceptions, cities and countries are grammatically feminine. Entire groups of people are grammatically masculine. Ninety-nine Roman women and one Roman man would still be called **Romani.**

Talkin' the Talk

Marcus is a young man visiting Rome for the first time from one of the provinces. Julia is the daughter of a Roman senator.

Marcus: **Salve!**
            suhl-way!
            Hello!

Julia:	**Salve! Esne civis?**
	sul-way! *ehs*-neh *kee*-wis?
	Hello! Are you a citizen?
Marcus:	**Sum civis.**
	sum *kee*-wis.
	I am a citizen.
Julia:	**Num es Romanus? Ubi habitas?**
	num ehs ro-*mah*-nus *oo*-bee *huh*-bih-tahs?
	You are not Roman, are you? Where do you live?
Marcus:	**Habito in Gallia. Cur?**
	huh-bih-to ihn *guhl*-lih-ah. kur?
	I live in France. Why?
Julia:	**Es puer Gallus, sum puella Romana. Vale!**
	ehs *pu*-ehr *guhl*-lus, sum pu-*ehl*-luh ro-*ma*-nuh *wuh*-lay!
	You are a French boy, I am Roman girl. Goodbye!
Marcus:	**Vale.**
	wuh-lay.
	Goodbye.

Asking Questions

In Latin, you can indicate that you're asking a question in a couple of ways: You can use an actual interrogative word, such as **cur** (kur; why) or **quo** (kwo; where), or you can attach the suffix **–ne** to the first word of a sentence.

Using –ne

Asking a question can be as simple as attaching the suffix **–ne** to the first word of the sentence. Since the Romans did not use marks of punctuation, this suffix is a clue that says, "Make your voice go up at the end because this is going to be a question."

A basic question might be

Esne civis? (*ehs*-neh *kee*-wis; Are you a citizen?)

In this question, the suffix **–ne** is attached to the "be" verb **es** (es; you are). Refer to the "Being There: Esse (To Be)" section earlier in this chapter for the conjugation of Latin verb **esse** (to be).

Here's a possible answer:

> **Non sum, sed ero.** (non sum, sehd *eh*-ro; I am not, but I shall be.)

Common question words

Following are some of the most commonly used interrogative words:

- ✔ **Ubi** (*oo*-bee; where? or when?): Use **ubi** to ask the location of a person or thing or to ask when something happened. Context usually helps you figure out which meaning is being used.

    Ubi es et ubi eris in Graecia?

    oo-bee ehs eht *oo*-bee *eh*-rihs ihn *grigh*-kih-ah?

    Where are you and when will you be in Greece?

- ✔ **Quo?** (kwo; where?): Use **quo** to ask where someone is going.

    Quo vadis?

    kwo *wah*-dis?

    Where are you going? (Legend has it that St. Peter said this to Jesus when he saw Him in a vision, and this expression became the title of a popular novel and movie.)

- ✔ **Cur?** (kur; why?) Use **cur** to ask the reason for an action.

    Cur eras in Gallia?

    kur *eh*-rahs ihn *guhl*-li-ah?

    Why were you in France?

- ✔ **Quomodo?** (*kwo*-moh-doh; how?) Use **quomodo** to ask in what manner something is done.

    Quomodo aquam portabis?

    kwo-moh-doh *uh*-kwuhm pohr-*tah*-bihs?

    How will you carry the water?

- ✔ **Quid?** (kwihd; what?) Use **quid** when asking about a thing.

    Quid est?

    kwihd ehst?

    What is it?

✔ **Quis?** (kwihs; who?) Use **quis** when asking about a person.

> **Quis est?**
>
> kwihs ehst?
>
> Who is it?

Keep in mind the two words that tell what kind of answer a person expects to receive. **Num** (num) expects the answer no, and **nonne** (*non*-neh) expects the answer yes. A disbelieving citizen might ask,

> **Num Hannibal non est ad portas?**
> num *huhn*-nih-buhl non ehst uhd *pohr*-tahs?
> Surely Hannibal is not at the gates, is he?

A more hopeful question is,

> **Nonne Scipio barbarum superabit?**
> *non*-neh *skee*-pih-oh *buhr*-buh-rum su-peh-*rah*-biht?
> Scipio will defeat the foreigner, won't he?

Words to Know

civis, civis, m/f	kee-wihs, kee-wihs	citizen
puella, puellae, f	pu-*ehl*-luh, pu-*ehl*-ligh	girl
puer, pueri, m	pu-ehr, pu-eh-ree	boy
habito, habitare, habitavi, habitatus	huh-bih-to, huh-bih-*tah*-reh, huh-bih-*tah*-wee, huh-bih-*tah*-tus	to live
salve	suhl-way	hello
vale	wuh-lay	goodbye
saluto, salutare, salutavi, salutatus	suh-loo-to, suh-loo-*tah*-reh, suh-loo-tah-wee, suh-loo-tah-tus	to greet
vir, viri, m	wihr, *wih*-ree	man
femina, feminae, f	fay-mih-nuh, fay-mih-nigh	woman
ubi	oo-bee	where/when
cur	kur	why

The Preposition Proposition

Using prepositions can show the relationship of one object to another. Unlike Latin nouns, Latin prepositions are not declined, so in this way, they're more like English. See Chapter 2 for more information about declensions and noun cases.

To express motion away from an object, general location, or accompaniment, use these prepositions with an ablative-case noun, that is, a noun ending in **–a, –is, –o, –e, –ibus, –u,** or **–ebus.**

- ✔ **ab** (uhb; away from)
- ✔ **ex** (ehks; out of)
- ✔ **de** (day; down from)
- ✔ **in** (ihn; in, on)
- ✔ **cum** (koom; with)

See the following brief example:

> **Cum amico in silva ambulo.**
>
> koom uh-*mee*-ko ihn *sihl*-wah *uhm*-bu-lo.
>
> I am walking with my friend in the forest.

Like the use of *a* or *an* before words beginning with consonants or vowels in English, Latin makes a similar distinction with prepositions. Use **a** (ah) and **e** (ay) before words beginning with consonants, but **ab** (uhb) and **ex** (ehks) before vowels.

If you want to express a spatial relationship or motion toward an object, use the following prepositions and a noun in the accusative case, that is, a noun ending in **–am, –as, –um, –os, –a, –em, –es, –us,** or **–ua.**

- ✔ **in** (ihn; into)
- ✔ **ad** (uhd; to, toward)
- ✔ **circum** (*kihr*-koom; around)
- ✔ **supra** (*su*-prah; above)

Taking all this preposition information together, you can understand something like this:

> **Ex silva ad villam festinabo et cum amico in cameram ambulabo.**
>
> ehks *sihl*-wah uhd *wee*-lum fehs-tee-*nah*-bo eht koom uh-*mee*-ko *kuh*-meh-ruhm uhm-bu-*lah*-bo.
>
> I shall hurry out of the forest toward the house and shall walk into the room with my friend.

City names work a little differently when it comes to prepositions. To show that you are in a particular city, use **–ae** for first-declension nouns and **–i** for second declension. When expressing motion toward a particular city, use **–am** for first declension, **–um** for second declension, and don't use a preposition. When expressing motion away, use **–a** for first declension, **–o** for second declension, and no preposition. Consider this example:

> **Syracusa Brundisium navigabo, sed Romae habito.**
>
> sihr-ah-*koo*-sah brun-*dih*-sih-um nah-wih-*gah*-bo, sehd *ro*-migh *huh*-bih-to.
>
> I shall sail from Syracuse to Brundisium, but I live in Rome.

Playing the Numbers

The ancient Romans were practical people, and while they left the more theoretical mathematics to the Greeks, they did use a numbering system that allowed them to keep track of everything from the slope of an aqueduct to the amount of taxes to be rendered unto Caesar. You can find their words that refer to numbers in the many English derivatives used today. As for Roman numerals, you can't read the copyright of a movie or television show without seeing them.

Counting it down: Cardinal numbers

In Latin, the first three cardinal numbers (one, two, and three) have multiple forms. What form of the number you use depends on the gender of the noun that accompanies it. A masculine noun takes a masculine cardinal number; a feminine noun takes a feminine cardinal number. Table 3-3 shows the forms of the Roman numbers one through three.

Table 3-3	Cardinal Numbers 1, 2, 3		
	Masculine	*Feminine*	*Neuter*
One	unus (*oo*-nus)	una (*oo*-nuh)	unum (*oo*-num)
Two	duo (*du*-oh)	duae (*du*-igh)	duo (*du*-oh)
Three	tres (trays)	tres (trays)	tria (*trih*-uh)

The word for "thousand" also has multiple forms, which, unlike the preceding, have nothing to do with gender. Instead, these forms (singular and plural) indicate how many thousands you're talking about:

✔ To indicate one thousand, you use **mille** (*mihl*-leh).

✔ To indicate more than one thousand, you use **milia** (*mihl*-lih-uh).

All the other number words just use one form, as shown in Table 3-4. (If you're a Latin teacher — or are trying to butter up a Latin teacher — you would say these numbers are *indeclinable*.)

Table 3-4	Cardinal Numbers 4 through 10	
Latin Number	*Pronunciation*	*Translation*
quattuor	*kwuht*-tu-ohr	four
quinque	*kween*-kweh	five
sex	sehks	six
septem	*sehp*-tehm	seven
octo	*ohk*-to	eight
novem	*noh*-wehm	nine
decem	*deh*-kehm	ten

The teen numbers are mostly combinations with **–decim** (*de*-kihm). **Undecim** (*un*-deh-kihm) is eleven, **duodecim** (du-*oh*-deh-kihm) is twelve, **et cetera** (eht *keh*-teh-ruh; and the rest). Interestingly, the words for eighteen and nineteen are **duodeviginti** (du-oh-day-wih-*gihn*-tee) and **undeviginti** (un-day-wih-*gihn*-tee), which literally mean "two down from twenty" and "one down from twenty," respectively.

The remaining numbers up to one hundred use compounds with the suffix **–ginta** (*gihn*-tah). Thirty-six would be **triginta sex** (tree-*gihn*-tah sehks), for example; forty-nine would be **quadraginta novem** (kwuh-drah-*gihn*-tah *noh*-wehm).

After **centum** (*kehn*-tum; one hundred), the numbers use compounds with the suffix **–centi** (*kehn*-tee). You would say, for example, **septingenti quinquaginta tres** (sehpt-*kehn*-tee kween-kwah-*gihn*-tah trays; seven hundred fifty-three) to express the year B.C. in which Rome was built.

"Rome was not built in a day," and this is true. Originally a small village of thatched huts along the Tiber River in central Italy, Rome grew over hundreds of years to become the Eternal City. Tradition has it, however, that the founding date of Rome was April 21, 753 B.C.

Putting things in order: Ordinal numbers

The ordinal numbers are all adjectives. (That is, you use them to describe nouns.) Table 3-5 lists the Latin ordinals and their declensions.

Table 3-5	Latin Ordinal Numbers		
Ordinal	*Masculine*	*Feminine*	*Neuter*
First	primus (*pree*-mus)	prima (*pree*-muh)	primum (*pree*-mum)
Second	secundus (seh-*kun*-dus)	secunda (seh-*kun*-duh)	secundum (seh-*kun*-dum)
Third	tertius (*tehr*-ti-us)	tertia (*tehr*-ti-uh)	tertium (*tehr*-ti-um)
Fourth	quartus (*kwuhr*-tus)	quarta (*kwuhr*-tuh)	quartum (*kwuhr*-tum)
Fifth	quintus (*kween*-tus)	quinta (*kween*-tuh)	quintum (*kween*-tum)
Sixth	sextus (*sehks*-tus)	sexta (*sehks*-tuh)	sextum (*sehks*-tum)
Seventh	septimus (*sehp*-tih-mus)	septima (*sehp*-tih-muh)	septimum (*sehp*-tih-mum)
Eighth	octavus (ohk-*tah*-wus)	octava (ohk-*tah*-wuh)	octavum (ohk-*tah*-wum)
Ninth	nonus (*no*-nus)	nona (*no*-nuh)	nonum (*no*-num)
Tenth	decimus (*deh*-kih-mus)	decima (*deh*-kih-muh)	decimum (*deh*-kih-mum)

You can see that many of the ordinal numbers are similar to the cardinal numbers, but an important difference exists: Whereas only a few of the cardinal numbers have different forms for gender, *all* the preceding ordinal numbers use different forms. So make sure that the gender of the ordinal number you use matches the gender of the noun it describes.

For most other ordinal numbers, use the suffix **–esimus** (eh-sih-mus). For example, a famous murder happened in the **septingentesimus decimus** (sehp-tehn-*keh*-sih-mus *deh*-kih-mus; seven hundred tenth) year from the founding of Rome. That was the year that Julius Caesar met his untimely death at the hands of his colleagues in the Roman senate. (So much for getting yourself named dictator for life. Guess the assassins decided to shorten the term of office.)

The "I's" have it: Roman numerals

Roman numerals are simply a combination of capitalized letters. After you know the letters and the basic rules for addition and subtraction, you're ready to go. Check out these "must know" numerals:

I=1, V=5, X=10, L=50, C=100, D=500, and M=1000

When two numerals stand next to each other, subtract the smaller if it's on the left, but add the smaller if it's on the right. The first Roman emperor, Augustus, lived from LXIII B.C. to A.D. XIV, that is, from 63 B.C. to A.D. 14.

50 (L) + 10 (X) + 3 (III) = 63

10 (X) + 4 (IV) = 14

Talkin' the Talk

In this scene, Publius and his wife Pompeia are talking about the wine business.

Pompeia: **Publi, quot amphoras vini e Foro portabas?**
pu-blee, kwoht *uhm*-foh-rahs *wee*-nee ay *fo*-ro
pohr-*tah*-bahs?
Publius, how many jars of wine were you carrying from the Forum?

Publius: **Duas amphoras porto, Pompeia, sed tres portabam.**
du-ahs *uhm*-foh-rahs *pohr*-to, pohm-*pay*-yuh sehd trays
pohr-*tah*-buhm.
I am carrying two jars, Pompeia, but I was carrying three.

Pompeia: **Ubi est amphora tertia?**
oo-bee ehst *uhm*-foh-ruh *tehr*-tih-uh?
Where is the third jar?

Publius: **Est in stomacho!**
ehst ihn stoh-*muh*-ko!
It is in my stomach!

Fun & Games

Can you identify the modern names for the following ancient locations?

1. Londinium   lohn-*dih*-nih-um   _____

2. Hispania   hih-*spah*-nih-uh   _____

3. Gallia   *guhl*-lih-uh   _____

4. Helvetia   hehl-*weh*-tih-uh   _____

Can you complete each sentence with the correct form of **esse?**

5. Romani _____(are) in Italia.

6. Ubi _____ (will you be?)

7. Quot pueri et puella _____(were) in Foro?

8. _____(I am) Graecus, sed _____ (you are) Aegypti.

See Appendix C for the answers.

Part II
Latin in Action

The 5th Wave   By Rich Tennant

"Stuart — would you like to come up and rap some Vergil for us?"

In this part . . .

You could learn a language without knowing much about the culture it came from, but why would you want to? That'd just be boring. Besides, the Romans were fascinating people who did fascinating things, the effects of which can still be seen and felt today. So to make learning Latin more interesting and fun, this part combines information about the language with info about the Romans. Want to know how the Romans lived, ate, worked, fought, and had fun? It's all right in this part, mixed in with a healthy dose of Latin.

Chapter 4

The Roman Family and Social Structure

*F*rom the modern world all the way back through history to antiquity, family relationships have had deep and abiding ties. When Julius Caesar was conquering the Gauls, he took special pleasure in defeating one tribe just because their people had killed his father-in-law's grandfather.

In fact, ancient family relationships were as complex as many today. Few people outside the upper class, business class, or the military traveled very much, so most people remained in contact with a wide range of family members. A large vocabulary was needed to describe these varied relationships.

Keeping It in the Family

Although the word **familia** (fuh-*mih*-lih-uh), the Latin word for "family," is a first-declension noun, many of the words for particular family members are from the third declension. See the following list to understand what you need to know about the third declension:

✔ Third declension contains nouns of all three genders: masculine, feminine, and neuter. (Head to Chapter 2 if you need a fast and easy explanation of grammatical gender.)

✔ Masculine and feminine nouns of the third declension use the same set of endings as shown in Table 4-1. (Again, if you need a quick explanation of what declensions are and how they work, Chapter 2's the place to go.)

✔ The neuter nouns use different endings (refer to Table 4-1).

Table 4-1	Third-Declension Case Endings			
	Masculine/Feminine		**Neuter**	
Case	**Singular**	**Plural**	**Singular**	**Plural**
Nominative	*	–es	*	–a
Genitive	–is	–um	–is	–um
Dative	–i	–ibus	–i	–ibus
Accusative	–em	–es	*	–a
Ablative	–e	–ibus	–e	–ibus

Here are a couple more things to know about the case endings for third-declension nouns:

✔ The nominative singular of third declension masculine and feminine nouns can have a variety of forms, including **–l, –n, –o, –r, –s,** and **–x.** (See Chapter 2 for an explanation of Latin noun cases.) Table 4-2 shows the complete declension of the masculine noun **pater** (*puh*-tehr; father).

✔ The neuter suffixes are much like the masculine/feminine endings, and the nominative singular has no set form.

To be sure what the correct nominative singular form is, you have to look the word up in a dictionary. The nominative singular is the first form shown in the dictionary entry.

✔ Here's one important difference with neuter endings: Whatever the nominative singular form turns out to be, the accusative singular form is the same. Table 4-3 shows the declension of the neuter word "time," which is **tempus, temporis,** n (*tehm*-pus, *tehm*-poh-rihs).

Table 4-2	Declining a Third-Declension Masculine Noun	
Case	**Singular**	**Plural**
Nominative	pater (*puh*-tehr)	patres (*puh*-trays)
Genitive	patris (*puh*-trihs)	patrum (*puh*-trum)

Case	Singular	Plural
Dative	patri (*puh*-tree)	patribus (*puh*-trih-bus)
Accusative	patrem (puh-trehm)	patres (*puh*-trays)
Ablative	patre (*puh*-treh)	patribus (*puh*-trih-bus)

Table 4-3	Declining a Third-Declension Neuter Noun	
Case	Singular	Plural
Nominative	tempus (*tehm*-pus)	tempora (*tehm*-poh-ruh)
Genitive	temporis (*tehm*-poh-rihs)	temporum (*tehm*-poh-rum)
Dative	tempori (*tehm*-poh-ree)	temporibus (tehm-*poh*-rih-bus)
Accusative	tempus (*tehm*-pus)	tempora (*tehm*-po-ruh)
Ablative	tempore (*tehm*-poh-reh)	temporibus (tehm-*poh*-rih-bus)

Familiarizing yourself with the familia

Several of the words used to identify family members just happen to be third-declension nouns, such as those that follow:

- **pater, patris,** m (*puh*-tehr, *puh*-trihs; father)
- **mater, matris,** f (*mah*-tehr, *mah*-trihs; mother)
- **frater, fratris,** m (*frah*-tehr, *frah*-trihs; brother)
- **soror, sororis,** f (*soh*-rohr, soh-*ro*-rihs; sister)
- **infans, infantis,** m/f (*een*-fahns, een-*fuhn*-tihs; baby)
- **nepos, nepotis,** m (*neh*-pos, neh-*po*-tihs; grandson)
- **neptis, neptis,** f (*nehp*-tihs, *nehp*-tihs; granddaughter)
- **uxor, uxoris,** f (*uks*-ohr, uks-*o*-rihs; wife)
- **coniunx, coniugis,** m (*kohn*-yoonks, *kohn*-yu-gihs; husband)

Here are a couple more folks in the family (these are not third-declension nouns):

- **filia, filiae,** f (*fee*-lih-uh, *fee*-lih-igh; daughter)
- **filius, fili,** m (*fee*-lih-us, *fee*-lee; son)

Keep a Latin dictionary on hand

If you check its dictionary entry, you can always determine the nominative singular form of a noun. The first form in the dictionary is the nominative singular. The second form is the genitive singular. The initial indicates gender. The dictionary entry for the noun "father" looks like this:

> **pater, patris, m** — father (*puh*-tehr, *puh*-trihs)

From this entry, you know that **pater** is the nominative singular form, **patris** is the genitive singular form, and the noun is masculine.

Another little trick: If you know the genitive singular case ending, you can also determine what declension the noun belongs to (information that you need to know if you want to decline nouns properly):

first declension	genitive singular	**–ae**
second declension	genitive singular	**–i**
third declension	genitive singular	**–is**

That's how you know that **pater** is a third-declension noun. (Unless, of course, you decide to memorize what nouns belong to what declension.)

Of course, a Roman family consists of more than just mom, dad, and a couple of kids. See the following listing for a few people outside the nuclear family. (If you've read any Roman history or watched *I, Claudius* or *Gladiator,* you know that they can be just as explosive.) Again, several of these are not third-declension nouns:

- **avia, aviae,** f (*uh*-wih-uh, *uh*-wih-igh; grandmother)
- **avus, avi,** m (*uh*-wus, *uh*-wee; grandfather)
- **amita, amitae,** f (*uh*-mih-tuh, *uh*-mih-tigh; paternal aunt)
- **patruus, patrui,** m (*puh*-tru-us, *puh*-tru-ee; paternal uncle)
- **matertera, materterae,** f (mah-*tehr*-teh-ruh, mah-*tehr*-teh-righ; maternal aunt)
- **avunculus, avunculi,** m (uh-*wun*-ku-lus, uh-*wun*-ku-lee; maternal uncle)
- **patruelis, patruelis,** m (puh-tru-*ay*-lihs, puh-tru-*ay*-lihs; paternal cousin)

Talkin' the Talk

A father (**pater;** *puh*-tehr) and mother (**mater;** *mah*-tehr) are discussing their family.

Pater: **Nepos noster uxorem cupit.**
                  neh-pos *nohs*-tehr uhks-*o*-rehm *ku*-piht.
                  Our grandson wishes for a wife.

Mater:	**Pater filio puellam aptam inveniet.**
	puh-tehr *eh*-yus *fee*-lih-o pu-*ehl*-luhm *uhp*-tuhm ihn-*veh*-nih-eht.
	His father will find his son a suitable girl.
Pater:	**Erat difficile fratri meo ubi coniugem filiae suae petebat.**
	eh-ruht dihf-*fihk*-ih-leh *frah*-tree *meh*-o *oo*-bee *fee*-lih-igh *soo*-igh peh-*tay*-buht.
	It was difficult for my brother when he was seeking a husband for his daughter.
Mater:	**Sed fratris tui filia est non pulchra!**
	sehd *frah*-trihs *tu*-ee ehst non *pul*-chruh!
	But your brother's daughter is not pretty!
Pater:	**Difficultas non erat in puellae pulchritudine.**
	dihf-fih-*kul*-tahs non *eh*-ruht ihn pu-*ehl*-ligh pul-chrih-*too*-dih-neh.
	The difficulty was not in the girl's beauty.
Mater:	**Erantne in urbe non viri?**
	eh-ruhnt-neh ihn *ur*-beh non *wih*-ree?
	Were there no men in the city?
Pater:	**Erant multi viri in urbe, sed in fratris sacculo non multa pecunia.**
	eh-ruhnt *mul*-tee *wih*-ree ihn *ur*-beh, sehd ihn *frah*-trihs *suhk*-ku-lo non *mul*-tuh peh-*koo*-nih-uh.
	There were many men in the city, but in my brother's money pouch there was not much money.

Dial C for murder

The verb **caedo, caedere, cecidi, caesus** (*kigh*-do, *kigh*-deh-reh, *keh*-kee-dee, *kigh*-sus) means to kill, and from it English derives many nouns with the suffix **–cide**. Another third-declension noun is **homo, hominis,** m (*hoh*-mo, *hoh*-mih-nihs), meaning "man" or "human." Combine these two words, and you get the technical term for murder, "homicide." This is a rather general word, however, and other terms are derived from some of the family words in the preceding list to describe particular acts of murder. For example, "patricide" is killing one's father, "fratricide" means to kill one's brother, and "matricide"? Every Latin student knows that's not harming your mattress but killing your mother. Of course, the police aren't likely to arrest you for murdering your bed anyway!

Words to Know

avia, aviae, f	*uh-wih-uh, uh-wih-igh*	grandmother
avus, avi, m	*uh-wus, uh-wee*	grandfather
filia, filiae, f	*fee-lih-uh, fee-lih-igh*	daughter
filius, fili, m	*fee-lih-us, fee-lee*	son
frater, fratris, m	*frah-tehr, frah-trihs*	brother
mater, matris, f	*mah-tehr, mah-trihs*	mother
pater, patris, m	*puh-tehr, puh-trihs*	father
soror, sororis, m	*soh-rohr, soh-ro-rihs*	sister

Gushy stuff: Love and marriage

The ancient Romans had laws and customs concerning marriage just as most cultures do today. For example, in ancient Rome, the bride's father gave a **dos** (dos; dowry) to the groom — one of the more well-known customs. In the case of **repudium** (reh-*pu*-dih-um; divorce), a husband often had to return the **dos** (dos) dowry. Some other terms associated with ancient marriage practices are

- ✔ **sponsalia** (spon-*sah*-lih-uh) the official engagement ceremony
- ✔ **flammeum** (*fluh*-meh-um) the bride's flame-colored veil
- ✔ **ubi tu Gaius, ego Gaia** (*oo*-bee too *gigh*-us *eh*-goh *gigh*-uh) an expression of the bride's submission to her husband. Using the names "Gaius" and "Gaia" like "John Doe" and "Jane Doe," it literally means, "Where you, Gaius [are], I, Gaia [am]."
- ✔ **deductio** (deh-*duk*-tih-o) escorted procession to the groom's house
- ✔ **epithalamium** (eh-pih-thuh-*luh*-mih-um) wedding song sung outside the groom's house
- ✔ **nova nupta** (*noh*-wus *nup*-tuh) bride (literally: new married woman)
- ✔ **novus maritus** (*noh*-wus muh-*ree*-tus) groom (literally: new husband)

Juno was the Roman deity responsible for marriages. For this reason, June was the most popular month for Roman weddings.

Throwing on Meaning with Adjectives

In both Latin and English, adjectives are those words that describe nouns. More literally, they throw more information at a noun. The word *adjective* is derived from the Latin **ad** + **iectus** (uhd + *yehk*-tus), meaning "thrown toward." Adjectives answer questions, such as *which?, what kind of?,* and *how many?*

Take the adjective *nice.* Now, I could wish you a nice day, you and I could enjoy a nice movie, and afterward we could meet our nice friends in a nice restaurant. Sounds nice, doesn't it? No matter what word that *nice* modifies, it never changes its spelling — in English, that is. Latin is different.

Because Latin is an inflected language, adjectives take on different forms to match the nouns they modify. In fact, adjectives must agree with nouns in three ways: gender, case, and number. For more information on gender and case, take a look at Chapter 2. As for the term *number,* don't worry, this isn't math class. *Number* is just the grammatical term that says whether a word is singular or plural.

Understanding first- and second-declension adjectives

Like nouns, adjectives are grouped into declensions. One class of adjectives is the first-and-second-declension type. A good example is the Latin word for "good," which in a dictionary looks like this. (The three forms shown for a Latin adjective represent the nominative singular form for the masculine, feminine, and neuter genders.):

bonus, bona, bonum — good

Adjectives of this type have a masculine form, such as **bonus** (*boh*-nus), a feminine form, such as **bona** (*boh*-nuh), and a neuter form, such as **bonum** (*boh*-num). Adjectives are not grammatical cross-dressers, but they have to be flexible enough in their forms to modify any noun. For example, a good daughter in Latin is **filia bona** (*fee*-lih-uh *boh*-nuh), and a good son is **filius bonus** (*fee*-lih-us *boh*-nus).

Bona Dea mama mia!

During the time of the Roman Republic (509–27 B.C.), the wife of the chief magistrate hosted an all-female festival in honor of the **Bona Dea** (*boh*-nuh *deh*-uh), the Good Goddess. In 62 B.C., this honor fell to Pompeia, the wife of Julius Caesar. A well-known man-about-town named Clodius, however, was apparently having an affair with one of the female guests. To be with her, Clodius dressed as a woman and crashed the party. The orator Cicero found out about it (one wonders how), and blabbed to everyone. Just in case his wife happened to be the target of those affections, Caesar divorced Pompeia shortly after the festival.

If you know that the gender, case, and number of adjectives and nouns must match each other, then you can figure out what would otherwise be some complicated sentences. Take a look at the following:

Servos malos regina timet.

sehr-wos *muh*-los ray-*gee*-nuh *tih*-meht.

This sentence means "The queen fears the bad slaves" or "The bad queen fears the slaves." Which sentence is right depends on what word — **servos** (slaves) or **regina** (queen) — that the adjective **malos** (bad) describes.

You know that the queen is doing the action, because the **–a** suffix is nominative singular, which makes queen (**regina**) the subject. You also know that the slaves (**servos**) are receiving the action, because the **–os** ending indicates accusative plural or the direct object. (Refer to Chapter 2 if this discussion of cases doesn't make sense to you.)

But what do you do with the adjective? **Malos,** a form of the word **malus, mala, malum** (*muh*-lus, *muh*-luh, *muh*-lum), meaning "bad," sits right in the middle of the two nouns. Because Latin word order is less important for understanding meaning than in English, where the adjective is in the sentence doesn't tell you what noun it modifies. So you have to look at its case, gender, and number.

As it turns out, **malos** is in the masculine gender, the accusative case, and the plural number, just like **servos.** Therefore, the sentence reads in English, "The queen fears the bad slaves."

Now, you may be thinking to yourself, "Hallelujah! I just have to look for endings that look the same to figure out which word an adjective modifies."

(**Malos** and **servos** both end in **–os,** after all.) Wrong. The words don't have to look the same; they have to have the same case, gender, and number. Sometimes, they'll look the same; sometimes they won't. Take a look at the following example:

> **Puella matrem bonam amat.**
>
> pu-*ehl*-luh *mah*-trehm *uh*-muht.
>
> The girl loves the good mother.

How do you know **bonam** modifies **matrem** (mother) and not **puella** (girl)? Although **bonam** and **matrem** don't look alike, they share the same case, gender, and number. The adjective **bonam** is the feminine accusative singular of the adjective **bonus, bona, bonum** (good). **Matrem** is the feminine accusative singular of the third-declension noun **mater, matris,** f (mother).

As you try to figure out adjectives, keep the following in mind:

- ✔ Masculine and neuter adjectives use the masculine and neuter endings from second declension.

- ✔ Feminine adjectives use the first-declension suffixes.

To see first- and second-declension endings, head to Chapter 2.

Adjectives don't have to look like the nouns they modify. Clearly **matrem** and **bonam** have two different suffixes. What counts in this case is that both words are feminine accusative singular. Beauty is in the eye of the beholder, the old saying goes, and in the eyes of Latin grammar, these two words match up beautifully.

Although word order is less significant for understanding Latin than it is for comprehending English, Latin does tend to fall into certain patterns. For example, nouns precede the adjectives that modify them.

Look over this helpful list of first- and second-declension adjectives to get yourself started.

- ✔ **bonus, bona, bonum** (*boh*-nus, *boh*-nuh, *boh*-num; good)

- ✔ **gratus, grata, gratum** (*grah*-tus, *grah*-tuh, *grah*-tum; pleasing)

- ✔ **longus, longa, longum** (*lohn*-gus, *lohn*-guh, *lohn*-gum; long)

- ✔ **magnus, magna, magnum** (*muhng*-nus, *muhng*-nuh, *muhng*-num; large)

- ✔ **malus, mala, malum** (*muh*-lus, *muh*-luh, *muh*-lum; bad)

- ✔ **multus, multa, multum** (*mul*-tus, *mul*-tuh, *mul*-tum; much, many)

✔ **novus, nova, novum** (*noh*-wus, *noh*-wuh, *noh*-wum; new)

✔ **parvus, parva, parvum** (*puhr*-wus, *puhr*-wuh, *puhr*-wum; small)

✔ **pulcher, pulchra, pulchrum** (*pul*-chehr, *pul*-chruh, *pul*-chrum; beautiful, handsome)

Using third-declension adjectives

You need to know one other basic type of adjective: the third-declension kind. Just as you can always recognize first- and second-declension adjectives by dictionary forms that end in **–a** and **–um,** you can spot third-declension adjectives by a dictionary form ending in **–is.** Keep in mind, though, that the **–is** ending doesn't always appear in the same place. As long as it's there, though, you've got yourself a third-declension adjective. Take a gander at these examples:

✔ **acer, acris, acre** (*ah*-kehr, *ah*-krihs, *ah*-kreh; sharp)

Adjectives like this have three nominative singular forms — masculine, feminine, and neuter — just as first- and second-declension adjectives do. Notice that the telltale **–is** suffix is on the feminine form.

✔ **fortis, forte** (*fohr*-tihs, *fohr*-teh; brave)

Adjectives like this have only two forms because the nominative singular masculine and feminine forms are exactly the same, so most dictionaries list them as just one form. Here the **–is** ending is on the first — masculine/feminine — form. The second entry is the nominative-singular-neuter form.

✔ **atrox, atrocis** (*uh*-troks, uh-*tro*-kihs; fierce)

Occasionally you'll see adjectives with only two dictionary forms, but with the **–is** suffix on the second word. When the **–is** is on the second of the two dictionary entries, it means that the nominative-singular-masculine, -feminine, and -neuter forms are exactly the same. The second entry is actually the genitive singular for all genders.

The suffixes for third-declension adjectives are similar to regular third-declension noun endings (refer Table 4-1) with just a few exceptions. Table 4-4 shows all possible third-declension adjective suffixes.

Table 4-4	Third-Declension Adjective Endings			
	Masculine/Feminine		**Neuter**	
Case	*Singular*	*Plural*	*Singular*	*Plural*
Nominative	*	–es	–e	–ia
Genitive	–is	–ium	–is	–ium

| | Masculine/Feminine | | Neuter | |
Case	Singular	Plural	Singular	Plural
Dative	–i	–ibus	–i	–ibus
Accusative	–em	–es	–e	–ia
Ablative	–i	–ibus	–i	–ibus

Remember that adjectives don't have to look like the nouns they modify. They only need to match according to gender, case, and number.

One third-declension adjective is **familiaris, familiare** (fuh-mih-lih-*ah*-rihs, fuh-mih-lih-*ah*-reh), which means "belonging to a family." English gets the derivative "familiar" from this adjective, and in Roman times, it came to be associated with a family's household slaves or with close friends of a family.

Talkin' the Talk

In this scene, Titus and Quinta are talking about new additions to their families.

Quinta: **Familiam felicem habemus. Familia nostra infantes novos hodie accipiet.**
fuh-*mih*-lih-um *fay*-lih-kehm huh-*bay*-mus.
fuh-*mih*-lih-uh *nohs*-truh ihn-*fahn*-tays *noh*-wos
ho-dih-ay uhk-*kih*-pih-eht.
We have a happy family. Our family will welcome new babies today.

Titus: **Suntne fili aut filiae?**
sunt-neh *fee*-lee owt *fee*-lih-igh?
Are they sons or daughters?

Quinta: **Patruus et amita mea filios geminos habebunt. Sunt patrueles parvi mei.**
pah-tru-us eht *ah*-mih-tuh *meh*-uh *fee*-lih-os
geh-mih-nos huh-*bay*-bunt. sunt puh-tru-*eh*-lays
puhr-wee *meh*-ee.
My uncle and aunt on my father's side will have twins. They are my little cousins.

Titus: **Avus et avia mea quoque hominem parvum accipiet.**
ah-wus eht *ah*-wih-uh *meh*-uh *kwoh*-kweh
hoh-mih-nehm *puhr*-wum uhk-*kih*-pih-eht.
My grandfather and grandmother will also welcome
a little person.

Quinta: **Materteram novam habebis?**
mah-tehr-*teh*-ruhm *noh*-wuhm huh-*bay*-bihs?
Will you have a new aunt?

Titus: **Minime. Avunculus meus e bello venit.**
mih-nih-meh. ah-*wun*-ku-lus *meh*-us ay *behl*-lo
weh-niht.
No. My uncle is coming from the war.

Quinta: **Avum ingentem habes, sed filius avi tui est parvulus.**
Est vere "avunculus."
ah-wum ihn-*gehn*-tehm *huh*-bays, sehd *fee*-lih-us *ah*-
wee ehst puhr-*woo*-lus. ehst *weh*-reh "ah-*wun*-kulus."
You have a big grandfather, but your grandfather's
son is quite small. He is truly your "little grandfather."

Words to Know

bonus, bona, bonum	*boh*-nus, *boh*-nuh, *boh*-num	good
gratus, grata, gratum	*grah*-tus, *grah*-tuh, *grah*-tum	pleasing
magnus, magna, magnum	*muhng*-nus, *muhng*-nuh, *muhng*-num	large
malus, mala, malum	*muh*-lus, *muh*-luh, *muh*-lum	bad
multus, multa, multum	*mul*-tus, *mul*-tuh, *mul*-tum	much, many
novus, nova, novum	*noh*-wus, *noh*-wuh, *noh*-wum	new
fortis, forte	*fohr*-tihs, *fohr*-teh	brave
atrox, atrocis	*uh*-troks, *uh*-tro-kihs	fierce

Perfecting the Past and the Future

In Chapter 2, you can read about three basic verb tenses: the present, the future, and a past tense called the imperfect. This section shows you the remaining three tenses in Latin, two more past tenses, and another future called the future perfect. Another future? And it's perfect? You probably never thought grammar could sound so hopeful!

Attaining perfection: Perfect tense

In Latin, the imperfect tense (see Chapter 2) shows incomplete action in the past. The perfect tense, on the other hand, shows completed past action. The difference between imperfect and perfect tenses is like the difference between a videotape and photograph. They both show actions that happened in the past, but the video shows ongoing activity, whereas the photo is a complete picture of what happened.

The perfect-tense endings are the same for all Latin verbs, as you can see in Table 4-5.

Table 4-5	Perfect-Tense Personal Endings		
Singular Ending	*Meaning*	*Plural Ending*	*Meaning*
–i	I	–imus	we
–isti	you	–istis	you
–it	he, she, it	–erunt	they

No matter what conjugation a verb belongs to (again, see Chapter 2 for details on verb conjugation), you go to the third dictionary entry to find the stem. Take the verb for "to take," whose principal parts are

capio, capere, cepi, captus (*kuh*-pih-o, *kuh*-peh-reh, *kay*-pee, *kuhp*-tus)

In the perfect tense, the conjugation of this word looks like this:

Singular	*Plural*
cepi	cepimus
cepisti	cepistis
cepit	ceperunt

Is this what the afterlife is all about?

In 63 B.C., the chief Roman magistrate Cicero put five citizens to death for their involvement in a conspiracy to overthrow the government. After they were strangled in the Tullianum, a dismal, subterranean execution chamber, Cicero proclaimed to the waiting crowd, **"Vixerunt!"** (weeks-*ay*-runt) **Vivo, vivere, vixi, victus** (*wee*-wo, *wee*-weh-reh, *weeks*-ee, *week*-tus) mean "to live," so his pronouncement in the perfect tense let everyone know, "The conspirators have lived!" By stating that the action of their lives has been completed, Cicero was politely saying, "They're dead!"

And speaking of the dead, the ancient Romans had interesting customs about honoring the dearly departed. One custom involved making a wax mask, an **imago** (ih-*mah*-go) of the deceased person. These masks were kept in the atrium of the house to remind you of your ancestors. The masks were then removed and carried in the funeral procession of the next family member to pass away, symbolizing the spirits of the ancestors who would welcome this new spirit to the underworld.

You can render the Latin perfect tense into English in several ways. You can use the helping words "has" and "have" — I have taken; you have taken, and so on — or you can use the simple English past tense — he took, they took, and so on. Notice in this next example how the imperfect tense differs from the perfect.

> **Aratrum trahebam ubi vocavisti.**
>
> uh-*rah*-trum truh-*hay*-buhm uh-bee woh-kah-*wihs*-tee.
>
> I was dragging the plough when you called.

Going beyond perfect: Pluperfect tense

Imagine a scene that goes like this: After the general had shouted, the soldiers fought. Can you see the action in your mind? Good. You have a scene completely set in the past, and you have two separate actions, shouting and fighting. Which happened first? The shouting, obviously, and that's what the pluperfect tense is all about — no, not shouting, but happening first.

The name of this tense provides the clue to its meaning. Combine the words **plus** (ploos; more) with **per** and **fectus,** and you get pluperfect, or the "more-than-perfect" tense. The pluperfect tense indicates an action that takes place *more* in the past or prior to another past action.

Like the perfect tense, the pluperfect tense uses the same set of personal endings for all verbs, regardless of their conjugations (see Table 4-6).

Table 4-6	Pluperfect-Tense Personal Endings		
Singular Ending	*Meaning*	*Plural Ending*	*Meaning*
–eram	I	–eramus	we
–eras	you	–eratis	you
–erat	he, she, it	–erant	they

Pluperfect forms use the third dictionary entry to form the stem. Consider the verb "to give," whose principal parts are as follows:

do, dare, dedi, datus (do, *duh*-reh, *deh*-dee, *duh*-tus)

Here's how this word is conjugated in the pluperfect tense:

Singular	*Plural*
dederam	dederamus
dederas	dederatis
dederat	dederant

A class action

Clodius was angry at Cicero for telling everyone that Clodius had dressed as a woman to crash the party of Caesar's wife. (Can you blame him?) When Cicero later executed several conspirators, he failed to give them a trial first, and Clodius found his revenge. Clodius was a patrician (of the highest social class), but he changed his status to plebeian so that he could get elected as a tribune and pass a bill calling for Cicero's exile. (See Chapter 9 for more on Roman government.)

This was a significant act for Clodius because social class meant everything in those days. Roman citizens fell into one of two basic classes: the *patricians,* who could trace their ancestry to the **patres** (*puh*-trays; fathers), founders of Rome, and the *plebeians*. One subdivision of the plebeians was the equestrian class comprised of wealthy business people. The equestrians were originally those rich enough to afford their own horse — **equus** (*eh*-kwus) — when fighting in the army.

Use the helping word *had* to render the pluperfect tense into English ("I had given," "you had given," "they had given," and so on). Watch the change of tenses carefully in this sentence:

Post Cicero Clodium e domu Caesaris expulerat, Clodius Ciceronem ex urbe expulit.

pohst *kih*-keh-ro *klo*-dih-um ay *doh*-moo *kigh*-suh-rihs ehks-*pu*-leh-ruht, *klo*-dih-us kih-keh-*ro*-nehm ehks *ur*-beh *ehks*-pu-liht.

After Cicero had driven Clodius from Caesar's house, Clodius drove Cicero from the city.

Finishing someday: Future-perfect tense

The last tense to talk about in Latin is the future perfect. This tense describes action to be completed in the future. It's different from the simple-future tense in that the future only makes a prediction about an action. Future perfect makes a statement about an action's fulfillment. For example, I can predict that you'll like this book. But I can be a bit more bold and say, "When you finish this book, you will have learned plenty about Latin." At least that's what the publisher hopes will happen!

One reason that the perfect, pluperfect, and future-perfect tenses are often presented together is that they all use the third dictionary entry to form the stem, and, given the tense, they all use the same set of personal endings no matter what conjugation the verb is. Take a look at the future-perfect endings in Table 4-7.

Table 4-7	Future Perfect Tense Personal Endings		
Singular Ending	**Meaning**	**Plural Ending**	**Meaning**
–ero	I	–erimus	we
–eris	you	–eritis	you
–erit	he, she, it	–erint	they

A sample verb in the future-perfect tense is the verb meaning "to conquer."

vinco, vincere, vici, victus (*wihn*-ko, *wihn*-keh-reh, *wee*-kee, *wihk*-tus)

Here is this verb conjugated:

Singular	*Plural*
vicero	vicerimus
viceris	viceritis
vicerit	vicerint

The helping words for future perfect in English are "shall have" and "will have," as in "I shall have conquered," "they will have conquered," and so on. The following dialogue helps you understand all six of the Latin verb tenses.

Talkin' the Talk

A Roman **frater** (*frah*-tehr; brother) and **soror** (*soh*-rohr; sister) discuss an upcoming journey. Notice how verb tense changes in this conversation.

Frater: **Cupiebasne ad villam aviae iter longum facere?**
ku-pih-ay-*bah*-sneh uhd *wee*-lum *uh*-wih-igh *ih*-tehr *lohng*-num *fuh*-keh-reh?
Were you wanting to make the long journey to grandmother's house?

Soror: **Illic proximo anno navigavi quod neptes omnes invitaverat.**
ihl-leek *prohks*-ih-mo *uhn*-no nah-wih-*gah*-wee kwohd *nehp*-tays *ohm*-nays ihn-wee-*tah*-weh-ruht.
I sailed there last year because she had invited all her granddaughters.

Frater: **Habesne in animo redire?**
huh-*bay*-sneh ihn *uh*-nih-mo reh-*dee*-reh?
Are you planning (literal: Do you have it in mind) to return?

Soror: **Redibo ubi officia mea hic confecero.**
reh-*dee*-bo *oo*-bee ohf-*fih*-kih-uh *meh*-uh heek kon-*fay*-keh-ro.
I shall return when I shall have completed my chores here.

Words to Know

iter, itineris, n	*ih-tehr, ih-tih-neh-rihs*	journey
imago, imaginis, f	*ih-mah-go, ih-mah-gih-nihs*	wax mask
omnis, omne	*ohm-nihs, ohm-neh*	all
do, dare, dedi, datus	*do, duh-reh, deh-dee, duh-tus*	to give
facio, facere, feci, factus	*fuh-kih-o, fuh-keh-reh, fay-kee, fuhk-tus*	to make
vinco, vincere, vici, victus	*wihn-ko, wihn-keh-reh, wee-kee, wihk-tus*	to conquer

Fun & Games

Play the dating game! Who is most likely to be married to each of the people listed?

1. avus

    a. filia   b. avia   c. matertera   d. neptis

2. matertera

    a. avunculus   b. frater   c. pater   d. nepos

3. pater

    a. neptis   b. filia   c. mater   d. matertera

4. uxor

    a. patruelis   b. pater   c. patruus   d. coniunx

See Appendix C for the answers.

Chapter 5

Food and Housing in Roman Life

· ·

In This Chapter

▶ Handling irregular verbs

▶ Understanding Roman dining practices

▶ Exploring typical Roman foods

▶ Understanding Roman housing

· ·

People often associate Italy with the finer things in life, such as high fashion, cultural treasures, and of course, Latin! Another association people make with Italy is food. You can find some of the best food in the world in tiny villages and major metropolitan locations throughout the Italian peninsula. On the other hand, not all Italian food is gourmet. On one particular student tour of Rome, Pompeii, and Florence, some adults, expecting to enjoy five-star quality food, were disappointed. Because it was a student tour, however, dinner often meant a pizza stand outside the Colosseum. Hey, you get what you pay for!

The situation was similar in the ancient world. You could enjoy rare delicacies, such as turbot fit for an emperor, or seek the strongest fish sauce you could find to cover up the taste of bad meat. Perhaps you might enjoy the finest dinner, complete with a drinking party at the end, or grab a bite at a fast-food stand in the Forum. Then, as now, quite a variety of foods was available along with different ways to eat them.

Living to Eat and Eating to Live

The Roman grammarian Quintillian wrote,

> **Non ut edam vivo, sed ut vivam edo.** (*Institutio Oratoria,* IX.3.85)
>
> non ut *eh*-duhm *wee*-wo sehd ut *wee*-wuhm *eh*-do.
>
> I do not live to eat, but I eat to live.

This is a great idea, but despite the Roman desire to keep things simple and frugal, luxury in food ended up right alongside the humble. In this section, you can find out all about food **ab ovo usque ad mala** (uhb *o*-wo *oos*-kweh uhd *mah*-luh) as the Romans used to say, "from the egg to the apples."

Living by bread alone

Vergil, the great Latin poet, told of Rome's beginnings in his *Aeneid:* Aeneas, the Trojan hero who had fled Troy in flames, and his soldiers relaxed around the cook fires and stretched out in the grass after dinner one night.

> **Implentur veteris Bacchi pinquisque ferinae.** (*Aeneid,* I.215)
>
> ihm-*plehn*-tuhr *weh*-teh-rihs *buhk*-chee pihn-*gwuihs* kweh feh-*ree*-nigh.
>
> They are filled with old wine and rich venison.

Sounds like a carnivore's dream, doesn't it? This picture is misleading, however, if you take it to mean that expensive wine and rich meat formed the basis of the ancient Roman diet. In fact, the cornerstone of the Roman diet was grain. From fodder for animals to porridge to cakes and breads, the grain stalk was literally the staff of life for the ancient Romans. Some of the basic words associated with this most basic of foods are

- **far, farris,** n (fahr, *fuhr*-rihs; wheat)
- **farina, farinae,** f (fuh-*ree*-nuh, fuh-*ree*-nigh; ground wheat)
- **puls, pultis,** f (puls, *pul*-tihs; wheat porridge)
- **hordeum, hordei,** n (*hohr*-deh-um, *hohr*-deh-ee; barley)
- **frumentum, frumenti,** n (froo-*mehn*-tum, froo-*mehn*-tee; grain)
- **placenta, placentae,** f (pluh-*kehn*-tuh, pluh-*kehn*-tigh; cake)
- **panis, panis,** m (*pah*-nihs, *pah*-nihs; bread)
- **mola, molae,** f (*moh*-luh, *moh*-ligh; sacrificial grain)

Although **mola** (sacrificial grain) had only ritual uses, **puls** (wheat porridge) was fit for both humans and sacrificial chickens. And just to show how essential grain was to the Roman diet, the word **frumentum,** which is the generic word for "grain," became synonymous with food itself.

Feeding veggies to an empire

For ordinary people, vegetables were the most common type of food along with grain-based products. Certain vegetables that the modern world takes for granted, however, were unknown to the Romans. Among these **holera incognita** (*hoh*-leh-ruh ihn-*kohg*-nih-tuh; unknown veggies) were the potato and the tomato.

Still, if **Petrus Cuniculus** (*peh*-trus ku-*nee*-ku-lus; Peter Rabbit), were to wear a toga, these would be some of his favorite foods:

- ✔ **holus, holeris,** n (*hoh*-lus, *hoh*-leh-rihs; vegetable)
- ✔ **caepa, caepae,** f (*kigh*-puh, *kigh*-pigh; onion)
- ✔ **beta, betae,** f (*bay*-tuh, *bay*-tigh; beet)
- ✔ **radix, radicis,** f (*rah*-deeks, rah-*dee*-kihs; radish)
- ✔ **alium, ali,** n (*ah*-lih-um, *ah*-lee; garlic)
- ✔ **phaselus, phaseli,** m (fuh-*say*-lus, fuh-*say*-lee; bean)
- ✔ **cicer, ciceris,** n (*kih*-kehr, *kih*-keh-rihs; chickpea)

In English slang, a "tomato" refers to an attractive woman. Some Latin vegetables also have unlikely double meanings. For example, the poet Catullus wrote about a boat called a **phaselus** (fuh-*say*-lus; bean), presumably because it was bean-shaped. And who was the greatest orator in first-century Rome? It was Mr. Chick-pea himself, Marcus Tullius **Cicero.**

Going whole hog with meat

On one trip to Italy, some Americans entered a restaurant and proceeded to order what they thought was a complete meal. One American ordered soup and pizza, another American ordered salad and pasta. A few minutes later, the waiter returned to convey the chef's confusion. Because all those items were considered appetizers and no one had ordered any meat, the chef didn't know what to fix first!

While the ancient Romans didn't consider meat to be the essential meal item that Italians do today, there was still quite a variety to choose from. One advantage to the lack of modern refrigeration meant that if you were going to eat meat, you were going to eat it fresh. (After all, the best that you could do to preserve food was to salt it, put it in a clay jar and let it sit in a cool stream, or if you were lucky, pack it in some snow). Among the more common items in the meat group were

- ✔ **pullus, pulli,** m (*pul*-lus, *pul*-lee; chicken)
- ✔ **ovum, ovi,** n (*o*-wum, *o*-wee; egg)
- ✔ **vitulina, vitulinae,** f (wih-too-*lee*-nuh, wih-too-*lee*-nigh; veal)

- **piscis, piscis,** m (*pihs*-kihs, *pihs*-kihs; fish)

- **mullus, mulli,** m (*mul*-lus, *mul*-lee; mullet)

- **ostrea, ostreae,** f (*ohs*-treh-uh, *ohs*-treh-igh; oyster)

The Romans referred to wild game in general as **fera, ferae,** f (*feh*-ruh, *feh*-righ) when it was still alive, but as **caro, carnis,** f (*kuh*-ro, *kuhr*-nihs) when it was on the dinner table. Likewise, as long as a pig could say **Oinc!** he was known as **porcus, porci,** m (*pohr*-kus, *pohr*-kee), but when he turned into dinner, he became **porcina, porcinae,** f (pohr-*kee*-nuh, pohr-*kee*-nigh).

Romans with a few more **denarii** (day-*nah*-rih-ee; a unit of money) in their pockets might spring for some of these fancier food items:

- **phasiana, phasianae,** f (fah-sih-*ah*-nuh, fah-sih-*ah*-nigh; pheasant)

- **perdix, perdicis,** m/f (*pehr*-deeks, pehr-*dee*-kihs; partridge)

- **coturnix, coturnicis,** f (koh-*tur*-neeks, koh-tur-*nee*-kihs; quail)

- **pavo, pavonis,** m (*pah*-wo, pah-*wo*-nihs; peacock)

- **grus, gruis,** m/f (groos, *gru*-ihs; crane)

Here's another Roman delicacy: stuffed dormouse, or **glis, gliris,** m (glees, *glee*-rihs). Yes, dormouse. As in rodent.

This is getting a little fruity

Fruits also played a major role in the eating habits of the Romans. They enjoyed native Italian fruits, such as figs and grapes, as well as fruit from other regions of their world and began growing them in Italy. The following list gives you a taste for some of the more common Roman fruits.

- **ficus, fici,** f (*fee*-kus, *fee*-kee; fig)

- **uva, uvae,** f (*oo*-wuh, *oo*-wigh; grape)

- **morum, mori,** n (*mo*-rum, *mo*-ree; mulberry)

- **pirum, piri,** n (*pih*-rum, *pih*-ree; pear)

- **palmula, palmulae,** f (*puhl*-mu-luh, *puhl*-mu-ligh; date)

- **cerasus, cerasi,** f (*keh*-ruh-sus, *keh*-ruh-see; cherry)

- **malum, mali,** n (*mah*-lum, *mah*-lee; apple)

- **malum Persicum, mali Persici,** n (*mah*-lum *pehr*-sih-koom *mah*-lee *pehr*-sih-kee; peach, literally: Persian apple)

Please pass the ketchup!

The ancient Romans loved to doctor the taste of food with little extras. For example, **garum, gari,** n (*guh*-rum, *guh*-ree) was a fermented fish sauce that could be put on just about anything. Simply let your fish sit in a stone pot for several days until it starts to liquefy, and you've got some good **garum.** Be sure to specify if you want extra chunky!

Then, as now, salt was an important condiment for flavoring and preserving. For the Romans, **sal, salis,** m (sahl, *suh*-lihs; salt) had more than just culinary uses. This word doubled for "wit," without which you couldn't have a good conversation. The poet Catullus invited his friend Fabullus to dinner, but only on the condition that Fabullus bring all the food and **sal.** Don't you think Fabullus used some "salty" language to talk about such a cheap friend?

Not only did the Romans like to spice it up a little, but they also liked it sweet, and by "it" I mean everything. They even liked to sweeten their wine! Of course, no little pink or blue packets of sugar sat on the table. Instead, they used **mel, mellis,** n (mehl, *mehl*-lihs; honey), to sweeten the deal.

Potent potables

You're sitting at a senator's dinner table, and the host has just asked your opinion on the emperor's new tax plan. Suddenly a piece of **pavo cum garo** (*pah*-wo koom *guh*-ro) — that's peacock with fish sauce to you and me — gets stuck in your throat. What do you do? Looks like it's time for a drink!

Chances are, you would reach for a glass of **vinum, vini,** n (*wee*-num, *wee*-nee), which is to say, a glass of wine. To drink **lac, lactis,** n (luhk, *luhk*-tihs), or milk, was to engage in low-class, almost barbaric behavior. Of course, you could always have water, or **aqua, aquae,** f (*uh*-kwuh, *uh*-kwigh) if the wine ran out.

Aawww . . . you're my little honeybee

Do you know anyone named Melissa? Is she as sweet as her name implies? This English name is actually a Latin spelling of a Greek word that means *honeybee*. For that matter, you probably know some other commonly used Latin names.

The name *Gregory,* for example, suggests someone who likes to be around herds (whether of animals or people is up to the individual). And Amanda? This Latin name literally means, "She who must be loved."

But what kind of wine? Wine aficionados today have hundreds of selections to choose from, and although the wine list wasn't so varied in ancient times, it still contained several options. You could choose between Greek wines and Italian wines. Here are a few more options:

- You could drink **mustum, musti,** n (*mus*-tum, *mus*-tee) young, unfermented wine.

- If you wanted to become inebriated in a hurry, you'd drink **merum, meri,** n (*meh*-rum, *meh*-ree), which was straight wine — that is, wine than hadn't been cut with water. (Most Romans usually drank wine mixed with water.)

- You could also choose from the expensive wines, which were known by the regions that produced them. Among some of the most noted were the **Setinum** (say-*tee*-num), wine from the town of Setia, **Caecubum** (*kigh*-ku-bum), wine that came from the Caecuban region south of Rome, and **Falernum** (fuh-*lehr*-num), wine from the region of northern Campania.

Following is the present-tense conjugation of the Latin word meaning "to drink."

Singular	Plural
bibo	bibimus
bibis	bibitis
bibit	bibunt

Through the literary device known as *metonymy,* a particular word or name comes to stand for another item. As the Roman god of wine, Bacchus, came to be synonymous with wine itself.

Talkin' the Talk

A **pistor** (*pee*-stohr; baker) helps an **ancilla** (*uhn*-kihl-luh; slave-girl) make a purchase for her mistress.

Ancilla:	**Domina mea me panem emere cupit.**
	doh-mih-nuh *meh*-uh may *pah*-nehm *eh*-meh-reh *ku*-piht.
	My mistress wants me to buy some bread.

Pistor:	**Quot homines cenabunt?**
	kwot *hoh*-mih-nays kay-*nah*-bunt?
	How many people will be having dinner?

Ancilla:	**Dominus epulas magnas donat. Viginti homines aderunt.** *doh*-mih-nus *eh*-puh-lahs *muhng*-nahs *do*-nuht. wee-*gihn*-tee *hoh*-mih-nays *ah*-deh-runt. The master is giving a great banquet. Twenty people will be there.
Pistor:	**Tibi panem et placentas cum melle vendam.** *tih*-bih *pah*-nehm eht pluh-*kehn*-tahs koom *mehl*-leh *wayn* duhm. I shall sell you bread and cakes with honey.
Ancilla:	**Bene. Tum vinum emam. Ubi Romani cenant, semper bibunt.** *beh*-neh. tuhm *wee*-num *eh*-muhm. *u*-bih ro-*mah*-nee *kay*-nahnt, *sehm*-pehr *bih*-bunt. Good. Then I shall buy some wine. When Romans dine, they always drink.

Words to Know

ancilla, ancillae, f	uhn-*kihl*-luh, uhn-*kihl*-ligh	slave-girl
domina, dominae, f	*doh*-mih-nuh, *doh*-mih-nigh	mistress
dominus, domini, m	*doh*-mih-nus, *doh*-mih-nee	master
bibo, bibere, bibi, bibitus	*bih*-bo, *bih*-beh-reh, *bih*-bee, *bih*-bih-tus	to drink
ceno, cenare, cenavi, cenatus	*kay*-no, kay-*nah*-reh, kay-*nah*-wee, kay-*nah*-tus	to dine
emo, emere, emi, emptus	*eh*-mo, eh-*meh*-reh, *ay*-mee, *ehmp*-tus	to buy

Dining Practices

With all those temptingly delectable items, like stuffed dormouse, or **glis, gliris,** m (glees, *glee*-rihs), and liquefied fish, you'd think that the Romans would have spent every waking hour stuffing themselves. But, of course, they didn't.

In this section, you can find out about Roman eating habits, including a good place to stop off for a drink the next time you travel back to the era of the Caesars.

Three squares a day

Like many folks in the western world today, the Romans ate three meals a day: breakfast, lunch, and dinner. Following is the future-tense conjugation of the Latin word meaning "to dine."

Singular	Plural
cenabo	cenabimus
cenabis	cenabitis
cenabit	cenabunt

The breakfast of (Roman) champions

If the Roman day began at all with food, it was usually a light meal called a **ientaculum, ientaculi,** n (*yayn*-tah-ku-lum, yayn-*tah*-ku-lee; breakfast). This usually consisted of no more than bread with **fructus, fructus,** m (*frook*-tus, *frook*-toos; fruit) and **caseus, casei,** m (*kah*-seh-us, *kah*-seh-ee; cheese).

The Latin lunch

Around midday, it was time for **prandium, prandi,** n (*pruhn*-dih-um, *pruhn*-ee), or lunch. Like breakfast, lunch was a light meal. A lunch menu would include such foods as eggs, fish, vegetables, and wine.

Feasting off the fercula — dinner

Evening saw the main meal of the day, called **cena, cenae,** f (*kay*-nuh, *kay*-nigh). A formal **cena** was comprised of three parts, beginning with **gustatio, gustationis,** f (gus-*tah*-tih-o, gus-tah-tih-*o*-nihs; appetizer). For this first course, the Romans enjoyed eggs, fish, and salad — **acetaria, acetariorum,** n (uh-kay-*tah*-rih-uh, uh-kay-tah-rih-*o*-rum), and they usually drank wine mixed with honey, a beverage known as **mulsum, mulsi,** n (*mul*-sum, *mul*-see).

Following the **gustatio** was the **cena** itself. A **ferculum, ferculi,** n (*fehr*-ku-lum, *fehr*-ku-lee) was a dinner tray, and the **cena** could involve as many as seven separate **fercula,** each carrying a specific food item. The **caput cenae** (*kuh*-puht *kay*-nigh), main dish (literally, head of the dinner), was often a whole roasted animal of some sort.

Secundae mensae (seh-*kun*-digh *mayn*-sigh; second tables) signaled the beginning of dessert. At this point, slaves brought in new **fercula** (trays) loaded with various **fructus** (fruits).

Some elaborate **cenae** involved one more event after the **secundae mensae.** This was the drinking party — the **comissatio, comissationis,** f (ko-mihs-*sah*-tih-o, ko-mihs-sah-tih-*o*-nihs). Unlike a college fraternity party, the object wasn't necessarily to become as inebriated as possible in the shortest amount of time. After a roll of the dice, a **magister bibendi** (muh-*gihs*-tehr bih-*behn*-dee) was chosen. By appointing a certain ratio of water to wine to be mixed in the cups, this so-called "master of the drinking" then decided the strength of the wine to be drunk.

A counterpart to the Latin **comissatio** was the Greek *symposium*. This, too, was a drinking party, but it often turned into a philosophical discussion.

Minding your manners around the mensa

Just like people today, the Romans ate some of their meals at home and ate others out.

Dining at home

Where in the home you ate depended on the occasion. If you were eating with the family, you would most likely take your meals in the **atrium, atri,** n (ah-*trih*-um, *ah*-tree) — the entry hall of the house. This would be comparable to eating in a breakfast nook in many homes today.

For more formal occasions, however, the slaves arranged **lecti** (*lehk*-tee; couches) in the dining room, called the **triclinium, triclini,** n (tree-*klee*-nih-um, tree-*klee*-nee). The Latin word **triclinium** comes from the fact that three people reclined on each couch, and there were usually three couches around each **mensa, mensae,** f (*mayn*-suh, *mayn*-sigh) — table. Slaves then brought dishes to and from the **culina, culinae,** f (ku-*lee*-nuh, ku-*lee*-nigh) — kitchen — where everything was prepared.

Only the men reclined at a formal Roman dinner. The women sat in chairs or ate in a separate room altogether.

Eating out

For the Roman on the go, other dining options were available. Excavations at the site of Pompeii, the city buried by the eruption of Mt. Vesuvius in A.D. 79, for example, have turned up fast-food restaurants, including petrified food remains! The **thermopolium, thermopoli,** n (thehr-moh-*po*-lih-um, thehr-moh-*po*-lee; hot food stand) involved large circular containers set into a marble counter, like a modern buffet, from which you could order what you wanted.

Those who traveled a lot could go to the **taberna, tabernae,** f (tuh-*behr*-nuh, tuh-*behr*-nigh). Although the English derivative of this word is "tavern," the **taberna** was more than a watering hole. It offered food and drinks, as well as a place to spend the night.

The poet Catullus wrote a poem addressed to and attacking a **salax taberna** (*suh*-lahks tuh-*behr*-nuh) — a "salacious tavern." The **taberna** incurred the wrath of his poison pen because it had become the hangout of Clodia Metella, the woman who dumped him.

Following is the present-tense conjugation of the Latin word for "to buy."

Singular	*Plural*
emo	emimus
emis	emitis
emit	emunt

Weapons of attack, or fun with forks

The preceding sections cover the basics of the Roman diet and dining habits, this section covers utensils. The word "utensil" itself comes from the Latin adjective **utensilis, utensile** (oo-*tayn*-sih-lihs, oo-*tayn*-sih-leh), meaning "useful," and what could be more useful for cutting up a tender **perdix** (*pehr*-deeks; ostrich) than a nice, sharp **cultellus** (kul-*tehl*-lus; knife)? The following words show you how to attack any Roman meal:

- **cultellus, cultelli,** m (kuhl-*tehl*-lus, kuhl-*tehl*-lee; knife)
- **furcilla, furcillae,** f (fuhr-*kihl*-luh, fuhr-*kihl*-ligh; fork)
- **cocleare, coclearis,** n (koh-kleh-*ah*-reh, koh-kleh-*ah*-rihs; spoon)
- **patella, patellae,** f (puh-*tehl*-luh, puh-*tehl*-ligh; plate)
- **cratera, craterae,** f (crah-*tay*-ruh, crah-*tay*-righ; bowl)
- **poculum, poculi,** n (*po*-ku-lum, *po*-ku-lee; cup)
- **urna, urnae,** f (*uhr*-nuh, *uhr*-nigh; water jar)
- **amphora, amphorae,** f (*uhm*-foh-ruh, *uhm*-foh-righ; wine jar)
- **linteum, lintei,** n (*lihn*-teh-um, *lihn*-teh-ee; napkin)

Apparently napkins were a big deal in the ancient world, at least to some people. The poet Catullus gets so worked up when Asinius steals his linen napkins that he threatens him if he does not return them. The threat? Catullus will write three-hundred lines of mean poetry about him.

To Be or To Eat: That's the Real Question

Shakespeare may concern himself with philosophical questions debating the nature of existence, but Latin students are a bit more practical. When a Roman says, **Morum esse cupio,** you need to know whether he means, "I want to eat a mulberry," or "I want to be a mulberry." It turns out that the verb **esse** means both "to eat" and "to be." The only difference is in pronunciation. If you want to eat a mulberry, you pronounce the verb "*ays*-seh." If you want to be a mulberry, call a psychiatrist. While the receptionist puts you on hold, pronounce the verb "*ehs*-seh."

The verb **sum, esse, fui, futurus** (suhm, *ehs*-seh, *fu*-ee, fu-*too*-rus) is the Latin verb "to be," and, just as in English, it's irregular because it does not follow the normal verb-tense patterns. To read more about this verb, see Chapter 3. Because this verb is such a common word, it has many compounds, the most common of which is **possum, posse, potui** (*pohs*-sum, *pohs*-seh, *poh*-tu-ee), which means "to be able." It's irregular in the present, imperfect, and future tenses only. Where forms of the base word **sum** have "s" as the first letter, forms of **possum** use "ss," and where forms of **sum** begin with "e," forms of **possum** use "te." The following table shows the present tense of **possum** to give you an idea of how this verb works.

Singular	*Plural*
possum	possumus
potes	potestis
potest	possunt

There are many other irregular verbs in Latin, with some being irregular in the dictionary entries and others showing irregularity in their actual tenses. The following sections list some common verbs that are irregular in their principal parts (some don't have the usual **–re** on the infinitive, for example, and others lack a fourth dictionary form) and in the present tense (the only tense in which these verbs are irregular).

For all other tenses, the following verbs function as third-conjugation verbs. For more on verb conjugation, see Chapter 2.

Volo (to wish)

Volo, velle, volui (*woh*-lo, *woh*-leh, *woh*-lu-ee) means "to wish." Following is this verb's conjugation in the present tense.

Singular	*Plural*
volo	volumus
vis	vultis
vult	volunt

Nolo (not to wish)

Nolo, nolle, nolui (*no*-lo, *no*-leh, *no*-lu-ee) means "not to wish." Following is the present-tense conjugation of this verb.

Singular	Plural
nolo	nolumus
non vis	non vultis
non vult	nolunt

Malo (to prefer)

Malo, malle, malui (*mah*-lo, *mah*-leh, *mah*-lu-ee) means "to prefer." Following is the present-tense conjugation of this verb.

Singular	Plural
malo	malumus
mavis	mavultis
mavult	malunt

In addition to **malo,** Latin has two other look-alike words: **malum, mali,** n (*mah*-lum, *mah*-lee), which means "apple," and the adjective **malus, mala, malum** (*muh*-lus, *muh*-luh, *muh*-lum), meaning "bad." (For more on this as an adjective, see Chapter 4.)

Fero (to bring or carry)

Fero, ferre, tuli, latus (*feh*-ro, *fehr*-reh, *tu*-lee, *lah*-tus) means "to bring or carry." The conjugation of this verb in the present tense is

Singular	Plural
fero	ferimus
fers	fertis
fert	ferunt

Eo (to go)

Eo, ire, ii, iturus (*eh*-o, *ee*-reh, *ih*-ee, *ih*-too-rus) means "to go." The following table shows the present-tense conjugation.

Singular	*Plural*
eo	imus
is	itis
it	eunt

Talkin' the Talk

A **coquus** (*koh*-kwus; cook) and his **dominus** (*doh*-mih-nus; master) talk about dinner plans. (As you read this, remember that the Latin word **sal** can mean both "salt" and "wit.")

Dominus: **Te parare cenam optimam volo, quod senatores eunt.**
tay puh-*rah*-reh *kay*-nuhm *ohp*-tih-muhm *woh*-lo, kwohd seh-nah-*to*-rays *eh*-unt.
I want you to prepare an excellent meal because the senators are coming.

Coquus: **Cibumne aut calidum aut frigidum senator mavult?**
kih-bum-ney owt *kah*-lih-dum owt *free*-gih-dum seh-*nah*-tor *mah*-wult?
Does a senator prefer hot or cold food?

Dominus: **Sum senator, ita respondere possum. Cibum cum sale malumus.**
sum seh-*nah*-tor, ee-tuh reh-spohn-*day*-reh *pohs*-sum. *kih*-bum koom *suh*-leh *mah*-lu-mus.
I am a senator, so I am able to answer. We prefer food with salt.

Coquus: **Tum in taberna, non in villa tua cenare debetis.**
tum ihn tuh-*behr*-nah, non ihn *wee*-la *tu*-uh kay-*nah*-reh deh-*bay*-tihs.
Then you ought to dine in a tavern, not in your house.

Dominus: **Nonne ferre salem ad cenam potes?**
non-neh *fehr*-reh *suh*-lehm uhd *kay*-nuhm *poh*-tehs?
Are you not able to bring salt to the food?

Coquus: **Ad cibum salem ferre possum sed non ad sermonem.**
uhd *kih*-bum *suh*-lehm *fehr*-reh *pohs*-sum sehd non uhd sehr-*mo*-nehm.
I can bring salt to the food but not to the conversation.

Words to Know

coquus, coqui, m	koh-kwus, koh-kwee	cook
cibus, cibi, m	kih-bus, kih-bee	food
sermo, sermonis, m	sehr-mo, sehr-mo-nihs	conversation
calidus, calida, calidum	kuh-lih-dus, kuh-lih-duh, kuh-lih-dum	hot
frigidus, frigida, frigidum	free-gih-dus, free-gih-duh, free-gih-dum	cold

Welcome Home!

For the Romans, the focus of their life was, quite literally, at home. The word **focus, foci,** m (*foh*-kus, *foh*-kee) meant "hearth," and as the source for warmth and cooking, it was not only the physical, but also the emotional, center of the home. But just as with food, housing posed several options. Certain dwellings were available to the rich, and others were accessible to the poor; some were inside the city, and some were in the country.

Living downtown

Ancient Rome offered two basic urban housing choices — the **insula** and the **domus:**

✔ **insula:** An apartment building was an **insula, insulae,** f (*een*-su-luh, *een*-su-ligh), which also meant "island." When you consider that an apartment building is just an island of people in the middle of the city, then this name makes sense. Though originally for those who couldn't afford single-family homes, **insulae** eventually became home to wealthy members of society, too.

✔ **domus:** For those who could afford it, however, the **domus, domus,** f (*doh*-mus, *doh*-moos; house) was the dwelling of choice. The **domus** was more elaborate than the **insula,** but you couldn't tell it from the outside. Buildings, **aedificia** (igh-dih-*fih*-kih-uh), had plain exteriors, with all the decoration reserved for those who lived inside. Following are some of the important features of a **domus:**

- **atrium, atri,** n (*ah*-trih-um, *ah*-tree; entry hall)
- **cubiculum, cubiculi,** n (ku-*bih*-ku-lum, ku-*bih*-ku-lee; bedroom)
- **compluvium, compluvi,** n (kohm-*plu*-wih-um, *kohm*-plu-wee; rectangular roof opening to let in rain and light)
- **impluvium, impluvi,** n (ihm-*plu*-wih-um, *ihm*-plu-wee; pool of rainwater below the **compluvium**)
- **peristylium, peristyli,** n (peh-rih-*stih*-lih-um, peh-*rih*-stih-lee; columned courtyard)
- **hortus, horti,** m (*hohr*-tus, *hohr*-tee; garden)

Venturing out to your villa

Those who wanted to escape the hustle and bustle of the city had several housing options in the country. A wealthy, gentleman-farmer lived in a **villa, villae,** f (*wee*-la, *wee*-ligh; farmhouse). This was the main dwelling for the family that owned a **fundus, fundi,** m (*fuhn*-dus, *fuhn*-dee; farm). Its general floor plan was similar to that of a **domus.** Those who did not have such means lived in simple **casa, casae,** f (*kuh*-suh, *kuh*-sigh; hut).

When traveling a long distance, it was customary to stay with a **hospes** (*hohs*-pehs) — a guest-friend. Formal ties of hospitality — **hospitium** (hohs-*pih*-tih-um) — were often established between families and lasted down through the generations. If, however, you had no such friends in the area, you could find a **taberna** (tavern) in which to spend the night.

I'm paying how much for this fleabag?

In the modern world of luxury hotels, apartments, and condominiums, the higher in elevation the room, the higher the price. Just the opposite was true, however, in ancient Rome. It was the wealthy who occupied the lowest floors of the **insulae,** while those of less means rented the upper levels. Why? Most of the buildings in ancient Rome were made of wood until the Emperor Nero improved standards in building materials. Fire was always a threat, and the only real protection was to have a quick exit . . . out the front door.

Sanitation departments were nonexistent in those days, so where did high-rise tenants throw their garbage? Out the window, of course! The poet Juvenal comments on the danger of just walking near such buildings, when pots fly from such a height out the windows that they crack the pavement below. And who picked up the garbage? Nobody. In Pompeii, for example, the streets sloped and led to the sea, suggesting that garbage was simply washed into the ocean. Rome had the Cloaca Maxima, originally an open sewer that was later enclosed.

Fun & Games

Can you come up with a menu for all three meals of the day? Write the following foods underneath the meal in which they would most likely be eaten. You may use some words more than once.

pullus, vinum, caseus, piscis, fructus, ova, holera, mulsum, mala, panis

Ientaculum

_____

_____

_____

Prandium

_____

_____

_____

Cena

_____

_____

_____

See Appendix C for the answers.

Chapter 6

The Roman Calendar

*E*astern standard time, daylight savings time, and Greenwich mean time — sometimes it seems that the *modern* world has a tough enough time trying to figure out the right time. But consider the year 46 B.C. By then, time, as the Romans figured it, was so out of whack that the calendar was three months ahead of the seasons. Your day planner may have said that the time had come to break out a lightweight tunic, but the weather outside said to bundle up in your woolen toga. Julius Caesar as **pontifex maximus** (*pohn*-tih-fehks *muhks-ih-mus*) — chief priest of all sacred things — created a 445-day year to make things right again, thus making that year **ultimus annus confusionis** (*ul*-tih-mus *uhn*-nus-kon-foo-sih-*o*-nihs) — the last year of confusion — according to the third century A.D. writer Censorinus.

But why was a priest responsible for fixing the calendar? For the Romans, the reckoning of time was linked to the gods, goddesses, and religious cere-monies. In this chapter, you find out about some of the major and not-so-major Roman deities, their festivals, and how to tell time, ancient-Roman style. You also discover some of the most important grammatical features of the language with clauses and something called subjunctive mood.

Planning Ahead with the Roman Calendar

For most of the modern world, Vergil's statement rings true:

Tempus inreparabile fugit. (*Georgics* III.284)

tehm-pus ihn-reh-puh-*rah*-bih-le *fu*-giht.

Time unrecoverable flees.

Despite this Roman poet's foresight into our agenda-filled lives, the Romans themselves were a bit more grounded. They didn't just mark the passage of time; they also marked the relationship of days to each other and to key events in their lives. Here are some basic words to get you started in understanding Roman time:

- **tempus, temporis,** n (*tehm*-pus, tehm-*poh*-rihs; time)
- **hora, horae,** f (*ho*-ruh, *ho*-righ; hour)
- **dies, diei,** m/f (*dih*-ays, dih-*ay*-ee; day)
- **mensis, mensis,** m (*mayn*-sihs, *mayn*-sihs; month)
- **annus, anni,** m (*uhn*-nus, *uhn*-nee; year)

Biding the hours and days

The Romans didn't regularly use the week as a unit of time, and the minute was referred to simply as **punctum temporis** (*poonk*-tum *tehm*-poh-rihs) — a point of time. The day, however, was one of the most important time units, and each twenty-four hour period had numerous divisions. Dawn was known as **prima luce** (*pree*-mah *loo*-keh) — first light. From there you simply reckoned time as **prima hora, secunda hora** (*pree*-muh *ho*-ruh, seh-*kun*-duh *ho*-ruh), which means "first hour, second hour." The hours of the night were more broadly divided into four watches — **vigiliae** (wih-*gih*-lih-igh).

When referring to a general, nonspecific day, the Romans used **dies** (*dih*-ays) in the masculine gender. When the Romans meant a particular or appointed day, they used the feminine version (**diei**). For example,

Die constituta, reus ad iudicium venit.

dih-ay kohn-stih-*too*-tah, *reh*-us uhd yoo-*dih*-kih-um *way*-niht.

On the established day, the defendant came to the trial.

Naming months

The month was another main unit of time, and originally, the year contained ten of them. The months usually had names that represented a particular deity honored in that month or that indicated the order in which that month fell during the year. The original Roman year looked like this:

- **Martius** (*mahr*-tih-us; March): A festival in March honored the god Mars, who was the father of Rome's founder, Romulus. This was the first month of the Roman year.

- **Aprilis** (uh-*pree*-lihs; April): The word **Aprilis** is derived from the verb **aperire** (uh-peh-*ree*-reh), which means "to open."

- **Maius** (*mah*-yus; May): May 1 and 15 were sacred to Maia, an earth goddess who was also the mother of the god Mercury.

- **Iunius** (*yoo*-nih-us; June): This month honored Juno, the queen of the gods.

- **Quinctilis** (kweenk-*tee*-lihs; Fifth Month): This month gained the name July — **Iulius** (*yoo*-lih-us) — in later years to honor Julius Caesar.

- **Sextilis** (seks-*tee*-lihs; Sixth Month): Like **Quinctilis,** this month was renamed **Augustus** (ow-*gus*-tus) in honor of Caesar's nephew and adopted son, the Emperor Augustus, who's name is preserved in the English month of August.

- **September** (sehp-*tehm*-behr; Seventh Month)

- **October** (ohk-*to*-behr; Eighth Month)

- **November** (noh-*wehm*-behr; Ninth Month)

- **December** (deh-*kehm*-behr; Tenth Month)

The Romans eventually added two more months to the beginning of the year, **Ianuarius** (yah-nu-*ah*-rih-us; January) to honor **Ianus** (*yah*-nus), the two-faced god of beginnings, and **Februarius** (feh-bru-*ah*-rih-us; February), in which certain purification rites, **februa** (*feh*-bru-uh), were held.

Nowadays, we think of month names as nouns. In Latin, however, the grammatical form of the month names is a masculine adjective that modifies the implied word for month, **mensis. Maius,** for example, is actually **Maius mensis,** the month May.

Flying by with the years

Figuring out the year in which an event took place is easier than figuring out the day. Sort of anyway. Over many centuries, the Romans used several systems for calculating a particular year. One early method was to note who the consuls or chief magistrates were for that year. (For more on consuls and Roman government, see Chapter 9.)

For example, the first Roman emperor, Gaius Julius Caesar Octavianus Augustus, was born **a.d. IX Kal. Oct. cos. Tullio et Antonio.** Without the abbreviations, this says he came into the world **ante diem IX Kalendas Octobres consulibus Tullio et Antonio** (*uhn*-teh *dih*-ehm *noh*-wehm kuh-*lehn*-dahs ohk-*to*-brays kon-*su*-lih-bus *tuhl*-lih-o eht uhn-*to*-nih-o), which means, "nine days before the Kalends of October when Tullius and Antonius were consuls." Of course, you know precisely when that was, right? An obvious flaw in this system was that if you wanted to date anything in the past, you needed to memorize a list of Roman government officials who changed every year.

A better system used the date when Rome was founded (traditionally believed to be April 21, 753 B.C.) and calculated how many years a particular year was from that date. The abbreviation used in this system was **A.U.C.**, which stood for **ab urbe condita** (uhb *ur*-beh *kon*-dih-tah) — from the founding of the city. In this system, the bouncing baby emperor was born **anno ab urbe condita sexcentesimo nonagesimo primo** (*uhn*-no uhb *ur*-beh *kohn*-dih-tah sehks-kehn-*tay*-sih-mo no-nah-*gay*-sih-mo *pree*-mo), the six hundred ninety-first year from the founding of the city.

Eventually, in the sixth century A.D., Dionysus Exiguus introduced a system of dates reckoned by the abbreviation **A.D.** — **Anno Domini** (*uhn*-no *doh*-mih-nee; in the year of the Lord).

You can easily convert the old A.U.C. system into the modern dating system. Because the date for the founding of Rome is April 21, 753 B.C., **1 A.U.C. = 753 B.C.** To find a B.C. date, simply subtract the A.U.C. date from the number 754. For all A.D. dates, just add 753 to the modern year.

Playing the dating game

You probably think that you simply use the Roman numbers (see Chapter 3) to figure a date. November 27, for example, would simply be **dies vicesimus et septimus Novembri** (*dih*-ays wee-*kay*-sih-mus eht *sehp*-tih-mus noh-*wehm*-bree) — literally, the twenty-seventh day of November, right? Wrong. Read on to find out why.

Who's in charge around here?

In 59 B.C., or 695 A.U.C., the consuls of Rome were Gaius Julius Caesar and Marcus Calpurnius Bibulus. Because Bibulus was by far the weaker of the two co-magistrates of the city, the people jokingly referred to that year not as "the consulship of Julius and Calpurnius," but as "the consulship of Julius and Caesar."

And speaking of alternative year references, consider this: In Rome's Mamertine Prison, a dreary, cavernous holding cell that numbers among its famous inmates the apostles St. Peter and St. Paul, you can find a Latin plaque that gives some of the prison's history. The modern year in which the plaque was dedicated is listed **ab orbis redemptione** (uhb *ohr*-bihs reh-dehmp-tih-*o*-neh; from the redemption of the world).

Fixed days: Kalends, Nones, and Ides

The Romans did not view time as an endless succession of days to be numbered one after the other. Instead, they calculated how far away a given day was from one of three fixed days in each month. Those fixed days were

- ✔ **Kalendae** (kuh-*lehn*-digh; Kalends): The **Kalendae** fell on the first day of each month, and this word seems to be etymologically related to the Greek word *kaleo,* meaning "to call out."

- ✔ **Nonae** (*no*-nigh; Nones): The word **Nonae** is a form of the ordinal number for "ninth." In the calendar, it signifies the ninth day before the Ides.

- ✔ **Idus** (*ee*-doos; Ides): This word indicates the thirteenth day of most months, but it falls on the fifteenth day in March, May, July, and October. (Thus, the Nones would be the fifth day of most months, but the seventh day in March, May, July, and October.)

Here's a little rhyme to help you remember the change of date for the Ides (and therefore, for the Nones):

In March, July, October, May

The Ides fall on the fifteenth day.

So how does knowing the three fixed days of every month help you get a date? Well, as long as you're not expecting this book to help your love life, read on.

Figuring out a date

The Romans reckoned a date by figuring out how many days it was before the next Kalends, Nones, or Ides, and they counted inclusively. Thus, November 27 would actually have been five days before the first — Kalends — of December (the 27, 28, 29, 30, and 1 = 5 days) and would have been written like this:

a. d. V Kal. Dec.

which stands for **ante diem V Kalendas Decembres** (*uhn*-teh *dih*-ehm *kween*-kweh kuh-*lehn*-dahs deh-*kehm*-brays) — five days before the Kalends of December. (And you thought it was hard to get a date in high school!)

The day before one of the fixed days was simply **pridie** (*pree*-dih-ay; the day before). Thus, historians who wrote about the nightmares that Caesar's wife had the day before his assassination would note that they occurred **prid. Id. Mart.,** which is to say **pridie Idus Martias** (*pree*-dih-ay ee-doos *mahr*-tih-ahs) — the day before the Ides of March.

Having a Roman holiday

In both the ancient and modern dating systems, religion has played a major role. In fact, so many holidays honored both major and minor deities that the poet Ovid began an epic poem called *Fasti* (*fah*-stee; calendar) just to describe the days of the Roman year. By dealing so closely with the important days, traditions, and celebrations of Roman life, this poem was Ovid's most patriotic. Unfortunately, he stopped halfway through in the month of June because he was exiled for not being a good Roman.

Take a look at some of the more common and most interesting of the ancient Roman holidays:

- **Lupercalia** (lu-pehr-*kah*-lih-uh), celebrated on February 15, was a fertility festival in honor of the god Faunus. Young men would run around naked and strike women with strips of goat skins to increase their fertility. (Obviously, this popular pastime eventually gave way to dinner and a movie.)

- **Parentalia** (puh-rehn-*tah*-lih-uh), celebrated February 13–21, honored dead family members. The Romans took a week for private family celebrations, ending with one day of public ceremony.

- **Saturnalia** (sah-tur-*nah*-lih-uh), celebrated on December 17, was a harvest festival to honor the god Saturn. The Saturnalia allowed slaves one day of freedom and involved the exchange of gifts and festive clothing.

- **Vestalia** (wehs-*tah*-lih-uh), celebrated June 9, was the time to honor Vesta, the goddess of the hearth. The attendants in her temple were young women known as *Vestal Virgins.*

- **Megalesia** (meh-gah-*lay*-sih-uh) was celebrated April 4 through 10. During this holiday, Romans celebrated the goddess Cybele, also known as **Magna Mater** (*muhng*-nuh *mah*-tehr; great mother). In keeping with sexless temple attendants, such as the Vestal Virgins, the attendants of Cybele were castrated males.

Oh, That Able Ablative!

Ablatives are to Latin grammar what black holes are to space: They suck in all matter and energy. Well, sort of. Actually, the ablative case is the case for all sorts of time and space-related uses. In other words, this case shows the following:

✔ The **time when** something happens or the time frame **within which** it happens.

✔ The **place where** or **place from which** an action takes place.

✔ How something was done, called the **Ablative of Means.**

✔ The way in which something was done, called the **Ablative of Manner.**

✔ **Ablative Absolute,** which is a basic adverbial clause that can show the time, circumstance, or cause of an event.

To see what ablatives are all about, check out the following sections. (And for a basic rundown of what noun cases are, see Chapter 2.)

If you're pretty comfortable with English grammar, thinking of ablatives as Latin's version of English adverbial clauses and phrases may help you. They perform practically the same function.

What time is it?

The ablative case shows the point of *time when* something happens or the time frame *within which* it happens. Although several ablative uses require a preposition, these time expressions don't. Consider these sentences:

✔ **Illo die ad urbem advenimus.**

ihl-lo *dih*-ay uhd *ur*-behm uhd-*way*-nih-mus.

On that day we arrived at the city.

✔ **Hostes vincemus diebus tribus.**

hoh-stays win-*kay*-mus dih-*ay*-bus *trih*-bus.

We shall conquer the enemy within three days.

Another space-time expression involves the accusative case and shows the *extent* of time or space in which something occurs. For example:

Menses duos et milia passuum innumerabilia altum navigaverunt.

mayn-says *du*-os eht *mee*-lih-uh *pahs*-su-um ihn-nu-meh-rah-*bih*-lih-uh *uhl*-tum nah-wih-gah-*weh*-runt.

For two months and countless miles they sailed the deep.

Quo Vadis? (Where are you going?)

You also use the ablative case to show the *place where* or *place from which* an action takes place. Unlike the time ablatives, these ablatives *do* require prepositions. (For more on prepositions, take a look at Chapter 3.) The basic prepositions that you use for these ablatives are

- **in** (ihn; in, on)
- **sub** (sub; under)
- **a, ab** (ah, uhb; from, away from)

  Note: Use **a** before consonants and **ab** before vowels.
- **e, ex** (ay, ehks; from, out of)

  Note: Use **e** before consonants and **ex** before vowels.
- **de** (day; down from)

The following sentence covers just about everything:

> **Sciurus in ramo sub umbra ab ave cucurrit et e fronde de arbore cecidit.**
>
> skih-*oo*-rus ihn *rah*-mo sub *um*-brah uhb *uh*-weh ku-*kur*-riht eht ay *frohn*-deh day-*uhr*-boh-reh *keh*-kih-diht.
>
> The squirrel on the branch under the shade ran away from the bird and fell out of the foliage down from the tree.

The adverb **quo** (kwo) is an interrogative word that asks "where?" in the sense of "to what place?" In general, however, when you want to show the *place to which* something is going, use the accusative case and a preposition such as **in** (ihn) meaning "into," or **ad** (uhd) meaning "to, toward:"

> **Avis ad nidum volabat.**
>
> *uh*-wihs uhd *nee*-dum woh-*lah*-buht.
>
> A bird was flying toward the nest.

Everything but the kitchen sink

The ablative case has many other uses, and you can explore some of them in Chapters 8 and 9. You need to know three other main uses, however, before leaving this chapter. After you understand the primary functions of the ablative case, you can sail through a vast array of classic Latin literature.

Hollywood toga party

Quo Vadis (literally, "Where are you going?) was one of a long list of Hollywood movies set in ancient Roman times. Many classics are still available:

- *Julius Caesar,* the film version of William Shakespeare's play.

- *Cleopatra,* the first flick ever in which an actor (in this case, leading lady Elizabeth Taylor) was paid a cool million.

- *Ben Hur* features a must-see chariot race.

- *Spartacus* showcases Kirk Douglas (that's Michael's father for you newer movie-goers) as the gladiator who led a rebellion against Rome.

- Of course, if you want a laugh, you can always watch *A Funny Thing Happened on the Way to the Forum* or Monty Python's *The Life of Brian.*

The most recent sword-and-sandal movie was the 2001 Academy Award winner for Best Picture, *Gladiator.* There have, however, been other recent, if lesser-known movies, such as the 1988 release *Norman's Awesome Experience,* which tells of a time-traveling trio's adventure back to ancient Rome. This movie even features some spoken Latin with English subtitles!

Ablative of means

The ablative of means doesn't require a preposition. It simply involves a word in the ablative case that shows how something was done. For example:

Deos deasque et carminibus et ludis honorabamus.

deh-os deh-*ahs*-kweh eht kuhr-*mih*-nih-bus eht *loo*-dees hoh-no-rah-*bah*-mus.

We were honoring the gods and goddesses with both songs and games.

The Romans had many ways of worshiping their gods, including games that involved athletics and dancing. The **Ludi Megalenses** (*loo*-dee meh-guh-*layn*-says) — Great Games — for example, were held in April to honor the fertility goddess Cybele, also known as **Magna Mater** (*muhng*-nuh *mah*-tehr), the Great Mother.

Ablative of manner

Similar to the ablative of means, the ablative of manner shows the way in which something was done. It always involves abstract nouns, such as *virtue, love, anger,* and so on. If no adjective is used, you must use the preposition **cum** (koom), which means "with:"

Templum cum reverentia intravi.

tehm-plum koom reh-weh-*rehn*-tih-ah ihn-*trah*-wee.

I entered the temple with reverence.

When adjectives are part of the phrase, then **cum** is optional:

> **Pontifex magna cum cura victimam obtulit.**
>
> *pohn*-tih-fehks *muhng*-nah koom *koo*-rah *wihk*-tih-muhm *ohb*-tu-liht.
>
> The priest offered the sacrifice with great care.

Latin usually pulls one word of a prepositional phrase out in front of the preposition itself. For example, if you graduate from college the highest in your class, you're honored **summa cum laude** (*sum*-mah koom *low*-deh). Even though the preposition is in the middle, this phrase still means "with highest praise."

Ablative absolute

English teachers always say not to use dangling participial phrases. If you never understood what that meant, don't worry. Latin uses them all the time with this construction. Basically, you take a couple of words in the ablative case with no preposition and stick them somewhere in a sentence. This clause is grammatically freed from (**ab** (uhb) from + **solutus** (soh-*loo*-tus) freed) the rest of the sentence, so they just sort of dangle there. Take a look:

> **Caesare pontifice maximo, Romani fastos novos obtinuerunt.**
>
> *kigh*-suh-reh pohn-*tih*-fih-keh *muhks*-ih-mo, ro-*mah*-nee *fahs*-tos *noh*-wos ohp-tih-noo-*ay*-runt.
>
> With Caesar as chief priest, the Romans obtained a new calendar.

You can usually get a rough idea of what an ablative absolute means when you translate using the word *with*. To smooth things out, however, try something like *when* or *because*. Of course, the clause "*because* Caesar was chief priest" is different from the clause "*when* Caesar was chief priest," but that just shows how every translation is in some ways an interpretation.

Talkin' the Talk

Gaius and Flavia are having a conversation about an upcoming holiday. (Watch for the different ablative uses in their chat.)

Gaius: **Feriis proximis, in calamitate sum.**
fay-rih-ees *prohks*-ih-mees, ihn kuh-luh-mih-*tah*-te sum.
With the holidays so close, I'm in trouble.

Flavia: **Sed hodie est ante diem III Nonas Decembres! Tibi multum temporis est ante Saturnalia.**
sehd *hoh*-dih-ay ehst *uhn*-teh *dih*-ehm trays *no*-nahs deh-*kehm*-brays! *tih*-bih *mul*-tum *tehm*-poh-rihs ehst *uhn*-teh sah-tur-*nah*-lih-uh.
But today is the third day before the Nones of December! You still have a lot of time before Saturnalia.

Gaius: **Mihi adiuvabis dono pro me emendo?**
may uhd-yu-*wah*-bihs *do*-no pro may eh-*mehn*-do?
Will you help me by buying a gift for me?

Flavia: **Tibi cum gaudio adiuvabo, sed non donum emam.**
tih-bih koom *gow*-dih-o uhd-yu-*wah*-bo, sehd non *do*-num *eh*-muhm.
I shall help you with joy, but I shall not buy a gift.

Gaius: **Hoc anno gaudium pro dono amicis dare non possum.**
hok *uhn*-no *gow*-dih-um pro *do*-no uh-*mee*-kees *dah*-reh non *pohs*-sum.
This year, I cannot give my friends joy in place of a gift.

Flavia: **Cur non?**
kur non?
Why not?

Gaius: **Quod sedecim diebus tardissimus ero cum dono Saturnale e consulibus Murena et Silano.**
kwohd *say*-deh-kihm dih-*ay*-bus tuhr-*dihs*-sih-mus koom *do*-no sah-tur-*nah*-leh ay kon-*su*-lih-bus moo-*ray*-nah eht see-*lah*-no.
Because within sixteen days, I shall be quite late with a Saturnalia gift from the consulship of Murena and Silanus.

Flavia: **Sed erat proximus annus!**
sehd *eh*-ruht *prohks*-ih-mus *uhn*-nus!
But that was last year!

Gaius: **Accurate!**
uhk-koo-*rah*-tay!
Exactly!

Words to Know

adiuvo, adiuvare, adiuvi, adiutus	uhd-yu-wo, uhd-yu-wah-reh, uhd-yoo-wee, uhd-yoo-tus	to help
donum, doni, n	do-num, do-nee	gift
feria, feriae, f	fay-rih-uh, fay-rih-igh	holiday
gaudium, gaudi, n	gow-dih-um, gow-dee	joy
obfero, obferre, obtuli, oblatus	ohb-feh-ro, ohb-fehr-reh, ohb-tu-lee, ohb-lah-tus	to offer
templum, temple, n	tehm-plum, tehm-plee	temple

Expressing Subjunctive Moodiness

Subjunctive mood is a distinction for verbs in both English and Latin. In English, the subjunctive often sounds like a plural verb form used with a singular subject. For example, "If I were in Rome, I would see the statues," is the correct way to express that thought, even though "was" may sound better to you. In this example, "were" is in the subjunctive mood.

Oh, great, you're thinking that you should have paid better attention in high school English class. Well, you probably should have, but that's beside the point. Subjunctive mood is rapidly disappearing from English usage, but it's a huge factor in Latin.

Latin has six basic verb tenses, which you can read more about in Chapters 2 and 4. The forms in those chapters are in the *indicative mood,* which means they're used to indicate things. Verbs in the indicative form are the most common because they're used for basic storytelling. The subjunctive forms are a little different. The following list tells what you need to know:

- ✔ The subjunctive mood contains only four of the tenses that the indicative mood has: present, imperfect, perfect, and pluperfect.

- ✔ For the most part, you find these subjunctive forms in subordinate clauses — SUBjunctive, SUBordinate . . . get it?

- ✔ Most of the time, subjunctive verb forms mean exactly the same thing as their indicative counterparts do, so perfect subjunctive translates just like perfect indicative.

My underwear is where?

An honored tradition among Latin students is the *howler,* a humorous and grammatically inaccurate sentence, one of the most famous of which is

O ubi, o ubi est meus sub ubi?

o *u*-bee o *u*-bee ehst *meh*-us sub *u*-bee?

Literally, it means "O where, o where is my under where?" Said quickly, however, this howler takes on a whole new meaning.

And speaking of being under, the Romans added a civilizing element to their city when they put in sewers. In fact, the **Cloaca Maxima** (kloh-*ah*-kuh *muhks*-ih-muh) — Greatest Drain — was built as far back as the sixth century B.C. during the reign of King Tarquinius Superbus.

What's the point in having two verb forms that say the same thing, you ask? Well, subjunctive forms carry a sense of not being completed or of depending on another action. They're also a good clue to a reader or listener that you're in a subordinate clause.

Understanding the present subjunctive

The subjunctive mood is simple to deal with, in that it's easy to recognize. If you know a verb's conjugation and recognize a signature vowel, you can spot a present-tense subjunctive form. (For more on conjugations, see Chapter 2.)

First-conjugation verbs use "e"

Here's an example, using the verb **laudo, laudare, laudavi, laudatus,** which means "to praise":

Singular	Plural
laudem	laudemus
laudes	laudetis
laudet	laudent

The present indicative for first-conjugation verbs uses **a** instead of **e.**

Second-conjugation verbs use "ea"

The following example uses the verb **exerceo, exercere, exercui, exercitus,** which means "to train":

Singular	Plural
exerceam	exerceamus
exerceas	exerceatis
exerceat	exerceant

The present indicative for second-conjugation verbs uses only **e** instead of **ea.**

Third-conjugation verbs use "a"

The following example shows the verb **cano, canere, cecini, cantus,** which means "to sing":

Singular	Plural
canam	canamus
canas	canatis
canat	canant

The present indicative for third-conjugation verbs uses **o, i,** or **u** instead of **a.**

Third–io- and fourth-conjugation verbs use "ia"

The following example uses the verb **accipio, accipere, accepi, acceptus,** which means "to receive":

Singular	Plural
accipiam	accipiamus
accipias	accipiatis
accipiat	accipiant

The present indicative for third–io- and fourth-conjugation verbs uses **i** and **u** instead of **ia.**

Although, most of the time, you can translate the subjunctive forms just like you would the indicative forms, you can also render the present subjunctive with the helping words *may* or *let.* To wish someone a long life, for example, you'd say something like this:

> **Serus in caelum redeas.** (Horace, *Sermones* I.2.45)
>
> *say*-ruhs ihn *kigh*-lum *reh*-deh-ahs.
>
> May you return late to heaven.

Here's a little something to help you remember the present-tense subjunctive forms: sh**E** r**EA**ds **A** d**IA**ry. This mnemonic device shows the present-subjunctive vowels in order by conjugation.

Understanding the perfect and not-so-perfect subjunctive tenses

The three remaining subjunctive tenses are the imperfect, the perfect, and the pluperfect. (For the basic meaning of these tenses, see Chapter 4.) Not only can you easily recognize these tenses, you don't have to worry about paying attention to what conjugation the verb is. The following sections list the subjunctive-spotting clues that apply even to irregular verbs.

Imperfect-subjunctive tense

The imperfect tense almost always has the letters **re** somewhere in the word. Basically, you take the infinitive (the second dictionary form) and add the personal endings. (See Chapter 2 for a chart of the personal endings.) When you translate, use helping words like *was, were,* and English past tense. Take a look at the following example of the imperfect subjunctive, using the verb **colo, colere, colui, cultus** (*koh*-lo, *koh*-leh-reh, *koh*-lu-ee, *kul*-tus), which means "to worship":

Singular	Plural
colerem	coleremus
coleres	coleretis
coleret	colerent

Perfect-subjunctive tense

The perfect subjunctive tense is another easy one to recognize. You can tell the difference through context clues in the story. If most of the other verbs are past tense, then a verb with **eri** in it is probably perfect subjunctive. This tense uses the third principal part for its stem, and the letters **eri** always appear before the personal endings. To translate these forms, use *has, have,* or English past tense. See the following example that uses the verb **salio, salire, salui, saltus** (*suh*-lih-o, suh-*lee*-reh, *suh*-lu-ee, *suhl*-tus), which means "to dance":

Singular	Plural
saluerim	saluerimus
salueris	salueritis
saluerit	saluerint

A group of dancing priests took their name, **Salii** (*suh*-lih-ee), from the verb meaning "to dance." Dressed in ancient military garb, they performed elaborate dances at festivals marking the beginning and ending of the war season in March and October.

Pluperfect-subjunctive tense

The last subjunctive tense is the pluperfect, which is also easy to recognize. If you find the letters **ss** attached to the third principal part of a verb, you have a pluperfect subjunctive. Translate these tenses just like the pluperfect indicative with the helping word *had.* Here's a quick example, using the verb **sero, serere, sevi, satus** (*seh*-ro, *seh*-reh-reh, *say*-wee, *suh*-tus), which means "to plant":

Singular	*Plural*
sevissem	sevissemus
sevisses	sevissetis
sevisset	sevissent

Pleading Insanity: The Insanity Clause

Most of the time, you find subjunctive verbs in *subordinate clauses.* Basically, a subordinate clause is a sentence that can't stand alone. It has a subject and a verb, but it doesn't express a complete thought. Check out these following examples:

> When you go to the store
>
> Because the dog ran away
>
> Who ran away with the spoon

Subordinate clauses describe actions, people, and/or things. In this way, English subordinate clauses function as adverbs (showing when, where, why, how, and the reason) or they modify nouns, describing who or which. Latin, on the other hand, has many different types of subordinate clauses. The following sections describe the most common.

Purpose clause

The purpose clause is one of the most common and easily recognized. It uses the introductory words **ut** (ut; so that) or **ne** (nay; so that . . . not). The purpose clauses use only the present or imperfect subjunctive, which are translated "may" and "might," respectively.

> **Romam navigavi ut statuas viderem.**
>
> *ro*-muhm nah-wih-*gah*-wee ut *stuh*-tu-ahs wih-*day*-rehm.
>
> I sailed to Rome so that I might see the statues.

Result clause

The result clause begins with **ut** (ut; that) or **ut non** (ut non; that . . . not). Because this clause looks a lot like the purpose clause, the Romans kindly threw some clue words in front of the result clause. (Refer to the preceding "Purpose clause" section for more on this.) Common signal words are **ita** (*ee*-tuh; so), **sic** (seek; so), **tam** (tuhm; so), **tot** (toht; so many), and **tantus** (*tuhn*-tus; so great).

> **Pompeius est tam fortis miles ut amici eum "Magnus" vocent.**
>
> pom-*pay*-yus ehst tuhm *fohr*-tihs *mee*-lehs ut uh-*mee*-kee *eh*-um "*muhng*-nus" *woh*-kuhnt.
>
> Pompey is such a brave soldier that his friends call him "The Great."

Characteristic clause

The characteristic clause begins with a form of the relative pronoun **qui** (kwee; who) and describes a type of person without necessarily saying anything factual.

> **Est vir qui docere amet.**
>
> ehst wihr kwee doh-*kay*-reh *uh*-meht.
>
> He is the sort of man who likes to teach.

If you want to talk about a man who actually does like to teach, then you need to use a regular indicative verb in a simple relative clause. An example would look like this:

> **Est vir qui docere amat.**
>
> ehst wihr kwee doh-*kay*-reh *uh*-muht.
>
> He is a man who likes to teach.

Clauses for indirect questions

Indirect questions are common and easy to recognize in Latin. Begin with a questioning verb, add some interrogative word, end with a subjunctive verb, and you have an indirect question. (For more on interrogative words, see Chapter 3.)

Rogavit in quot bellis dux pugnavisset.

roh-*gah*-wiht ihn kwot *behl*-lees duks pung-nah-*wihs*-seht.

She asked in how many wars the general had fought.

Introducing clauses with cum

The word **cum** (koom), when used with a subjunctive verb, can introduce one of three different types of clauses. The translation of **cum** depends on the type of clause.

✔ In a *circumstantial clause,* **cum** means "when."

✔ In a *causal clause,* it means "because."

✔ In a *concessive clause,* it means "although."

Context clues in the sentence or story can usually help you decide which translation to use. Consider the following, which shows a concessive clause:

Cum alium ames, te amo.

koom *uh*-lih-um *uh*-mays, tay *uh*-mo.

Although you love another, I love you.

Talkin' the Talk

A **Romanus** (ro-*mah*-nus; Roman) talks with a visiting **Aegyptius** (igh-*gihp*-tih-us; Egyptian) about the temple of Janus, which was open only during war.

Aegyptius: **Templa visitare amo. Estne templum Iani apertum aut clausum?**
tehmp-luh wee-sih-*tah*-reh *uh*-mo. *ehst*-neh *tehmp*-lum *yah*-nee uh-*pehr*-tum owt *klow*-sum?
I love to visit the temples. Is the temple of Janus open or closed?

Romanus: **Cum bellum non geramus, est clausum.**
koom *behl*-lum non geh-*rah*-mus, ehst *klow*-sum.
Because we are not waging war, it is closed.

Aegyptius: **Ianumne Romani honorant ut bellum gerant?**
yah-*num*-neh ro-*mah*-nee hoh-*no*-ruhnt ut *behl*-lum *geh*-ruhnt?
Do the Romans honor Janus so that they may wage war?

Romanus: **Minime, sed Ianus est tam potens ut nobis victoriam ferat.**
mih-nih-may, sehd *yah*-nus ehst tuhm *poh*-tayns ut *no*-bees wihk-*to*-rih-uhm *feh*-ruht.
No, but Janus is so powerful that he brings us victory.

Aegyptius: **Gratia pacis, Ianus est deus qui non laborando optime laboret.**
grah-tih-uh *pah*-kihs, *yah*-nus ehst *deh*-us kwee non lih-bo-*rahn*-do *ohp*-tih-may lah-*bo*-reht.
For the sake of peace, Janus is the sort of god who works best by not working.

Words to Know

alius, alia, aliud	*uh*-lih-us, *uh*-lih-uh, *uh*-lih-ud	other, another
aperio, aperire, aperui, apertus	uh-*peh*-rih-o, uh-*peh*-ree-reh, uh-*peh*-ru-ee, uh-*pehr*-tus	to open
caelum, caeli, n	*kigh*-lum, *kigh*-lee	heaven, sky
claudo, claudere, clausi, clausus	*klow*-do, *klow*-deh-reh, *klow*-see, *klow*-sus	to close
doceo, docere, docui, doctus	doh-*keh*-o, doh-*kay*-reh, doh-*koo*-ee, *dohk*-tus	to teach
dux, ducis, m	duks, *du*-kihs	general, leader
laboro, laborare, laboravi, laboratus	luh-*bo*-ro, luh-bo-*rah*-reh, luh-bo-*rah*-wee, luh-bo-*rah*-tus	to work

He Seems Like a God! Roman Deities

The poet Catullus once wrote:

> **Ille mi par esse deo videtur . . . (*Carmen* 51.1)**
>
> *ihl*-leh mee pahr *ehs*-seh *deh*-o *wih*-deh-tur . . .
>
> He seems like a god to me . . .

Turns out that Catullus loved a woman from afar; his verse refers to her husband. Apparently, Catullus felt that just being next to this woman made a man
appear as a god. Catullus went on to curse her with some of the most vicious
poetry ever, but such are the side effects of Cupid's arrows. Whether using
the concept of deity as literary metaphor or truly believing in humanlike gods
and goddesses, religion played a major role in the lives of the ancient
Romans. Some, such as Julius Caesar's co-consul Bibulus, were so superstitious that they refused to leave the house without checking the omens. Even
those who only paid lip service to the state religions often sought out one of
the many philosophies of the time to give life meaning.

The Big Twelve

Many people are familiar with the major Greek and Roman gods and goddesses who make their way into everything from classic English poetry to
Saturday morning television cartoons. If you study mythology a bit, you can
see that, although the Greek and Roman deities had many similarities, they
weren't simply the same beings with different names. Table 6-1 lists the
twelve major deities, shows their area of influence, and explains what symbol
commonly represented them.

Do your friends call you "Juppy"?

Some of the Roman gods acquired last names,
which were really titles associated with a particular function. For example, one temple was
devoted to Jupiter **Stator** (*stuh*-tor; one who
stops), referring to when Jupiter stopped the
Romans from running away during battle.
Another temple for Jupiter included the sur-
name **Optimus et Maximus** (*ohp*-tih-mus eht
muhks-ih-mus) — Best and Greatest.

Another temple was dedicated to Juno **Moneta**
(moh-*nay*-tuh; one who warns). Juno received
this name when her sacred geese began honk-
ing and alerted the guards that the city was
under attack. Eventually her temple turned into
the Roman mint. The English word *money*
comes from the name **Moneta**, which the
Romans gave to Juno.

Table 6-1	Greco-Roman Gods and Goddesses		
Greek	*Roman*	*Area*	*Symbol*
Zeus	Jupiter	sky	lightning bolt
Hera	Juno	marriage	peacock
Poseidon	Neptune	sea	trident
Hades	Pluto	underworld	bident
Aphrodite	Venus	love	sea foam
Athena	Minerva	wisdom	owl
Apollo	Apollo	sun, music	lyre
Demeter	Ceres	grain	stalks of wheat
Hephaestus	Vulcan	fire	anvil
Ares	Mars	war	weaponry
Artemis	Diana	hunt	moon
Hermes	Mercury	messengers	winged sandals, caduceus

Housecleaning with the gods

The Roman gods and goddesses were arranged in a sort of hierarchy. The gods of the household fell somewhere below the major twelve gods, described in "The Big Twelve" section in this chapter. Household gods were divided into two sets:

- The **lares** (*luh*-rays) represented the spirits of a family's deceased ancestors.
- The **penates** (peh-*nah*-tays) were the guardian spirits of a family's food pantry.

The Romans worshiped these gods in a private chapel in the house, called a **lararium** (luh-*rah*-rih-um). Families often kept small figurines to represent their **lares** and **penates.**

On a more personal level, each male was supposedly born with a **genius** (*geh*-nih-us; guardian spirit). Although all men had a **genius,** only the spirit of the **paterfamilias** (puh-tehr-fuh-*mih*-lih-ahs; head of the family) received honor in the **lararium.** The female counterpart to the **genius** was a spirit named for the queen of the gods, **Iuno** (*yoo*-no).

Oh, and the god of mildew? That was **Robigus** (ro-*bee*-gus), whose festival was on April 25.

Knocking on wood: Superstitions

The Romans were not only polytheistic (believing in many gods), but they were pantheistic as well, which means they believed a divine spirit existed in just about everything. In fact, the practice of knocking on wood for good luck hearkens back to the Roman belief of divine spirits dwelling in trees. Following are just a few examples to show how widespread the Roman divinities roamed:

- **Aeolus** (*igh*-oh-lus): god of wind
- **Egeria** (ay-*geh*-rih-uh): goddess of fountains and childbirth
- **Fornax** (*fohr*-nahks): goddess of ovens
- **Pales** (*puh*-lays): goddess of herds and shepherds
- **Picus** (*pee*-kus): god of woodlands

Polytheistic Epicureans or good ol' Stoic monotheists?

Despite how much of a role the gods and goddesses seemed to play in everyday life, many Romans did not truly believe in these gods. Historian Edward Gibbon noted in his *The Decline and Fall of the Roman Empire,* "The various modes of worship, which prevailed in the Roman World, were all considered by the people as equally true; by the philosopher, as equally false; and by the magistrate, as equally useful."

Basically, this meant that you always participated in the public festivals, but privately, you might have followed one of a variety of philosophical outlooks on life. Among the most common were

Epicureanism: According to this belief, the main goal of life was pleasure of the soul. Though originally meant a lack of disturbance for the soul, Epicureanism came to mean indulgence in just about everything.

Stoicism: The Stoics believed that virtue was based on knowledge, and that therefore, the only good was to live in harmony with reason. Stoics are often seen as not getting too bent out of shape, whether through excessive joy or excessive sadness.

Mithraism: This belief was popular among the Roman military. These men (no women were allowed into the cult) followed an ancient Iranian god of light and truth (Mithras) and passed through several grades of initiation beginning with **Corax** (*koh*-ruhks; raven) and ending with **Pater** (*puh*-tehr; father). Little else is known about this philosophy.

Platonism: Named for one of the most famous Greek philosophers, this belief centered on the notion that everything you see is just a copy of the perfect "form" existing someplace else.

Fun & Games

See if you can figure out the following dates, using the ancient A.U.C. method.

1. June 8, 1991

2. January 17, 1878

3. December 2, 72 B.C.

If you were in ancient Rome, to which god would you make sacrifice to solve the following problems?

1. relationship trouble   a. Mercury

2. bread won't rise   b. Robigus

3. e-mail isn't working   c. Venus

4. gym socks are mildewing   d. Fornax

See Appendix C for the answers.

Chapter 7

The Roman Army

* *

In This Chapter

▶ Finding out about how the Romans organized for war

▶ Understanding military rank and weaponry

▶ Working with fourth- and fifth-declension nouns

▶ Using pronouns of all types

* *

One of the most enduring images of ancient Rome is that of the red-crested soldier with metal plates encasing his torso, sword at his side, spear in his hand. The ancient Roman military has fascinated historians and military enthusiasts down through the centuries, and why not? The march of their hobnailed boots brought conquest to countless nations from Britain to Egypt, from Spain to the Black Sea. Much of western culture, based as it is on the culture of the Romans, exists primarily because it followed the dust of Rome's legions.

This chapter takes you inside the once mighty army of the Roman Empire to see some of its people, structures, and practices. You can also learn the last two groupings of Latin nouns, not to mention all about pronouns. So snap a salute and say **Ave, dux!** (*uh*-way duks) — "Hail, general!"

You're in the Army Now

The great Latin poet Vergil told of Aeneas, the Trojan hero, and Rome's beginnings. When Aeneas visited his father in the Underworld, the old man gave Aeneas a glimpse of the future and his famous descendants, who would become the renowned leaders of the Roman Empire. Then he added this admonition:

> **Tu regere imperio populos, Romane, memento**
>
> **hae tibi erunt artes, pacisque imponere morem,**
>
> **parcere subiectis et debellare superbos.** (*Aeneid,* VI.851-853)

too *reh*-geh-reh ihm-*peh*-rih-o *poh*-pu-los ro-*mah*-neh meh-*mehn*-to

high *tih*-bih *eh*-runt *uhr*-tays pah-*kihs*-kweh ihm-*po*-neh-reh *mo*-rehm,

puhr-keh-reh sub-*yehk*-tees eht day-behl-*lah*-reh su-*pehr*-bos.

Roman, remember, with power to rule over nations is your fate —

These will be your private arts — and to place on them habits of good will,

Sparing the vanquished and casting down arrogant souls as you wage war.

Rome didn't impose peace and civilization through haphazard fighting. Roman conquests came as a result of a professional, well-organized, and highly trained military force. For starters, you may want to take a look at the organizational structure of these famous warriors.

Exercising the right to fight

The Latin word for *army* is **exercitus, exercitus,** m (ehks-*ehr*-kih-tus, ehks-*ehr*-kih-toos), but it's important to know that this word is a derivative of the verb **exercere** (ehks-ehr-*kay*-reh) meaning "to train or exercise." As you can see in the following sections, the two main divisions of this highly trained and skilled army were made up of the **pedes, peditis,** m (*peh*-dehs; *peh*-dih-tihs; foot soldier, infantryman) and the **eques, equitis,** m (*eh*-kwehs; *eh*-kwih-tihs; horse soldier, cavalryman).

Organizing a Roman legion

The strength of the Roman infantry rested with a unit called the **legio** (*leh*-gih-o; legion). An army could be made up of several **legiones** (leh-gih-o-nays), which gave the Romans an advantage. Giving a commander a much greater range of strategies, a legion contained several smaller units that could be broken off and sent in different directions.

When battling a barbarian army that fought as one massed horde, the legion's structure proved deadly. Although a full **legio** supposedly contained 6,000 **milites** (*mee*-lih-tays; soldiers), it often carried much smaller numbers. The legions in Julius Caesar's army, for example, numbered approximately 3,600 men each. The following list shows the divisions and enrollments for a legion at full strength.

✔ **legio, legionis,** f (*leh*-gih-o, leh-gih-*o*-nihs; legion) 6,000 **milites**

✔ **cohors, cohortis,** f (*koh*-hohrs, koh-*hohr*-tihs; cohort) 600 **milites**

✔ **manipulus, manipuli,** m (muh-*nih*-pu-lus, muh-*nih*-pu-lee; maniple) 200 **milites**

✔ **centuria, centuriae,** f (kehn-*tu*-rih-uh, kehn-*tu*-rih-igh; century) 100 **milites**

Over time the words **legio** in Latin and *legion* in English have come to indicate a large number of anything. When Jesus once asked a possessed man what his name was, the man replied,

> **Legio mihi nomen est, quia multi sumus.** (*Biblia Vulgata, Marcum* 5:9)
>
> *leh*-gih-o *mih*-hih *no*-mehn ehst, *kwih*-uh *mul*-tee *su*-mus.
>
> My name is Legion, because we are many.

Calling out the cavalry

In addition to well-trained foot soldiers, the Romans also had a highly effective **equitatus, equitatus,** m (eh-kwih-*tah*-tus, eh-kwih-*tah*-toos; cavalry). The Roman cavalry was made up of the following divisions:

- **ala, alae,** f (*ah*-luh, *ah*-ligh; wing) 300 to 400 **equites**

  The term **ala** ("wing") for the main unit of the cavalry shows its place in battle. The cavalry usually formed on the right and left wings of the main body of infantry.

- **turma, turmae,** f (*tur*-muh, *tur*-migh; squadron) 30 to 40 **equites**

- **decuria, decuriae,** f (deh-*ku*-rih-uh, deh-*ku*-rih-igh; division) 10 **equites**

Originally, **equites** were simply cavalrymen in the army. Because only the rich could afford their own horses, eventually this term came to apply to the wealthy business class of Rome.

Fighting alongside foreigners

In addition to the two main divisions of the **exercitus** (army) — the foot soldiers and the calvary — Roman armies used a number of other types of fighters. Many of these were foreigners whom the Romans employed because of their skill with a certain type of weaponry. The Romans didn't put their main trust in these fighters, though, because they saw their tactics as somehow un-Roman. (Hey, whatever gets the job done.) Noncombatants also performed other functions that were useful to the operation of an army camp.

- **calo, calonis,** m (*kah*-lo, kah-*lo*-nihs; aide-de-camp)

- **sagittarius, sagittari,** m (suh-giht-*tah*-rih-us, suh-giht-*tah*-ee; archer)

- **speculator, speculatoris,** m (speh-ku-*lah*-tohr, speh-ku-lah-*to*-rihs; spy)

- **explorator, exploratoris,** m (ehks-plo-*rah*-tohr, ehks-plo-rah-*to*-rihs; scout)

- **funditor, funditoris,** m (*fun*-dih-tohr, fun-dih-*to*-rihs; slinger)

- **mulio, muliones,** m (*moo*-lih-o, moo-lih-*o*-nihs; mule driver)

- **mercator, mercatoris,** m (mehr-*kah*-tohr, mehr-kah-*to*-rihs; trader)

- **faber, fabri,** m (*fuh*-behr, *fuh*-bree; engineer)

Take this!

Sometimes archaeologists make interesting discoveries. Take, for example, the skull of a Roman enemy that had indentations across the forehead. The clue to deciphering these marks was found on a small stone, the kind of stone that a **funditor** (*fun*-dih-tohr; slinger) would use. In raised letters on the stone were the words, "CAPE HOC" (*kuh*-peh hohk), which in Latin means "Take this!"

Other products of the Roman army didn't have to await excavation to come to modern attention. The **fabri** (*fuh*-bree; engineers) were responsible for building much of the Roman road system that extended throughout the empire and can still be seen today. In fact, the Romans surfaced enough roads to encircle the entire globe twice.

Saluting men of rank

In describing Queen Dido's heroic rescue of her people from tyranny, Vergil says of her,

> **Dux femina facti.** (*Aeneid* I.364)
>
> duks *fay*-mih-nuh *fuhk*-tee.
>
> The leader of this act was a woman.

Not even the skillfully trained Roman army could function without leaders, including the one best known in modern times, the centurion. The following list shows the basic chain of command from highest to lowest rank in the **exercitus.**

- ✔ **imperator, imperatoris,** m (ihm-peh-*rah*-tohr, ihm-peh-rah-*to*-rihs; general of an army after his first victory)

- ✔ **dux, ducis,** m (duks, *du*-kihs; general of an army)

- ✔ **legatus, legati,** m (lay-*gah*-tus, lay-*gah*-tee; commander of a legion)

- ✔ **centurio, centurionis,** m (kehn-*tu*-rih-o, kehn-tu-rih-*o*-nihs; commander of a century — military unit of 100 soldiers)

- ✔ **miles, militis,** m (*mee*-lehs, *mee*-lih-tihs; soldier)

The Roman army did have two other easily distinguished and important positions: the **signifer, signiferi,** m (sihng-nih-fehr, sihng-*nih*-feh-ree; standard bearer for the maniple) and the **aquilifer, aquiliferi,** m (uh-*kwihl*-ih-fehr, uh-kwihl-*ih*-feh-ree; the standard bearer for the legion). Each man carried into battle a tall pole with symbols to identify his maniple or legion.

✔ The standard that the **signifer** carried bore the image of a hand, which was appropriate if you consider that **manus, manus,** f (*muh*-nus, *muh*-noos; hand) is the root of the word **manipulus,** the Latin word for *maniple.*

✔ A golden eagle stood on the top of the standard that an **aquilifer** carried. This also made sense because the word for *eagle* is **aquila, aquilae,** f (*uh*-kwih-luh, *uh*-kwih-ligh).

With the use of standard bearers, changes of troop movement were simple to make. If you were the general, you would simply tell one of your standard bearers to go to a different part of the battle, and his men would follow him. For this reason, soldiers knew to protect their standard bearer at all costs.

The tools of the trade: Arma and tela

Vergil opens his war epic with the words,

> **Arma virumque cano . . .** (*Aeneid* I.1)
>
> *uhr*-muh wih-*rum*-kweh *kuh*-no . . .
>
> I sing of arms and a man . . .

And when it comes to battle, you really can't have one without the other. Caesar is famous for observing that all of Gaul was divided into three parts, and the same can be said of the Roman army. Its successes over most of the known world stemmed from the superior training, organization, and weaponry of the Roman army. The following is a rundown of the weapons that the Romans used:

✔ **arma, armorum,** n (*uhr*-muh, uhr-*mo*-rum; weapons, including armor)

✔ **telum, teli,** n (*tay*-lum, *tay*-lee; weapon)

✔ **pilum, pili,** n (*pee*-lum, *pee*-lee; spear)

✔ **hasta, hastae,** f (*huh*-stuh, *huh*-stigh; javelin — smaller and lighter than the **pilum**)

✔ **gladius, gladi,** m (*gluh*-dih-us, *gluh*-dee; sword)

✔ **pugio, pugionis,** m (*pu*-gih-o, puh-gih-*o*-nihs; dagger)

✔ **scutum, scuti,** n (*skoo*-tum, *skoo*-tee; shield)

✔ **galea, galeae,** f (*guh*-leh-uh, *guh*-leh-igh; helmet)

✔ **lorica, loricae,** f (lo-*ree*-kuh, lo-*ree*-kigh; breastplate)

✔ **tunica, tunicae,** f (*tu*-nih-kuh, *tu*-nih-kigh; tunic)

✔ **caligae, caligarum,** f (*kuh*-lih-gigh, kuh-lih-*gah*-rum; boots)

Drop and give me twenty!

Discipline in the Roman army was notoriously strict. When Caesar's Uncle Marius made reforms requiring the soldiers to carry their own equipment, which weighed around 70 pounds, the soldiers earned the nickname "Marius's Mules." If an individual soldier got out of line, his **centurio** quickly brought him back in. The vine staff that the **centurio** carried to deliver quick punishments identified him.

A more serious punishment was **decimatio** (deh-kih-*mah*-tih-o; decimation) the execution of every tenth man in the legion. A legion earned this punishment for a major military offense, such as when a legion deserted a battle.

Most pieces of weaponry had both an offensive and defensive function. For example, a **pilum** (*pee*-lum) was a heavy-shafted spear with a narrow neck made of lead. When the spear pierced an enemy's shield (or an enemy himself), the weight of the shaft bent the lead neck, making it useless to throw back at the Romans. The **scutum** (*skoo*-tum; shield) was rimmed in bronze and bore a large, bronze hemisphere called an **umbo** (*um*-bo; boss) in the middle. Besides protecting nearly the whole body of a soldier, the **scutum** could be rammed into an enemy's stomach, slammed down on his foot, or thrust upward to crush his jaw. Several soldiers could also band together, holding their **scuta** above them and to their sides, making an impenetrable shell called a **testudo** (tehs-*too*-do), which was perfect for advancing on a heavily defended, walled city. Even the color of a soldier's **tunica** had a function beyond fashion. This war shirt was dyed red so that, if a soldier was hit, he wouldn't notice his own blood and stop fighting.

The third emperor of Rome was a man named Gaius Julius Caesar Germanicus. As a little boy, he used to hang around the army camp of his father, the general Germanicus. The boy wore a small army uniform complete with imitations of his daddy's big **caligae** (*kuh*-lih-gigh; boots). The soldiers thought it was cute and gave him the nickname "Little Boots." That's how one of the most cruel and perverse emperors of Rome came to be known as Caligula.

Fourth- and Fifth-Declension Nouns

The word for *army* is **exercitus, exercitus,** m, which at first glance may look like a second-declension noun, but it isn't. (Chapters 2 and 4 tell you all about noun declensions.) Because you use the genitive singular (second dictionary form) of a noun to discover its declension, you know that **exercitus** isn't a second-declension noun. The genitive singular ending of second-declension noun is **–i.** The genitive singular for army, **exercitus,** obviously ends with **–us.** So welcome to the world of fourth- and fifth-declension nouns, the last two noun declensions in Latin.

Understanding fourth-declension nouns

Like second- and third-declension nouns, nouns in the fourth declension use one set of endings for the masculine and feminine genders and another set for the neuters. (Don't understand grammatical gender? Head to Chapter 2 for a quick explanation.) Table 7-1 shows the endings for fourth-declension masculine and feminine nouns.

Table 7-1	Fourth-Declension Masculine/Feminine Endings	
Case	*Singular*	*Plural*
Nominative	–us	–us
Genitive	–us	–uum
Dative	–ui	–ibus
Accusative	–um	–us
Ablative	–u	–ibus

A good example of a fourth-declension masculine noun is **exercitus, exercitus,** m, the word that seems to be marching through this chapter. You can tell that **exercitus** is a fourth-declension noun because of the genitive singular form ending in **–us.** Using **exercitus** as an example, Table 7-2 shows you how to decline fourth-declension masculine (and feminine) nouns.

Just tell me where to stand

The typical arrangement for a Roman line of battle was actually the **triplex acies** (*trih*-plehks *uh*-kih-ays; triple battle line). As the name implies, three lines of soldiers stretched across the field of combat, one in front of the other. The more inexperienced soldiers formed the front line, the main corps of the army stood in the middle, and the veterans — **triarii** (trih-*ah*-rih-ee; third liners) held the back. To say that a matter had gone **ad triarios** (uhd trih-*ah*-rih-os) became proverbial for critical situation.

The other common arrangement for soldiers was the **agmen, agminis,** n (*uhg*-mehn, *uhg*-mih-nihs), which was the column formation used for marching.

Table 7-2	Declining a Fourth-Declension Masculine Noun	
Case	*Singular*	*Plural*
Nominative	exercitus (ehks-*ehr*-kih-tus)	exercitus (ehks-*ehr*-kih-toos)
Genitive	exercitus (ehks-*ehr*-kih-toos)	exercituum (ehks-ehr-*kih*-tu-um)
Dative	exercitui (ehks-ehr-*kih*-tu-ee)	exercitibus (ehks-ehr-*kih*-tih-bus)
Accusative	exercitum (ehks-*ehr*-kih-tum)	exercitus (ehks-*ehr*-kih-toos)
Ablative	exercitu (ehks-*ehr*-kih-too)	exercitibus (ehks-ehr-*kih*-tih-bus)

The neuter endings in fourth declension are similar to the masculine/feminine endings. Table 7-3 lists them.

Table 7-3	Fourth-Declension Neuter Endings	
Case	*Singular*	*Plural*
Nominative	–u	–ua
Genitive	–us	–uum
Dative	–u	–ibus
Accusative	–u	–ua
Ablative	–u	–ibus

A good word to call your attention to fourth-declension neuter nouns is **cornu, cornus,** n (*kohr*-noo, *kohr*-noos), which means "horn." A **cornicen** (*kohr*-nih-kehn; horn-blower) would sound a horn to draw an army to attention. Using **cornu** as an example, Table 7-4 shows you how to decline a fourth-declension neuter noun.

Table 7-4	Declining a Fourth-Declension Neuter Noun	
Case	*Singular*	*Plural*
Nominative	cornu (*kohr*-noo)	cornua (*kohr*-nu-uh)
Genitive	cornus (*kohr*-noos)	cornuum (*kohr*-nu-um)
Dative	cornu (*kohr*-noo)	cornibus (*kohr*-nih-bus)
Accusative	cornu (*kohr*-noo)	cornua (*kohr*-nu-uh)
Ablative	cornu (*kohr*-noo)	cornu (*kohr*-nih-bus)

Clearly, the main vowel in the fourth declension is **–u;** with neuter nouns, the **–u** is actually used in four separate cases. To tell which case is being used in a particular sentence, use context clues. Take a look at this example:

Ut milites convenirent, cornicen cornu inflavit.

ut *mee*-lih-tays kohn-weh-*nee*-rehnt, *kohr*-nih-kehn *kohr*-noo een-*flah*-wiht.

So that the soldiers might assemble, the horn-blower sounded the horn.

Understanding fifth-declension nouns

The final group of nouns in Latin is fifth declension. As in first declension, none of these nouns have a neuter gender, and masculine and feminine nouns share the same set of endings shown in Table 7-5.

Table 7-5	Fifth-Declension Masculine/Feminine Endings	
Case	*Singular*	*Plural*
Nominative	–es	–es
Genitive	–ei	–erum
Dative	–ei	–ebus
Accusative	–em	–es
Ablative	–e	–ebus

A typical field of battle saw the Roman army drawn up in a long battle line called **acies, aciei,** f (*uh*-kih-ays, uh-kih-*ay*-ee). The genitive singular ending of **–ei** shows this word to be a fifth-declension noun. Table 7-6 shows how to decline a fifth-declension noun.

Table 7-6	Declining a Fifth-Declension Noun	
Case	*Singular*	*Plural*
Nominative	acies (*uh*-kih-ays)	acies (*uh*-kih-ays)
Genitive	aciei (uh-kih-*ay*-ee)	acierum (uh-kih-*ay*-rum)
Dative	aciei (uh-kih-*ay*-ee)	aciebus (uh-kih-*ay*-bus)
Accusative	aciem (*uh*-kih-ehm)	acies (*uh*-kih-ays)
Ablative	acie (*uh*-kih-ay)	aciebus (uh-kih-*ay*-bus)

Proceeding with Pronouns

Pronouns are those little words in English and Latin that stand in the place of and rename nouns. Although they are often tiny words, pronouns are some of the most important words in the language, and the following sections introduce you to the most common ones.

I, I, I! — using personal pronouns

The personal pronouns in Latin are the words for *I, you, we,* and *us.* Tables 7-7 and 7-8 list them. (For those of you who may not remember what "person" means in the context of pronouns, first-person pronouns are *I* and *me* for the singular and *we* and *us* for the plural. The second-person pronoun is *you,* which can be singular or plural.)

If you're wondering where the third-person pronoun is, Latin doesn't have one. Instead, it uses the demonstrative pronoun **is, ea, id,** which you can read about in the next section, "This or that? Demonstrative pronouns."

Table 7-7	First-Person Pronouns	
Case	*Singular*	*Plural*
Nominative	ego (*eh*-go)	nos (nos)
Genitive	mei (*meh*-ee)	nostrum (*noh*-strum)
Dative	mihi (*mih*-hih)	nobis (*no*-bees)
Accusative	me (may)	nos (nos)
Ablative	me (may)	nobis (*no*-bees)

Table 7-8	Second-Person Pronouns	
Case	*Singular*	*Plural*
Nominative	tu (too)	vos (wos)
Genitive	tui (*tu*-ee)	vestrum (*weh*-strum)
Dative	tibi (*tih*-bih)	vobis (*wo*-bees)
Accusative	te (tay)	vos (wos)
Ablative	te (tay)	vobis (*wo*-bees)

The personal endings of Latin verbs show who is doing the action, so you may think Latin has no need for separate personal pronouns. Having these words in your vocabulary, however, allows you to put more emphasis on a verb. It's like shouting, only silently and on paper. This example can help you sort it out:

Pacem amo, sed bellum amas.

pah-kehm *uh*-mo, sehd *behl*-lum *uh*-mahs.

Ego pacem amo, sed tu bellum amas.

eh-go *pah*-kehm *uh*-mo, sehd too *behl*-lum *uh*-mahs.

Although both sentences look the same in translation — "I like peace, but you like war" — the first simply notes a difference of opinion. The second sentence, adding **ego** and **tu,** makes the contrast between the two people more noticeable.

This or that? Demonstrative pronouns

Demonstrative pronouns are pronouns that demonstrate (point out) a particular thing. Instead of identifying *a* table, for example, you identify *this* table. In addition to *this,* the other demonstrative pronouns in English are *these, that,* and *those.* (Just in case high school English let you down, remember that *this* and *that* refer to singular nouns, and *these* and *those* refer to plural nouns.)

In Latin, these pronouns look like adjectives because they show gender: masculine, feminine, and neuter. What gender they use depends on the noun they point to. A masculine noun, for example, takes a masculine pronoun. In this way, Latin can say with specificity something like, "this boy," "this girl," or "this rock." Tables 7-9 and 7-10 show how the demonstrative pronouns appear in the various genders.

Table 7-9	Hic, Haec, Hoc — *This* and *These*	
Case	*Singular (M/F/N)*	*Plural (M/F/N)*
Nominative	hic, haec, hoc (heek, hike, hok)	hi, hae, haec (hee, high, hike)
Genitive	huius, huius, huius (*hoo*-yus, *hoo*-yus, *hoo*-yus)	horum, harum, horum (*ho*-rum, *hah*-rum, *ho*-rum)
Dative	huic, huic, huic (*hu*-ihk, *hu*-ihk, *hu*-ihk)	his, his, his (hees, hees, hees)
Accusative	hunc, hanc, hoc (hunk, huhnk, hok)	hos, has, haec (hos, hahs, highk)
Ablative	hoc, hac, hoc (hok, hahk, hok)	his, his, his (hees, hees, hees)

Table 7-10	Ille, Illa, Illud — *That* and *Those*	
Case	*Singular (M/F/N)*	*Plural (M/F/N)*
Nominative	ille, illa, illud (*ihl*-leh, *ihl*-luh, *ihl*-lud)	illi, illae, illa (*ihl*-lee, *ihl*-ligh, *ihl*-luh)
Genitive	illius, illius, illius (ihl-*lee*-us, ihl-*lee*-us, ihl-*lee*-us)	illorum, illarum, illorum (ihl-*lo*-rum, ihl-*lah*-rum, ihl-*lo*-rum)
Dative	illi, illi, illi (*ihl*-lee, *ihl*-lee, *ihl*-lee)	illis, illis, illis (*ihl*-lees, *ihl*-lees, *ihl*-lees)
Accusative	illum, illam, illud (*ihl*-lum, *ihl*-luhm, *ihl*-lud)	illos, illas, illa (*ihl*-los, *ihl*-lahs, *ihl*-luh)
Ablative	illo, illa, illo (*ihl*-lo, *ihl*-lah, *ihl*-lo)	illis, illis, illis (*ihl*-lees, *ihl*-lees, *ihl*-lees)

Latin usually uses forms of **hic** (this) for nouns that are closer to the speaker, and **ille** (that) for nouns that are farther away. Because these words have gender, they can also mean "he," "she," "it," and "they" when they stand alone and don't modify any particular noun. Consider this example:

> **Milites in castris parant. Hi tela acuunt, illi cibum parant, et hic litteras scribit.**
>
> *mee*-lih-tays ihn *kuhs*-trees *puh*-ruhnt. hee *tay*-luh *uh*-ku-unt, *ihl*-lee *kih*-bum *puh*-ruhnt, eht heek *liht*-teh-rahs *skree*-biht.
>
> The soldiers are getting ready in the camp. These sharpen their weapons, those prepare food, and he is writing a letter.

From the use of the pronouns, you can tell that the soldiers sharpening weapons and the one guy writing a letter are closer to the speaker than those who are getting food ready.

One other demonstrative pronoun, **is** (ihs), can have all the meanings of **hic** and **ille:** *this, these, that, those, he, she, it,* and *they* (see Table 7-11). Because it's not as strong a demonstrative, this word can also be a third-person personal pronoun.

Table 7-11	Is, Ea, Id — This, These, That, and Those	
Case	*Singular (M/F/N)*	*Plural (M/F/N)*
Nominative	is, ea, id (ihs, *eh*-uh, ihd)	ei, eae, ea (*eh*-ee, *eh*-igh, *eh*-uh)
Genitive	eius, eius, eius (*ay*-yus, *ay*-yus, *ay*-yus)	eorum, earum, eorum (eh-*o*-rum, eh-*ah*-rum, eh-*o*-rum)

Case	Singular (M/F/N)	Plural (M/F/N)
Dative	ei, ei, ei (*eh*-ee, *eh*-ee, *eh*-ee)	eis, eis, eis (*eh*-ees, *eh*-ees, *eh*-ees)
Accusative	eum, eam, id (*eh*-um, *eh*-uhm, ihd)	eos, eas, ea (*eh*-os, *eh*-ahs, *eh*-uh)
Ablative	eo, ea, eo (*eh*-o, *eh*-ah, *eh*-o)	eis, eis, eis (*eh*-ees, *eh*-ees, *eh*-ees)

Who's who? Relative pronouns

Another important pronoun to know is the relative pronoun. In English, these pronouns are *who, whom, whose, which,* and *that.* Table 7-12 shows you the Latin versions.

The word *who* only refers to people and can only be the subject of a clause. In other words, it can translate any nominative case form. *Whom* also indicates people only, but it's an object form in English, thus it can translate any case but nominative. *Whose* shows possession for people or things, and therefore can only be used to translate the genitive case. Traditionally, *which* referred only to things, and *that* to people or things, but this distinction has almost disappeared from English. No matter how you slice it, though, you can use both of these words to translate any of the five Latin cases.

Table 7-12	Relative Pronouns	
Case	*Singular (M/F/N)*	*Plural (M/F/N)*
Nominative	qui, quae, quod (kwee, kwigh, kwohd)	qui, quae, quae (kwee, kwigh, kwigh)
Genitive	cuius, cuius, cuius (*koo*-yus, *koo*-yus, *koo*-yus)	quorum, quarum, quorum (*kwo*-rum, *kwah*-rum, *kwo*-rum)
Dative	cui, cui, cui (*ku*-ih, *ku*-ih, *ku*-ih)	quibus, quibus, quibus (*kwih*-bus, *kwih*-bus, *kwih*-bus)
Accusative	quem, quam, quod (kwehm, kwhuhm, kwohd)	quos, quas, quae (kwos, kwahs, kwigh)
Ablative	quo, qua, quo (kwo, kwah, kwo)	quibus, quibus, quibus (*kwih*-bus, *kwih*-bus, *kwih*-bus)

A relative pronoun takes its gender (masculine/feminine/neuter) and number (singular/plural) from its antecedent (the noun it renames) but gets its *case* (nominative, genitive, and so on) from how it's used in its own clause. Consider the following sentence:

The general whom we loved earned the title "Imperator."

The word *whom* renames *general,* so in Latin you need a masculine singular pronoun because *general* is masculine and singular. In the clause *whom we loved,* the word *whom* functions as a direct object, so it must be in the accusative case, even though the word it renames (*general*) is in the nominative case as the subject of the sentence. The complete Latin sentence looks like this:

Dux quem amavimus nomen "Imperator" meruit.

duks kwehm uh-*mah*-wih-mus *no*-mehn "ihm-peh-*rah*-tohr" *meh*-ru-iht.

Talkin' the Talk

A **mater** (*mah*-tehr; mother) and her **filius** (*fee*-lih-us; son) discuss the Roman general Pompey. (Notice the different pronouns used in this conversation.)

Mater: **Fili, mihi librum fer.**
fee-lee, *mih*-hih *lih*-brum fehr.
Son, bring me the book.

Filius: **Cupisne hunc librum de Caesare?**
ku-*pihs*-neh hunk *lih*-brum day *kigh*-suh-reh?
Do you want this book about Caesar?

Mater: **Minime. Illum in mensa legebam.**
mih-nih-may. *ihl*-lum ihn *mayn*-sah leh-*gay*-buhm.
No. I was reading that one on the table.

Filius: **Magister meus de Pompeio docuit, qui erat dux magnus.**
muh-*gihs*-tehr *meh*-us day pohm-*pay*-yo *doh*-ku-iht, kwee *eh*-ruht duks *muhng*-nus.
My teacher taught about Pompey, who was a great general.

Mater:	**Sine dubio. Et tu es eius consanguineus.** *sih*-neh *du*-bih-o. eht too ehs *ay*-yus kon-suhn-*gwih*-neh-us. Without a doubt. And you are his relative.
Filius:	**Fortasse ego exercitum ducam.** fohr-*tuhs*-seh *eh*-go ehks *ehr*-kih-tum *du*-kuhm. Perhaps I shall lead an army.
Mater:	**Fortasse, sed primum mihi illum librum fer!** fohr-*tuhs*-seh, sehd *pree*-mum *mih*-hih *ihl*-lum *lih*-brum fehr! Perhaps, but first bring me that book!

Words to Know

dubium, dubi, n	du-bih-um, du-bee	doubt
fortasse	fohr-tuhs-seh	perhaps
lego, legere, legi, lectus	leh-go, leh-geh-reh, lay-gee, lehk-tus	to read
liber, libri, m	lih-behr, lih-bree	book
magister, magistri, m	muh-gihs-tehr, muh-gihs-tree	teacher
mensa, mensae, f	mayn-suh, mayn-sigh	table
mereo, merere, merui, meritus	meh-reh-o, meh-ray-reh, meh-ru-ee, meh-rih-tus	to earn
nomen, nominis, n	no-men, no-mih-nihs	name
scribo, scribere, scripsi, scriptus	skree-bo, skree-beh-reh, skreep-see, skreep-tus	to write

Fun & Games

If you're a soldier, you need to know who to gripe to when things go wrong. Pick the person most likely to solve your problem in the following situations:

1. A horse did its business right outside your tent.

   A. eques   B. dux   C. funditor   D. cornicen

2. You need an arrow to go hunt your dinner.

   A. explorator   B. imperator   C. sagittarius   D. miles

3. You had trouble seeing the eagle standard during the battle.

   A. centurio   B. aquilifer   C. signifer   D. faber

4. You want secret information about a cute barbarian in the town you just sacked.

   A. legatus   B. triarius   C. mercator   D. speculator

See Appendix C for the answers.

Chapter 8

Roman Entertainment and Sports

• •

In This Chapter

▶ Recognizing the comparative and superlative adjective forms

▶ Understanding gladiatorial games

▶ Exploring Roman athletics

▶ Appreciating Roman drama

• •

*F*or some people, entertainment is going to a movie, taking in a play, or enjoying a concert. Others prefer something a bit more high-energy, such as sports or writing a Latin book. Most cultures across the world and throughout history have had various forms of entertainment. The flourishing of arts and athletics is a sign of civilization. After all, having time to engage in these pastimes means that your culture has tamed the elements, and you don't have to worry about finding food (or running from something that wants to eat you).

As one of the first great multicultural societies, the Roman Empire understood something about entertainment. From cathartic tragedies to bawdy comedies to the sands of the arena, the Romans knew how to put on a good show.

Let the Games Begin!

Juvenal was a first century A.D. Roman satirist who enjoyed poking fun at his own society. He observed that his countrymen had become content with two things: **panem et circenses** (*Saturae*, X.78) (*pah*-nehm eht kihr-*kayn*-says; bread and circus games). By Juvenal's day, athletic contests had become a favorite means of escape from the realities of life, but in the beginning, they had another purpose.

Sacred games

Organized athletic competitions had their origins in funerals, particularly of those who died in battle. These competitions were a way to honor the dead with activities taken from the lives they had just left. Many of the contests involved skills necessary in war. For example, in Book 5 of the *Aeneid,* the hero Aeneas holds funeral games that include a boat race, a footrace, javelin throwing, and boxing. Glory itself was the main prize in such games, and the visible award was a simple **palma** (*puhl*-muh; palm wreath).

These **ludi** (*loo*-dee; games) became a part of various religious celebrations and were connected with different holidays; eventually the Romans celebrated more than forty varieties of games throughout the year.

Athletic competition for its own sake was more of a Greek concept than a Roman one. Although the Romans occasionally engaged in Olympic-style contests, the concept of fun for fun's sake — at least in sporting events — never really caught on with most Romans. For athletic entertainment, the gladiatorial shows were by far the most popular.

Not for the squeamish: Gladiatorial games

The word *gladiator* literally means "one who uses a sword." **Gladius, gladi,** m (*gluh*-dih-us, *gluh*-dee) is the word for "sword." But Roman gladiators were much more than just sword fighters, and gladiatorial games were much more than just two men fighting to the death.

One on one

Of course, the sport did include that whole fighting-to-the-death thing, so perhaps that's the place to begin. A **gladiator** (gluh-dih-*ah*-tohr) was a trained killer. Whether a prisoner of war, a condemned criminal, a slave, or a freeman who had sworn the **auctoramentum gladiatorium** (owk-to-rah-*mehn*-tum gluh-dih-ah-*to*-rih-um; gladiator's oath), these men were sent to training schools run by a **lanista** (luh-*nih*-stuh; trainer). In these schools, they received instruction in how to fight with a variety of weapons. Knowing how to kill was important, but they also had to know how to put on a good show. Fighting in the **amphitheatrum** (uhm-phih-theh-*ah*-trum; amphitheater), which was almost identical in construction to the modern stadium, they had to put on a killing display for as many as 50,000 people. The following list shows some of the basic types of gladiators and what distinguished one from another:

- **murmillo, murmillonis,** m (mur-*mihl*-lo, mur-mihl-*lo*-nihs): Heavily armored with an oblong shield, a short sword, and a full-face protection, these warriors could also be recognized by a crest on their helmets in the shape of a fish.

- **retiarius, retiari,** m (ray-tih-*ah*-rih-us, ray-tih-*ah*-ree): The **retiarius** had minimal armor and fought with a trident and **rete** (*ray*-teh; net).

- **Thrax, Thracis,** m (thrahks, *thrah*-kihs): You could spot a Thracian from his small, round shield and curved scimitar. These weapons were also symbols of his homeland, Thrace.

- **Samnis, Samnitis,** m (*suhm*-nees, suhm-*nee*-tihs): Like the **murmillo,** the Samnite was a heavily-armored warrior, fighting with a short sword and helmet with a visor. His name indicated he was from Samnium, a region in central Italy.

Unlike modern boxing where opponents of similar weights fight each other, gladiatorial contests often featured mismatched pairs. A lightly armed **retiarius,** for example, might go up against a heavily armed **murmillo.** Part of the excitement came from seeing whether speed or brute strength would win the day.

The Noah's Ark of entertainment

In addition to men fighting each other, the Romans also liked to watch a **venatio** (way-*nah*-tih-o) — a staged hunt. Although people often think of martyrs being fed to the lions (which did in fact occur), a proper **venatio** involved **bestiarii** (bays-tih-*ah*-rih-ee; beast hunters) tracking and killing wild animals in the arena.

Thumbs up or down?

If you've seen enough "sword and sandal" movies, you know that a winning gladiator didn't immediately kill the defeated opponent. He waited for a signal from the emperor, who based his decision on the will of the crowd. If the crowd liked the fallen gladiator, they might cheer for him to be spared so they could see him fight another day.

So what was the signal? According to Hollywood and modern convention, thumbs up indicated life, and thumbs down meant death. The phrase used in Latin is **pollice verso** (*pohl*-lih-keh *wehr*-so), which literally means "with thumb turned." No one knows which direction was really used to indicate life or death. Many think that thumbs up or pointing toward the heart meant death, and thumbs down (pointing toward the sand) meant to throw the weapon away and let your opponent live.

I thought this was PG-13

The bloodlust inherent in the gladiatorial games was unavoidable. Although the crowd may have rewarded a good fight by allowing the loser to live, the whole object of this sport was death. In fact, any modern sports facility called an *arena* takes its name from the Latin **arena, arenae,** f (uh-*ray*-nuh, uh-*ray*-nigh), the word for *sand,* which covered the floor where gladiators fought; its purpose wasn't to cushion the falls; it was to soak up the blood. In an effort to make gladiatorial games a bit more family-friendly,

women and children had to sit in the highest seats so that they would be farther away from the actual killing.

And if you think modern soccer matches can get out of hand, consider this. In A.D. 59, the citizens of Nuceria went to the games at Pompeii. Violence got so out of hand among the spectators that the Emperor Nero, himself no candidate for a Nobel Peace Prize, banned games in Pompeii for ten years.

Imitation hunting areas were set up to add realism, and part of the thrill was in seeing exotic animals. (Zoos hadn't been invented yet.) These hunts became so popular that when the Flavian Amphitheatre (better known as the Colosseum) was dedicated in A.D. 80 under the Emperor Titus Flavius Vespasianus, 9,000 animals, both tame and wild, were slaughtered.

The Flavian Amphitheater became known as the Colosseum because of its proximity to a giant statue of the Emperor Nero called **Colossus** (koh-*lohs*-sus; giant statue), which was itself named for one of the so-called Seven Wonders of the Ancient World, the Colossus at Rhodes. In the Colosseum, the Romans also held mock naval battles called **naumachiae** (now-*muh*-khih-igh). The entire floor was flooded, and gladiators fought it out from ships that sailed around the arena. Julius Caesar first gave such a display to the Romans, but that was in 46 B.C., nearly ninety years before the Colosseum was completed. For his **naumachiae,** he used an artificial lake just outside the city.

Free at last

In the modern world, the popular athlete is the one who signs a contract for millions. In ancient Rome, the superstar gladiator was the one who simply survived. And if you lived through enough contests, you could win your freedom. A gladiator's symbol of freedom was a wooden sword, the **rudis** (*ru*-dihs), which meant that he no longer had to fight. Knowing how to do little else, however, some returned to the training schools as **lanistae,** and others became bodyguards for the rich and famous.

The government provided the gladiatorial games, but up-and-coming politicians would sometimes add their own money to make the games even more spectacular. They did this to plant themselves firmly in the minds of voters.

Round and round we go: Chariot racing

The Roman chariot race, another ancient form of athletic entertainment, has been immortalized in such films as *Ben-Hur.* **Circenses** (kihr-*kayn*-says), which is the Latin term for these races, took place on an oval track called a **circus** (*kihr*-kus), with the **Circus Maximus** (*kihr*-kus *muhks*-ih-mus) in Rome being the largest racetrack, holding around 250,000 spectators. A **spina** (*spee*-nah; spine) ran down the middle, and a typical race consisted of anywhere from four to twelve chariots running for seven laps, which were marked by turning a series of egg and dolphin emblems on a pole.

The egg symbol was sacred to the mythological twins Castor and Pollux (who were supposedly placed in the heavens as the constellation Gemini by Zeus), and the dolphin was connected with Neptune. The Romans associated all three of them with horses.

The teams, **factiones** (fuhk-tih-*o*-nays), raced under different colors, and people were fiercely loyal to their favorites. Betting was a major part of this sport, and one way to show your dislike of the emperor was to bet against his favorite color. Originally, chariot races had two **factiones,** the **russae** (*ruhs*-sigh; reds) and the **albae** (*uhl*-bigh, whites). Over time, the **prasinae** (*pruh*-sih-nigh; greens) and the **venetae** (*weh*-neh-tigh; blues) joined the field, and for a brief period, the **purpureae** (pur-*pur*-eh-igh; purples) and the **auratae** (ow-*rah*-tigh; golds) participated.

Takin' a bath

Believe it or not, going to the **thermae** (*thehr*-migh; public baths) was another form of entertainment. Bathing may sound like a chore to you, but in ancient Rome, it was quite a treat. The **thermae** were like modern day athletic clubs. You could go to work out, talk business or politics, or even read. The **thermae,** built by the Emperor Caracalla (A.D. 212–217), had a Greek library on one end and a Latin library on the other. The baths were one place where upper- and lower-classes mingled because the price for admittance was pretty cheap: just a **quadrans** (*kwuh*-drahns) or a fourth of an **as** (ahs), the **as** being just an ounce of bronze.

Typical **thermae** had an **apodyterium** (uh-poh-dih-*tay*-rih-um; changing room), **palaestra** (*puh*-ligh-struh; exercise ground), and then a series of rooms for cleaning, steaming, and cooling down: the **tepidarium** (teh-pih-*dah*-rih-um; warm room), the **caldarium** (kuhl-*dah*-rih-um; hot room), and the **frigidarium** (free-gih-*dah*-rih-um; cold room).

Talkin' the Talk

Titus and Marcus are sitting in the **thermae** (*thehr*-migh; public baths), discussing their further entertainment options.

Titus: **Gladiator Eudamus in amphitheatro pugnabit. Eumne vides?**
gluh-dih-*ah*-tohr yoo-*dah*-mus ihn um-phih-theh-*ah*-tro pung-*nah*-biht. eh-*um*-neh *wih*-days?
The gladiator Eudamus will fight in the amphitheater. Do you want to see him?

Marcus: **Eudamus est murmillo optimus, sed retiarios malo.**
yoo-*dah*-mus ehst mur-*mihl*-lo *ohp*-tih-mus, sehd ray-tih-*ah*-rih-os *mah*-lo.
Eudamus is the best *murmillo*, but I prefer *retiarii*.

Titus: **Tum circenses spectemus. Venetae equos celerrimos habent.**
tum kihr-*kayn*-says spehk-*tay*-mus. *weh*-neh-tigh *eh*-kwos keh-*lehr*-rih-mos *huh*-behnt.
Then let's watch the chariot races. The blues have the fastest horses.

Marcus: **Venetas non amo, et ubi circenses spectavi, lutum me semper spargebat.**
weh-neh-tas non *uh*-mo, eht *u*-bee kihr-*kayn*-says spehk-*tah*-wee, *lu*-tum may *sehm*-pehr spuhr-*gay*-buht.
I do not like the blues, and whenever I have watched chariot races, mud always splattered me.

Titus: **Tum quid agere vis?**
tum kwihd *uh*-geh-reh wees?
Then what do you want to do?

Marcus: **In bibliothecam Graecam intrantes puellas pulchras vidi. Libros legamus!**
ihn bih-blih-oh-*thay*-kuhm *grigh*-kuhm ihn-*trahn*-tays pu-*ehl*-lahs *pul*-chrahs *wee*-dee. *lih*-bros leh-*gah*-mus!
I saw some cute girls entering the Greek library. Let's read some books!

Words to Know

amphitheatrum, amphitheatri, n	um-fih-theh-ah-trum, um-fih-theh-ah-tree	amphitheater
arena, arenae, f	uh-ray-nuh, uh-ray-nigh	sand, arena
circus, circi, m	kihr-kus, kihr-kee	race course
gladiator, gladiatoris, m	glhu-dih-ah-tohr, gluh-dih-ah-to-rihs	gladiator
gladius, gladi, m	gluh-dih-us, gluh-dee	sword
intro, intrare, intravi, intratus	ihn-tro, ihn-trah-reh, ihn-trah-wee, ihn-trah-tus	to enter
panis, panis, m	pah-nihs, pah-nihs	bread
pulcher, pulchra, pulchrum	pul-kher, pul-khruh, pul-khrum	beautiful, handsome
spargo, spargere, sparsi, sparsus	spuhr-go, spuhr-geh-reh, spahr-see, spahr-sus	to sprinkle, splatter
verto, vertere, verti, versus	wehr-to, wehr-teh-reh, wehr-tee, wehr-sus	to turn

Good, Better, Best: Never Let It Rest!

"Good, better, best — never let it rest 'til your good is better, and your better, best!" So goes the children's rhyme teaching the correct forms of these adjectives. What this little ditty is really getting at is something called the *comparison of adjectives.* The simplest form of an adjective is one that has been placed (**positus;** *poh*-sih-tus) next to a word to give the most basic information about it. This form is the *positive degree.* Words like *good, bad, pretty, ugly,* and *sesquipedalian* are all positive-degree adjectives. (To read more about adjectives, check out Chapter 4.) Using the other degrees (comparative and superlative, explained in the following sections) is how you indicate something is better (or best), worse (or worst), prettier (or prettiest), and so on.

Comparative-degree adjectives (–er)

Pretend that you're sitting with your friend in the Colosseum and you see a gladiator. "So what?" says your friend. "There are plenty of gladiators." Not to be put off, you add a positive-degree adjective, and say that you see a *tall* gladiator. But this doesn't really help your friend identify which gladiator has caught your eye, so you try again. "I see a gladiator taller than you." Because your friend is a six footer, this is useful information. You made a comparison using a *comparative-degree* adjective.

In English, comparative adjectives usually end in **–er** or use an adverb, such as *more*. In Latin, comparative-degree adjectives have **ior** somewhere in the word or have **–ius** on the end. Here are a couple of other things you need to know about comparative-degree adjectives in Latin:

✔ They always use third-declension endings. (See Chapter 4 for a chart of these endings by themselves.)

✔ They use one set of suffixes for masculine and feminine forms and another set of endings for neuter.

For a rather lofty example, consider the positive-degree adjective **altus, alta, altum** (*uhl*-tus, *uhl*-tuh, *uhl*-tum; tall). Tables 8-1 and 8-2 show its comparative forms.

Table 8-1	Masculine/Feminine Comparative-Degree Adjectives	
Case	**Singular**	**Plural**
Nominative	altior (*uhl*-tih-ohr)	altiores (uhl-tih-*o*-rays)
Genitive	altioris (uhl-tih-*o*-rihs)	altiorum (uhl-tih-*o*-rum)
Dative	altiori (uhl-tih-*o*-ree)	altioribus (uhl-tih-*o*-rih-bus)
Accusative	altiorem (uhl-tih-*o*-rehm)	altiores (uhl-tih-*o*-rays)
Ablative	altiore (uhl-tih-*o*-reh)	altioribus (uhl-tih-*o*-rih-bus)

Table 8-2	Neuter Comparative-Degree Adjectives	
Case	**Singular**	**Plural**
Nominative	altius (*uhl*-tih-us)	altiora (uhl-tih-*o*-ruh)
Genitive	altioris (uhl-tih-*o*-rihs)	altiorum (uhl-tih-*o*-rum)

Case	Singular	Plural
Dative	altiori (uhl-tih-*o*-ree)	altioribus (uhl-tih-*o*-rih-bus)
Accusative	altius (*uhl*-tih-us)	altiora (uhl-tih-*o*-ruh)
Ablative	altiore (uhl-tih-*o*-reh)	altioribus (uhl-tih-*o*-rih-bus)

Usually when you compare two nouns, you want to finish the comparison with an expression that uses the word *than.* Someone is faster, prettier, or smarter *than* someone else. In Latin, you have two ways to express this. You can use the word **quam** (kwuhm), which, when following a comparative adjective means "than," or you can put the noun with which you are making the comparison in the ablative case. In a use known as the **ablative of comparison,** you simply translate an ablative following a comparative adjective with the word "than." Take a look at these examples:

> **Hic auriga est celerior quam ille.**
>
> heek ow-*ree*-guh ehst keh-*leh*-rih-ohr kwuhm *ihl*-leh.

> **Hic auriga est celerior illo.**
>
> heek ow-*ree*-guh ehst keh-*leh*-rih-ohr *ihl*-lo.

Both of these sentences say the same thing: "This charioteer is faster than that one."

One other use of the ablative case, called the **ablative of degree of difference,** often goes with a comparative-degree adjective. To emphasize how different the items being compared are, just throw in a quantity word, such as *much, little,* and so on, in the ablative case.

> **Pugil est multo fortior solus quam cum adversario.**
>
> *pu*-gihl ehst *mul*-to *fohr*-tih-ohr *so*-lus kwuhm koom uhd-wehr-*sah*-rih-o.
>
> The boxer is much braver alone than with an opponent.

Superlative-degree adjectives (–est)

The comparative-degree adjective, explained in the preceding "Comparative-degree adjectives (–er)" section, is useful because it relates one noun to another, giving more information than a simple positive-degree adjective. If you want to identify something without a shade of doubt, however, you need the superlative degree. In English, these forms use the suffix **–est** or get help from the word *most,* and they describe a unique noun. To say that someone is the tallest athlete is technically to say that no taller athlete exists anywhere in the world.

Superlative-degree adjectives are easy to recognize in Latin. They all have a double consonant in the middle. Here are other things to know about superlative-degree adjectives:

- Most adjectives use the suffix **–issimus.** The superlative of **altus,** for example, is **altissimus** (uhl-*tihs*-sih-mus; tallest).

- Adjectives that have **–er** for their masculine form use **–rimus** for the superlative. The superlative of **celer** (*keh*-lehr; fast) is **celerrimus** (keh-*lehr*-rih-mus; fastest).

- A few adjectives with **–lis** on the masculine form use **–limus** in the superlative degree. For example, the word for "easy," **facilis** (*fuh*-kih-lihs), has **facillimus** (fuh-*kihl*-lih-mus; easiest) for its superlative form.

All superlative-degree adjectives use first-declension endings for the feminine gender and second-declension endings for the masculine and neuter. To review what those endings are, head to Chapter 2.

The word **quam** also makes its way into phrases with superlative-degree adjectives. A phrase made up of **quam** plus a superlative translates to "as (whatever) as possible."

Quam ferocissimus leo bestiarium oppugnavit.

kwuhm feh-ro-*kihs*-sih-mus *leh*-o bays-tih-*ah*-rih-um ohp-pung-*nah*-wiht.

As fierce a lion as possible attacked the beast-fighter.

Irregular comparisons

Children and people learning English as a second language often make the mistake of sticking "–er" or "–est" on every adjective when they want to show degree. The comparison forms of *good,* for example, end up being *gooder* and *goodest* instead of *better* and *best.* Of course, this is just one of the many places where English doesn't follow its own rules; it has irregular forms instead.

Turns out that Latin has irregular comparative and superlative forms, too. The following chart shows the three degrees for several important adjectives. (Just as Latin dictionaries do, this list shows the abbreviated feminine and neuter forms for the positive and superlative degrees. The first of the two comparative forms listed is the masculine/feminine form, and the other is the neuter.) This chart can be a big help, unless you really want to sound like a barbarian by saying **bonior** to mean "better."

Table 8-3	Irregular Comparison of Adjective	
Positive Degree	**Comparative Degree**	**Superlative Degree**
bonus, –a, –um (good)	melior, melius (better)	optimus, –a, –um (best)
malus, –a, –um (bad)	peior, peius (worse)	pessimus, –a –um (worst)
superus, –a, –um (high)	superior, superius (higher)	summus, –a, –um (highest)
inferus, –a, –um (low)	inferior, inferius (lower)	imus, –a, –um (lowest)
magnus, –a, –um (big)	maior, maius (bigger)	maximus, –a, –um (biggest)
parvus, –a, –um (small)	minor, minus (smaller)	minimus, –a, –um (smallest)

Standing Room Only: Roman Plays

The Romans enjoyed plays, or **ludi scaenici** (*loo*-dee *skigh*-nih-kee; theatrical games). As with the athletic games (see the earlier section "Let the Games Begin!"), these plays were usually performed in connection with a religious celebration. Unlike modern movies, which you can see at any time of the day or night, Roman plays happened much less often, partly because of their association with particular sacred celebrations and partly because of the elements. Most plays were performed in open-air buildings or auditoriums with temporary wooden stages being erected in the Forum or even the Circus Maximus. Without sound or lighting equipment, the cast needed Mother Nature's cooperation. In fact, by the end of the first century B.C., Romans could enjoy a drama on only fifty-five days — little more than 15 percent of the year.

Long before the days of special effects, Roman drama relied primarily on the script and the actors' performances to deliver the message. Here's how they did it:

- **The props:** The basic set in a Roman **theatrum** (theh-*ah*-trum; theater) was a backdrop depicting a house with three doors. These doors represented various entrances to one house or to neighboring homes, but the majority of the play was acted out in front of this simple set. An exit off stage to the right indicated the direction to a town or market, and an exit left suggested the way to a harbor or the countryside.

- **The actors:** Like Greek actors, the Romans wore **personae** (pehr-*so*-nigh; masks) when performing. Similar to the set appearance of one of the Three Stooges or Laurel and Hardy, these masks helped audiences identify the stock characters in a Roman comedy. Comic actors also wore a low-cut shoe called a **soccus** (*sohk*-kus) to distinguish themselves from the tragic actors, who wore a high boot or buskin called a **cothurnus** (ko-*thur*-nus).

Except for in the mimes (farces, explained in the section "Laughing 'til it hurts"), which predated Roman comic plays, actors in ancient Rome were men. Unlike today's big stars, who enjoy all sorts of perks and pleasures, actors back then were slaves or freedmen considered too low class even to vote. (For more information on mimes, see the section "Laughing 'til it hurts.")

A tragic story

In his **De Natura Deorum** (day nah-*too*-rah deh-*o*-rum; about the nature of the gods), Cicero quoted the tragedian Seneca's line, **maior mihi moles, maius miscendumst malum** (III.26.38) (*migh*-ohr *mih*-hih *mo*-lays *migh*-us mihs-*kehn*-dumst *muh*-lum), which is to say, "I must stir up greater trouble, an even greater evil." Sounds pretty ominous. (Can you spot the comparative-degree adjectives? If you can't — or don't know what comparative-degree adjectives are, head to the "Good, Better, Best: Never Let It Rest!" section.)

Tragedy, as Cicero's quotation shows, is drama on the dark side. On the really, *really* dark side. But if you want plenty of tragedy, you have to go to the Greeks, who wrote a whole slew of plays in which parents killed children (*Medea* by Euripides, for example); children killed parents (*Oedipus Rex* by Sophocles), and general mayhem and revenge plots abounded (*Antigone* by Sophocles and *Agamemnon* by Aeschylus).

Although the Romans had tragic playwrights, such as Livius Andronicus, who first adapted Greek tragedies for a Latin-speaking audience in 240 B.C., they just never really became popular. In fact, only a few Roman tragedians from the third century B.C. are even known. No great Roman tragedian really took the stage until Seneca did in the reign of Nero during the first century A.D., and several of his plays were retellings of the classical Greek tragedies, such as *Medea* and *Agamemnon,* for example.

That's gratitude for you

In addition to writing Roman tragedies, Lucius Annaeus Seneca worked as a tutor to the infamous Emperor Nero. Despite Seneca's best advice, Nero ended up murdering his relatives and allowing (or causing) half of Rome to burn. Seneca died of what at that time was practically considered a natural cause: suicide at the order of the emperor. **Vita artem imitatur!** (*wee*-tuh *uhr*-tehm ih-mih-*tah*-tur) Life imitates art!

According to Nero's biographer Suetonius, the emperor was quite fond of performing himself. Nero would order that no one leave his performances, which — unfortunately for the audience — were so long that pregnant women gave birth and some men faked death just for an excuse to escape.

Laughing 'til it hurts

The Roman poet and satirist Horace once quipped,

> **Quid rides? Mutato nomine fabula de te narratur.** (*Sermo* I.1.69–70)
>
> kwihd *ree*-days? moo-*tah*-to *no*-mih-ne *fah*-bu-luh day tay *nahr*-ruh-tur.
>
> What are you laughing at? With the name changed, the story is told about you.

True enough, and a good warning perhaps, but that didn't stop the Romans from enjoying comedy, especially when the laughter came at someone else's expense.

In the second and third centuries B.C., comic playwrights Plautus and Terence set the stage for humor with their lively reworking of Greek originals. Although Terence won greater critical acclaim for his work (the intellectual elite liked him), most Romans preferred Plautus. Why? Because they wanted sex jokes and puns, and Plautus's plays obliged.

Perhaps the Romans preferred broader, crude humor because they were used to a type of performance called **mimus** (*mee*-mus; mime). Unlike the white-faced, silent performers called *mimes* today, **mimi** in ancient Rome were short, crude comic sketches performed by both men and women. They featured, as did the plays of Plautus, stock characters in routine situations: husband and cheating wife, rich father and playboy son, and a crowd-pleasing favorite, the tricky slave who manages to save the day by outwitting everyone.

Twenty-one plays from Plautus survive in one form or another today. Only six of Terence's survive.

Talkin' the Talk

A **femina** (*fay*-mih-nuh; woman) and **vir** (wihr; man) talk about going to the theater.

Vir:	**Plautus comoediam iocosissimam scripsit.** *plow*-tus ko-*moi*-dih-um yoh-ko-*sihs*-sih-muhm *skreep*-siht. Plautus has written the funniest comedy.
Femina:	**Estne iocosior illa Terenti?** *ehst*-neh yoh-ko-sih-or *ihl*-lah teh-*rehn*-tee? Is it funnier than Terence's?

Vir:	**Plautus est multo melior quam Terentius.**
	plow-tus ehst *mul*-to *meh*-lih-or kwuhm teh-*rehn*-tih-us.
	Plautus is much better than Terence.
Femina:	**Sed ioci eius sunt tam humiles, et servus dolosus semper vincit.**
	sehd *yoh*-kee *ay*-yus sunt tuhm *hu*-mih-lays, eht *sehr*-wus doh-*lo*-sus *sehm*-pehr *wihn*-kiht.
	But his jokes are so low class, and the tricky slave always wins.
Vir:	**Et iuvenis puellam pulcherrimam semper invenit, sic ego te inveni.**
	eht *yu*-weh-nihs pu-*ehl*-luhm pul-*chehr*-rih-muhm *sehm*-pehr *ihn*-weh-niht, seek *eh*-goh tay ihn-*way*-nee.
	And the young man always finds the most beautiful girl, just as I found you.
Femina (**discedens** (dihs-*kay*-dayns) departing):	**Tu es mendax peior, mi amice, et Plauto et Terentio!**
	too ehs *mehn*-dahks *pay*-yohr, mee uh-*mee*-keh, eht *plow*-to eht teh-*rehn*-tih-o!
	You are a worse liar, my friend, than both Plautus and Terence!

Words to Know

celer, celeris, celere	keh-lehr, keh-leh-rihs, keh-leh-reh	fast
fabula, fabulae, f	fah-bu-luh, fah-bu-ligh	story
facilis, facile	fuh-kih-lihs, fuh-kih-leh	easy
ludus, ludi, m	loo-dus, loo-dee	game, play
oppugno, oppugnare, oppugnavi, oppugnatus	ohp-pung-no, ohp-pung-nah-reh, ohp-pung-nah-wee, ohp-pung-nah-tus	to attack
persona, personae, f	pehr-so-nuh, pehr-so-nigh	dramatic mask

Fun & Games

Can you complete each of these Latin sentences to show where you would go for each activity?

1. **Ludos gladiatorios _____ spectamus.**

    A. in theatro   B. in amphitheatro   C. in socco   D. in circo

2. **Factio russa equos celeriores habet quam prasina _____.**

    A. in Colosseo   B. in arena   C. in circo   D. in ludo

3. **Quadrantem habeo. Cupisne ire _____?**

    A. ad thermas   B. ad theatrum   C. ad lanistam   D. ad circenses

Draw a line connecting the correct adjective with the English sentence whose italicized word best defines it.

4. That gladiator is *taller* than the other one.   A. maior

5. He has the *biggest* shield in the world!   B. facillimus

6. Latin is *easier* than any other language.   C. altissimus

7. One chariot is *bigger* than the other.   D. facilior

8. This is the *tallest* arch I have ever seen.   E. altior

9. The *easiest* game is the one you're prepared for.   F. maximus

See Appendix C for the answers.

Chapter 9

Roman Government

. . . .

In This Chapter

▶ Recognizing passive-voice verbs

▶ Working with gerunds

▶ Understanding participles

▶ Investigating Roman government

. . . .

Pax Romana (pahks ro-*mah*-nuh). The Roman Peace. Although the world's deadliest army advanced this ideal, governments throughout the world have maintained the same ideal ever since. Many people think of emperors when they think of ancient Rome, and the Eternal City certainly had them during part of its history, but Rome's government and Roman politics were more varied than that. Rome enjoyed a democratic form of rule called a republic, which had written law and elected officials. Many countries today base their governments on the model of the Roman Republic. Rome ruled its physical world for more than twelve hundred years, but nearly three millennia after Romulus first founded the little city on the Tiber River, Rome's influence continues to spread across the globe.

This chapter introduces you to all three periods of ancient Roman history: the kingdom, the republic, and the empire. Along the way, you can find out about some of the most famous and influential Roman leaders, whose names have become synonymous with power and influence. You also get a look at an important verb form called passive voice, as well as participles and gerunds.

Ruling the World

When the ancient Romans wanted to refer to the world, they said **orbis terrarum** (*ohr*-bihs tehr-*rah*-rum), which literally means "circle of lands." Yes, the ancients knew the world was round long before Christopher Columbus went off on his adventures. But the real world for the Romans was the Mediterranean world. Imagine a map. In your mind, draw a line from England to Babylon (the ancient city located in the middle of Iraq), then draw another line from southern Spain to the Caspian Sea, and you have an idea of what the world really meant for the Romans. And right there almost in the middle of the X was Rome itself. Of course, even a mighty empire has to start somewhere.

Hometown boys

Tullus Hostilius waged a battle in which the Romans conquered the hometown of Romulus and Remus, Alba Longa. In that battle, a set of triplet brothers known as the Horatii fought in the Roman army, and a set of triplets called the Curiatii fought in the Alban army. The leaders from each side agreed that the two sets of triplets would fight each other. The outcome of the battle between the brothers would determine the outcome of the war.

In the fight, five of the six brothers ended up dead. The last man standing was from the Horatii, and so Rome gained control of its parent city. This story became the subject of a famous painting by eighteenth-century French artist Jacques-Louis David.

King for a day: The kingdom

According to the Roman historian Livy, Rome began when two brothers, Romulus and Remus, set out with some people from the Italian town of Alba Longa to build a new city. Because Romulus and Remus were twins (and the same age), they couldn't figure out who should be king. So they decided to watch the birds for a sign from the gods. Almost immediately, Remus saw six vultures. Shortly after, Romulus saw twelve. Again the quandary: Who should rule? The brother who saw the birds first or the one who saw more?

Apparently, Romulus thought the king should be the one who saw more birds, and so he started to build. Remus, annoyed when he saw the defensive wall of his brother's city going up, began to tease Romulus by jumping back and forth over the wall. Romulus, not getting the joke, drew his sword and killed his brother, effectively settling the dispute.

For almost 250 years, seven men with the title of **rex** (rayks; king) ruled the small community on the banks of the Tiber River in central Italy, watching it grow in size and influence. Here they are, with a little something to distinguish each one:

- ✔ **Romulus:** The first king of Rome, Romulus was the one who brought women into the new city. He invited neighboring communities to a festival, where, at an arranged signal, each Roman man kidnapped a girl. Some of the prettiest girls were reserved for the leaders of Rome.

- ✔ **Numa Pompilius:** The second king of Rome, Numa was known for establishing early Roman laws and religious practices. He created the office of the Vestal Virgins, for example. Chosen when they were between 6 and 10 years old, these girls kept the fire burning in the temple of Vesta, the goddess of hearth and home, and served for thirty years. A Vestal who didn't remain chaste (virginal) was buried alive.

- ✔ **Tullus Hostilius:** Much more aggressive than Numa, this third Roman king waged many wars and added plenty of land to Roman territory.

- ✔ **Ancus Marcius:** The fourth king of Rome was the grandson of Numa Pompilius, and like his grandfather, he revived Roman interest in religious practices. One of his most memorable accomplishments was building one of the first bridges over the Tiber River, the **Pons Sublicius** (pons suh-*blih*-kih-us) — literally, "the bridge made of wooden piles."

- ✔ **Tarquinius Priscus:** The fifth Roman king is known for building the Circus Maximus, the great chariot-racing course. One of Ancus Marcius's sons, who considered him an outsider and resented his taking the throne after their father, murdered the king.

- ✔ **Servius Tullius:** The sixth king of Rome was a rags-to-riches story. (See the sidebar "Behind every great man . . ." later in this chapter for details). When two sons of Ancus Marcius murdered Tarquinius, Servius became king. He organized the citizens into groups (called *centuries*) based on wealth so everyone would know how much they should contribute in times of war.

- ✔ **Tarquinius Superbus:** Helped by his wife, Tullia (daughter to King Servius), Tarquinius Superbus became Rome's seventh and last king by arranging the king's murder. (That's how he earned the nickname **superbus** (su-*pehr*-bus), which means "proud" or "arrogant.")

Behind every great man . . .

A couple of women figure prominently in the lives of at least three of Rome's kings: **Tanaquil,** the wife of Rome's fifth king (Tarquinius Priscus), and **Tullia,** daughter of Rome's sixth king (Servius Tullius) and wife of its seventh (Tarquinius Superbus).

Tanaquil and Tarquinius Priscus had left their home in Etruria partly because he wanted to live a better life and partly because she didn't want to be married to a loser of a husband. On the way to Rome, an eagle swooped down, plucked Tarquinius' hat from his head, and set it back down again. Tanaquil, very superstitious, interpreted this as a sign that her husband would be crowned king of Rome. Sure enough, that's what happened.

Tanaquil — with her tendency to see signs — also saw great things in Servius Tullius. He grew up as a slave in her household. One night, Servius's head caught fire, but he didn't get burned. Tanaquil interpreted this to mean that the gods favored Servius. So she ordered that he be raised with the best of everything, including a royal education and the king's own daughter for his wife.

Tarquinius Superbus, who was Tanaquil's and Tarquinius Priscus's son, married King Servius Tullius's daughter Tullia. Tullia's ambition was even worse than Tanaquil's. She conspired with her husband to overthrow her own father. At a senate meeting, the young Tarquinius picked up the elderly Servius Tullius and threw him into the street. As the old man staggered back to his palace, his daughter's assassins did him in.

From rhymes to reason

Having trouble keeping the stories straight? Can't remember which king did what? The following verses can help you.

For the Romulus versus Remus story:

Did Remus murder Romulus or was the killing in reverse?
To help remember who slew whom, just memorize this little verse:
'Twas Romulus killed Remus, and lent his name to a tiny dream
That grew to rule the western world, and thus we study Rome not Reme.

For remembering which king did what:

Now Romulus was Rome's first king, he was the start of everything.
Numa Pompilius beat the odds by sacrificing to the gods.
Tullus Hostilius was third, who made men cringe with just a word.
The fourth was Ancus Marcius, who bridged the Tiber first for us.
The fifth was Tarquin, surnamed "First," whose wife's ambition was the worst.
Servius Tullius followed these, dividing Rome into centuries.
Tarquin the Proud ended the race of kings by leaving in disgrace.

By the people, for the people: The republic

King Tarquinius Superbus' son, **Sextus Tarquinius,** brought the kingdom to an end through disgrace. According to Livy, Sextus raped a noble woman named Lucretia, who in turn told her husband about the offense. She then took her own life rather than live with the shame of what had happened. Seeing this as one more in a list of intolerable acts by oppressive rulers, the Romans decided to run the royal family out of town. In place of the kings, they elected their own rulers, and in 509 B.C., Rome became a **res publica** (rays *poo*-blih-kuh), which literally means "a public state." The modern world knows this era of history as the republic.

During the Roman Republic, the Romans began writing down their laws, and the concept of **lex, legis,** f (layks, *lay*-gihs; codified law) came into practice. After the abuses of the kings, the people wanted to know what the actual laws were and what rights they actually had.

The foundation of law for the Romans was the will of the gods or **fas** (fahs). This comes from the verb **fari** (*fah*-ree), meaning "to speak." In other words, what the gods spoke was law. At a different level was the concept of **ius, iuris,** n (yoos, *yoo*-rihs), which indicated personal rights or justice.

In fact, if you remember that the letters *i* and *j* in Latin are basically the same letter, you can see in this word such derivatives as "justice" and "jury."

Early on in this new era of government, the Romans went to Athens, famous for its democracy, to get a copy of the laws that the Greeks had written down. Then the Romans appointed the **decemviri** (*deh*-kehm-*wih*-ree; board of ten men) to draft a set of laws for Rome. Published in the years 451 to 450 B.C., the **XII Tabulae** (du-*oh*-deh-kihm *tuh*-bu-ligh; Twelve Tables) formed the foundation of Roman law and government. Under these laws, the republic flourished for hundreds of years.

To be elected to lead the people was quite an honor, and the system of public offices was known as the **cursus honorum** (kur-sus hoh-*no*-rum; course of honors.) The following list shows the main offices of the **cursus honorum** in the order in which you had to be elected.

- ✔ **quaestor, quaestoris,** m (*kwigh*-stohr, kwigh-*sto*-rihs; quaestor): These were Rome's financial officers. When elected **quaestor,** a person automatically became a **senator, senatoris,** m (seh-*nah*-tohr, seh-nah-*to*-rihs; senator). The **quaestor** was something like a treasurer. No wonder senators are the only ones who can vote themselves pay raises!

- ✔ **praetor, praetoris,** m (*prigh*-tohr, prigh-*to*-rihs; praetor): These officials oversaw aspects of Roman justice, could command an army, and were in charge of the city when the consuls were away. The simplest equivalent in the modern world would be a judge. A **praetor** could also command an army, giving whole new meaning to the phrase "judge, jury, and executioner."

- ✔ **consul, consulis,** m (*kon*-sul, *kon*-su-lihs; consul): These were the chief magistrates of the city. They led all civil matters, presided over the senate, and regularly commanded armies. A counterpart in the United States of America would be the president, who is also commander in chief of the armed forces.

- ✔ **censor, censoris,** m (*kayn*-sohr, kayn-*so*-rihs; censor): The censor oversaw the census of the Roman citizens every five years. He also reviewed the list of senators and could remove anyone from office who had acted illegally or against Roman morality. Modern censors, fortunately, keep themselves busy with song lyrics. Can you imagine if they had power over Capitol Hill?

While these were the main positions, many other opportunities for government service existed. The following were also important leadership positions:

- ✔ **tribunus, tribuni,** m (trih-*boo*-nus, trih-*boo*-nee; tribune): This office was open only to plebeians or the lower class of Roman citizens. The **tribunus** enjoyed the power of veto over other magistrates. This was the forerunner to the system of checks and balances seen in the legislative, judicial, and executive branches of governments.

> ✔ **aedilis, aedilis,** m (igh-*dee*-lihs, igh-*dee*-lihs; aedile): Aediles were in charge of public works, such as temple repair, and the maintenance of aqueducts and roads. They also became responsible for public games, and from this responsibility, ambitious politicians often launched their careers. The more spectacular the games were that you put on, the more people would remember you when you ran for other offices. In other words, the **aedilis** was the ancient ancestor of Don King.

Rendering unto Caesar: The empire

In the last century before Christ, the Roman Republic began to show signs of stress. Wars and rumors of wars abounded. Shortly after defeating his own countryman and former son-in-law Pompey the Great in a civil war, Gaius Iulius Caesar managed to get himself appointed dictator for life, which from that point proved to be short. Six months later, revolutionaries who wanted a return to the values of the Roman Republic assassinated Iulius Caesar, and he fell at the foot of the statue of his former foe, Pompey.

Two great personalities arose during this confused period, **Marcus Antonius** (known nowadays as "Mark Antony"), who had served in Caesar's army, and **Gaius Iulius Caesar Octavianus** (known as "Octavian"), the nephew and adopted son of the murdered dictator. Together, these two men avenged Iulius Caesar's death by waging war on the conspirators, but they were not destined for a long association.

In 31 B.C., Antony and Octavian squared off against each other in a naval battle in Greece. Octavian was the victor. For all practical purposes, the 32-year-old Octavian was in charge of Rome. Four years later, the senate voted Octavian numerous honors, including the title of **Augustus** (ow-*gus*-tus; revered one), by which name he is known to history as the first emperor of Rome.

Roman adventure stories

Some of the best Roman adventure stories come from the early days of the republic. The historian Livy records how the Tarquinius family tried to regain the throne by allying themselves with another local king. Out of this war come famous Roman heroes, such as Horatius Cocles and Mucius Scaevola. Horatius and two of his friends kept the entire enemy army at bay while the Romans chopped down the Pons Sublicius, the wooden bridge over the Tiber, to keep the enemy out of the city. With similar heroism, Mucius attempted to assassinate the foreign king, but was caught and ordered to tell the details of his conspiracy. To show that they could not even torture the information out of him, Mucius thrust his right hand into the fire and burned it off, hence his nickname **scaevola** (*skigh*-woh-luh) — lefty.

Following Augustus, a series of men led the Roman Empire, calling themselves **princeps** (*preen*-kehps; first citizen.) At times, the distinction between a **princeps** and a **rex** seemed negligible, although the Romans continued to abhor the title of king. Many of the colorful personalities from ancient history come from this period, including the emperor **Caligula,** who made his horse a senator, and **Commodus,** who thought of himself as the incarnation of Hercules and decided to compete as gladiator, but his own advisors assassinated him before he got the chance.

Getting Out of the Verbal Trap

Verbals are verb forms that function as another part of speech. So when aren't verbs verbs? When they're parading around as adjectives or nouns, that's when.

Here's an example that may make this concept clearer. Consider the word *train* in these sentences:

> We train for the Olympics.
>
> We went to training camp.
>
> We saw a trained bear.
>
> Training for a marathon is hard work.

In the first sentence, *train* is the verb, conveying action. In the second and third sentences, *training* and *trained* (both verb forms) aren't functioning as verbs. In these sentences, they're functioning as adjectives (that is, describing the nouns *camp* and *bear*). In the last sentence, *training* functions as a noun; in fact, it's the subject of that sentence.

Verbal is a generic term describing verbs that don't behave like verbs. You have two types of verbals:

- ✔ **Participles:** When a verbal functions as an adjective, it's a *participle* — easy to remember if you just keep in mind that a PARTiciple is PART verb and PART adjective. In English, words like *running, copied,* and *taught* are participles. Because they are part verb, they show some action, but because they are part adjectives, they modify nouns, as in "the runnng athlete," "a copied poem," and "the taught lesson."

  Although Latin has six verb tenses (for a refresher on what those look like, check out Chapters 2, 4, and 6), it only has three participle tenses: present, perfect, and future.

✔ **Gerunds:** When a verbal functions as a noun, it's called a gerund. A gerund is part verb and part noun. In English, gerunds usually end in **–ing,** which means that you may get them confused with present participles, which also end in **–ing.** But how the word is used in a sentence clearly lets you know whether it's functioning as a participle (adjective) or gerund (noun). In the sentence, "The running girl enjoys running," the first use of *running* is as a present participle because it describes the girl. The second use of *running* is as a gerund, because it's a direct object showing what the girl enjoys.

The following sections explain how you can identify and decline participles and gerunds in Latin.

Presenting present participles

The present participle in Latin is easy to recognize. Just as the suffix **–ing** identifies the present participle in English (running, jumping, singing, and so on), in Latin, the letters **–ns** and **–nt** identify the present participle.

✔ The **–ns** suffix appears on the nominative singular form of the participle

✔ The letters **–nt** appear in the middle of all the other forms

Because participles function as adjectives, they must have adjective endings. All present participles take their endings from the third declension.

Take a look at the present participles from the verb **censeo, censere, censui, census** (*kayn*-seh-o, kayn-*say*-reh, *kayn*-su-ee, *kayn*-sus; to vote) in Tables 9-1 and 9-2, and notice that present participles use the same set of endings for the masculine and feminine genders and a separate set for the neuters.

Table 9-1	Declining a Masculine/Feminine Present Participle	
Case	*Singular*	*Plural*
Nominative	censens	censentes
Genitive	censentis	censentium
Dative	censenti	censentibus
Accusative	censentem	censentes
Ablative	censente	censentibus

Take a look at the following example showing the present participle, **censentes:**

> **Consul ad Curiam senatores censentes convocavit.**
>
> *kon*-sul uhd *koo*-rih-uhm seh-nah-*to*-rays kayn-*sehn*-tays kohn-wo-*kah*-wiht.
>
> The consul has called the voting senators to the Senate House.

Table 9-2	Declining a Neuter-Present Participle	
Case	*Singular*	*Plural*
Nominative	censens	censentia
Genitive	censentis	censentium
Dative	censenti	censentibus
Accusative	censens	censentia
Ablative	censente	censentibus

The word *present* has the letters **nt** in it, as do most of the present participle forms in Latin. The only form that does not use **nt** is the **n**ominative **s**ingular, which ends in **ns.**

Understanding perfect participles

You already know the perfect participle. Don't think so? It's just the fourth dictionary form of a verb. Consider the verb **rego, regere, rexi, rectus** (*reh*-go, *reh*-geh-reh, *rayks*-ee, *rayk*-tus; to rule). In truth, that last dictionary form is the perfect participle, whose complete forms are **rectus, recta, rectum** (*rayk*-tus, *rayk*-tuh, *rayk*-tum; ruled). Table 9-3 shows you how to decline this verb form. The same is true in English. For the verb *sing, singing, sang, sung,* the perfect participle is *sung.* Most of the time, though, English uses the suffix **–ed** for this participle, as in *ruled.* The Latin forms of the perfect participle use first-declension endings for the feminine gender and second declension for masculine and neuter.

Table 9-3	Declining a Perfect Participle	
Case	*Masculine/Feminine/Neuter Singular*	*Masculine/Feminine/Neuter Plural*
Nominative	rectus, recta, rectum	recti, rectae, recta
Genitive	recti, rectae, recti	rectorum, rectarum, rectorum

(continued)

Table 9-3 *(continued)*

Case	Masculine/Feminine/Neuter Singular	Masculine/Feminine/Neuter Plural
Dative	recto, rectae, recto	rectis, rectis, rectis
Accusative	rectum, rectam, rectum	rectos, rectas, recta
Ablative	recto, recta, recto	rectis, rectis, rectis

Notice the difference between the present and perfect participles in this sentence:

Cives recti a regibus magistratus censentes iuste agere cupiverunt.

kee-ways *rayk*-tee ah *ray*-gih-bus muh-*gihs*-*trah*-toos kayn-*sehn*-tays *yoos*-tay *uh*-geh-reh ku-pee-*way*-runt.

The citizens ruled by kings wanted the voting magistrates to act justly.

In the preceding sentence, **recti** (ruled) is the perfect participle describing **cives** (citizens), and **censentes** (voting) is the present participle describing **magistratus** (magistrates).

Participles, especially the perfect participles, often sound best in English as clauses (structures that have subjects and verbs). For example, you can translate the phrase **cives recti** as "the citizens who had been ruled" rather than "ruled citizens."

Using present-future participles

Voice is a grammatical term applied to verbs, and it tells whether a verb or a verbal is active or passive. You can read all about passive-voice verbs later in this chapter in the section "Passive (Aggressive) Voice," but you need to know something about active and passive voice in general here.

Simply put, active voice means that the subject of the verb or the noun modified by the participle is doing the action. Take a look at this sentence:

The running girl finished the race.

In this sentence, the word *running* is a present *active* participle because the girl (which running describes) is the one doing the action.

In passive voice, just the opposite is true. With a passive verb or participle, the subject or modified noun receives the action as in the following sentence:

The injured king was murdered in the street.

In that sentence, *injured* is a perfect *passive* participle because the king received the action, in this case a violent one.

The reason why this info on active and passive voice is important here is because, in Latin, present participles are active voice, and perfect participles are passive voice. The future participles, however, can be active *or* passive.

Future-active participle

The future-active participle looks like the perfect participle with the letters **–ur** inserted before the ending. (See the earlier section "Perfect participles presented" for information on what perfect participles look like.) Like the perfect participle, this verbal uses first-declension endings for the feminine gender and second declension for masculine and neuter (see Table 9-4).

The perfect participle is the same as the fourth dictionary form of a verb. Also, the word *future* has the letters **–ur** in the middle as do the future active participles in Latin.

Table 9-4	Declining a Future-Active Participle	
Case	*Masculine/Feminine/Neuter Singular*	*Masculine/Feminine/Neuter Plural*
Nominative	recturus, rectura, recturum	recturi, recturae, rectura
Genitive	recturi, recturae, recturi	recturorum, recturarum, recturorum
Dative	recturo, recturae, recturo	recturis, recturis, recturis
Accusative	recturum, recturam, recturum	recturos, recturas, rectura
Ablative	recturo, rectura, recturo	recturis, recturis, recturis

Here's an example using the future-active participle **recturi** (rule).

Aquila in capite viri Romam recturi petasum deposuit.

uh-kwih-luh ihn *kuh*-pih-teh *wih*-ree *ro*-muhm *rayk*-tu-ree *peh*-tuh-sum day-*poh*-su-iht.

An eagle placed a hat on the head of the man about to rule Rome.

You can translate the future-active participle into English as "about to [whatever]." Still, a clause sometimes sounds better. The phrase **viri Romam recturi** also means "of the man who was about to rule Rome."

Future-passive participle: The gerundive

The future-passive participle looks different from the future active. In fact, it's so different that it gets its own special grammatical name, the *gerundive*. One thing that future passive shares with its active relative, though, are identifying letters somewhere in the word. In this case, the letters are **–nd.** Another shared trait among the gerundive, future active, and perfect participles is the use of first- and second-declension endings for the three genders.

Table 9-5 shows the gerundive forms for **porto, portare, portavi, portatus** (*pohr*-to, pohr-*tah*-reh, pohr-*tah*-wee, pohr-*tah*-tus; to carry).

Table 9-5	Declining a Gerundive	
Case	*Masculine/Feminine/Neuter Singular*	*Masculine/Feminine/Neuter Plural*
Nominative	portandus, portanda, portandum	portandi, portandae, portanda
Genitive	portandi, portandae, portandi	portandorum, portandarum portandorum
Dative	portando, portandae, portando	portandis, portandis, portandis
Accusative	portandum, portandam, portandum	portandos, portandas, portandos
Ablative	portando, portanda, portando	portandis, portandis, portanda

An easy way to recognize gerundives is to remember that the word *geruNDive* has the letters **nd** in the middle as do the Latin forms themselves.

Notice the difference between the future-active and future-passive participles in the following sentence:

Servus nuntium portandum ad regem portaturus in flumen cecidit.

sehr-wus *noon*-tih-um pohr-*tuhn*-dum uhd *ray*-gehm pohr-tah-*too*-rus ihn *floo*-mehn *keh*-kih-diht.

The slave about to carry the message to be carried to the king fell into the river.

A basic way to translate the gerundive is "to be [whatever]," but this translation often results in awkward English as illustrated in the English translation in the preceding example. Because the gerundive carries a sense of obligation or necessity, you can usually render it with a clause using the words *must, ought, had,* or *should.* Using clauses for both participles in the preceding example, you get

> The slave <u>who was about to carry</u> the message <u>that had to be carried</u> to the king fell into the river.

The first underlined clause is a translation of the future-active participle. The second underlined clause is a translation of the gerundive.

Passive periphrastic

Because the gerundive implies obligation or necessity, it can function in a special construction called the *passive periphrastic.* Don't let the word *periphrastic* scare you. It just means a round-a-bout way of saying something. Basically, the passive periphrastic is a gerundive plus some form of the linking verb **sum, esse, fui, futurus** (sum, *ehs*-seh, *fu*-ee, fu-*too*-rus; to be). Take a look at this:

> **Aqua portanda est.**
>
> *uh*-kwuh pohr-*tuhn*-duh ehst.
>
> The water must be carried.

Just as when you translate a gerundive by itself, you can use the helping words *must, ought, had,* or *should* to make a smooth reading.

To show who must do the action with a passive periphrastic, Latin uses the dative case in a function called **dative of agent.** Putting an agent — **tibi** (*tih*-bih; by you) — with the previous example, you get

> **Aqua tibi portanda est.**
>
> *uh*-kwuh *tih*-bih pohr-*tuhn*-duh ehst.
>
> The water must be carried by you.

Running with gerunds

A gerund is a verbal that functions as a noun in the sentence. Here's what you need to know about Latin gerunds:

> ✔ Latin gerunds can appear in the genitive, dative, accusative, and ablative cases.

✔ Latin gerunds don't have a nominative, or subject, case. That is, they can't be subjects in sentences. Latin makes up for this by using the present infinitive, which is the second dictionary entry for verbs. Thus you have this famous expression:

Errare est humanum.

ehr-*rah*-reh ehst hoo-*mah*-num.

Literally, this means "To make a mistake is human," but a gerund translation in **–ing** works just as well, "Making a mistake is human."

✔ Latin gerunds have one form for both singular and plural.

✔ The gerund (like the gerundive — see the preceding section) uses the letters **–nd** somewhere in its forms.

✔ As a noun, the gerund is always second-declension neuter in form.

Table 9-6 shows the gerund forms of the verb **erro, errare, erravi, erratus** (*ehr*-ro, ehr-*rah*-reh, ehr-*rah*-wee, ehr-*rah*-tus; to wander, make a mistake).

Table 9-6	Declining a Gerund
Case	*Singular and Plural*
Nominative	****
Genitive	errandi
Dative	errando
Accusative	errandum
Ablative	errando

Latin gerunds don't have a nominative case per se. Instead, they use the present infinitive, which is the second dictionary entry for verbs.

Consider this example:

Aeneas errandum non amavit et Venerem matrem consuluit.

igh-*nay*-ahs ehr-*ruhn*-dum non uh-*mah*-wiht eht *weh*-neh-rehm *mah*-trehm kon-*su*-lu-iht.

Aeneas did not like wandering and consulted Venus, his mother.

If you find the terms *gerund* and *gerundive* confusing, you can always tell which is which by remembering that the gerundive is a future-passive participle or verbal adjective. Thus, the gerundIVE is an adjectIVE.

Another use for the gerund (and the gerundive as well for that matter) is the purpose construction. A basic way to express purpose is with the purpose clause, which you can read more about in Chapter 6. Of course, who wants to say something the same way every time? The Romans liked variety, and the following constructions show different ways to express purpose in Latin:

- **Genitive of purpose:** This construction involves the words **gratia** (*grah*-tih-ah) or **causa** (*kow*-sah), both of which can mean "for the sake of" and genitive-case gerund or gerundive.

  > **Princeps gratia belli prohibendi laboravit.**

  > *preen*-kehps *grah*-tih-ah *behl*-lee pro-hih-*behn*-dee luh-bo-*rah*-wiht.

  > The emperor worked for the sake of stopping war.

- **Dative of purpose:** Here you just need a dative-case gerund or gerundive, which can translate simply "to [whatever]."

  > **Princeps bello prohibendo laboravit.**

  > *preen*-kehps *behl*-lo pro-hih-*behn*-do luh-bo-*rah*-wiht.

  > The emperor worked to stop war.

- **Accusative of purpose:** For this construction look for the preposition **ad** (uhd), meaning "for the purpose of" and an accusative gerund or gerundive.

  > **Princeps ad bellum prohibendum laboravit.**

  > *preen*-kehps uhd *behl*-lum pro-hih-*behn*-dum luh-bo-*rah*-wiht.

  > The emperor worked for the purpose of stopping war.

You can translate any purpose construction quite simply with the word "to." Thus, all three of the preceding examples can mean "The emperor worked to stop war."

Whether an author uses a gerund or gerundive depends on whether a noun needs to be modified. Consider this pair of sentences:

> **Nero ad cantandum advenit.**

> *nay*-ro uhd kuhn-*tuhn*-dum uhd-*way*-niht.

> **Nero ad carmina cantanda advenit.**

> *nay*-ro uhd *kuhr*-mih-nuh kuhn-*tuhn*-duh uhd-*way*-niht.

The first sentence uses a gerund and means, "Nero came to sing." The gerundive in the second sentence modifies the word **carmina** (songs), thus giving the translation "Nero came to sing songs."

Talkin' the Talk

A **patricius** (puh-*trih*-kih-us; patrician) and a **plebeius** (play-*bay*-yus; plebeian) discuss the upcoming election.

Plebeius: **Romani bellum gesturi magistratus fortes cupiunt.**
ro-*mah*-nee *behl*-lum gehs-*too*-ree muh-gihs-*trah*-toos *fohr*-tays *ku*-pih-unt.
Romans about to wage war desire strong magistrates.

Patricius: **Sic, et praetor ab hominibus laudatus, consulatum peto.**
seek, eht *prigh*-tohr uhb hoh-*mih*-nih-bus low-*dah*-tus, kon-su-*lah*-tum *peh*-to.
Yes, and as a praetor praised by the people, I am seeking the consulship.

Plebeius: **Amici tui sed non omnes te laudant.**
uh-*mee*-kee *tu*-ee sehd non *ohm*-nays tay *low*-duhnt.
Your friends praise you but not everyone.

Patricius: **Romani viros pugnantes amant, et ego multis in proeliis pugnavi.**
ro-*mah*-nee *wih*-ros pung-nahn-tays *uh*-muhnt, eht eh-go mul-tees ihn proi-lih-ees pung-nah-wee.
Romans love fighting men, and I have fought in many battles.

Plebeius: **Virum qui vincit amant, et proelia tua sunt cum uxore, non hostibus.**
wih-rum kwee *wihn*-kiht *uh*-muhnt, eht proi-*lih*-uh *tu*-uh sunt koom uks-o-reh, non *hohs*-tih-bus.
They love the man who wins, and your battles are with your wife, not the enemy.

Patricius: **Me insultando tuo vexas.**
may een-sul-*tuhn*-do *tu*-o *wehks*-ahs.
You annoy me with your taunting.

Plebeius: **Tribunus sum, et te vetando peius vexabo.**
trih-*boo*-nus sum, eht tay weh-*tuhn*-do *pay*-yus wehks-*ah*-bo.
I am a tribune, and I shall annoy you worse by vetoing.

Words to Know

cado, cadere, cecidi, casurus	*kuh*-do, *kuh*-deh-reh, *keh*-kih-dee, *kah*-sus	to fall
laudo, laudare, laudavi, laudatus	*low*-do, low-*dah*-reh, low-*dah*-wee, low-*dah*-tus	to praise
nuntius, nunti, m	*noon*-tih-us, *noon*-tee	messenger
proelium, proeli, n	*proy*-lih-um, *proy*-lee	battle
rex, regis, m	*rayks, ray*-gihs	king
verbum, verbi, n	*wehr*-bum, *wehr*-bee	word

Passive (Aggressive) Voice

English teachers often caution against using passive voice, but it plays a regular part in Latin literature. With an active-voice verb, the subject does the action; with a passive-voice verb, the subject receives the action. Take a look at these two sentences:

> Romulus ruled Rome.
>
> Rome was ruled by Romulus.

The first sentence is active. Romulus, the subject doing the action (ruling Rome). In the second sentence, the subject, Rome, receives the action.

Latin authors use passive voice to convey specific connotations. The two preceding sample sentences say essentially the same thing, but each has a different focus. The first sentence puts the emphasis on Romulus and his activity of ruling. It carries the sense of, "Romulus and no one else, especially not Remus, ruled Rome." The second sentence conveys the same basic information, but the focus is on the city itself. The connotation in the second sentence might be that despite Romulus's being part of the royal family from Alba Longa, it was Rome that benefited from his guiding hand.

Present, imperfect, and future passive

For the present, imperfect, and future indicative tenses in Latin, as well as the present and imperfect subjunctive, the passive voice personal endings are all the same. (To review the active-voice endings, head over to Chapter 2.) Table 9-7 shows what you need to know.

Table 9-7	Passive-Voice Personal Endings		
Singular Ending	**Meaning**	**Plural Ending**	**Meaning**
–r	I	–mur	we
–ris	you	–mini	you
–tur	he, she, it	–ntur	they

The same rules apply about how to recognize the different tenses for the various verb conjugations: Basically you have to pay attention to the verb's ending. (If you need a refresher on all that, head to Chapter 2.) The following sentences can help make sense of this:

> **Roma, quae a consulibus regitur et semper sapientia regetur, a regibus regebatur.**
>
> *ro*-muh, kwigh ah kon-*su*-lih-bus *reh*-gih-tur eht *sehm*-per suh-pih-*ehn*-tih-ah reh-*gay*-tur, ah *ray*-gih-bus reh-*gay*-buh-tur.
>
> Rome, which is ruled by consuls and will always be ruled by wisdom, was ruled by kings.

Notice that five of the six passive-voice endings use the letter **–r,** which makes this a good clue to recognizing the passive-voice forms for these tenses.

The dative of agent often goes with the passive periphrastic (refer the earlier section "Passive periphrastic") to show who is actually doing the action. With regular passive-voice verbs, you need the *ablative of agent,* which uses the preposition **a** (ah) before consonants or the preposition **ab** (uhb) before vowels and a noun in the ablative case. In the preceding, **a consulibus** and **a regibus** are both ablatives of agent. The noun in an ablative of agent construction is always a living being, such as *consuls* and *kings*. Because *wisdom* isn't a person, the word **sapientia** doesn't need a preposition. It's functioning as an ablative of means. For more on the different ablative uses, see Chapter 6.

Perfect, pluperfect, future perfect passive

English uses compound verbs all the time. In the sentence "Rome was being ruled by Romulus," the verb is actually three separate words: *was being ruled.* Latin starts concocting compound verbs for the passive voice of the perfect, pluperfect, and future-perfect tenses. For all four of these tenses, you start off with the perfect participle, followed by a form of the verb **sum, esse, fui, futurus** (sum, *ehs*-seh, *fu*-ee, fu-*too*-rus; to be). Because these are the only compound forms in the whole Latin language, they're always easy to recognize.

Tables 9-8 through 9-10 show the perfect, pluperfect, and future-perfect passive forms for the verb **rego, regere, rexi, rectus** (*reh*-go, *reh*-geh-reh, *rayks*-ee, *rayk*-tus; to rule).

Table 9-8	Perfect-Passive Indicative
Singular	*Plural*
rectus, –a, –um sum	recti, –ae, –a sumus
rectus, –a, –um es	recti, –ae, –a estis
rectus, –a, –um est	recti, –ae, –a sunt

The perfect participle functions as an adjective, so it can have all three gender endings. For example, "He has been ruled" would be **Rectus est,** and "She has been ruled" would be **Recta est.** The perfect participle part of these compound verbs must always match the subject in gender, case, and number.

Table 9-9	Pluperfect-Passive Indicative
Singular	*Plural*
rectus, –a, –um eram	recti, –ae, –a eramus
rectus, –a, –um eras	recti, –ae, –a eratis
rectus, –a, –um erat	recti, –ae, –a erant

Table 9-10	Future-Perfect-Passive Indicative
Singular	*Plural*
rectus, –a, –um ero	recti, –ae, –a erimus
rectus, –a, –um eris	recti, –ae, –a eritis
rectus, –a, –um erit	recti, –ae, –a erunt

The following sentence is a monster that brings together all three of these passive tenses. Perhaps it describes villagers relaying water buckets to help put out a fire.

Aqua, quae a puellis portata erat, a pueris portata est et paucis horis ab omnibus portata erit.

uh-kwuh, kwigh ah pu-*ehl*-lees pohr-*tah*-tuh *eh*-ruht, ah *pu*-eh-rees pohr-*tah*-tuh ehst eht *pow*-kees *ho*-rees uhb *ohm*-nih-bus pohr-*tah*-tuh *eh*-riht.

The water, which had been carried by the girls, has been carried by the boys and within a few hours will have been carried by everyone.

Remember that Latin has only four subjunctive tenses. (Chapter 6 tells you all about the subjunctive mood.) Present and imperfect subjunctive use the same passive endings as the present- and imperfect-indicative forms. Perfect- and pluperfect-subjunctive passive are similar to their indicative counterparts because they're compounds, but they do look a little different as Tables 9-11 and 9-12 show.

Table 9-11	Perfect-Passive Subjunctive
Singular	*Plural*
rectus, –a, –um sim	recti, –ae, –a simus
rectus, –a, –um sis	recti, –ae, –a sitis
rectus, –a, –um sit	recti, –ae, –a sint

Table 9-12	Pluperfect-Passive Subjunctive
Singular	*Plural*
rectus, –a, –um essem	recti, –ae, –a essemus
rectus, –a, –um esses	recti, –ae, –a essetis
rectus, –a, –um esset	recti, –ae, –a essent

Talkin' the Talk

In this imaginary conversation, Julius Caesar advises his adopted son Octavian about the art of ruling.

Caesar: **Roma a viris infirmis diutissime gubernata est.**
ro-muh ah *wih*-rees een-*fihr*-mees di-oo-*tihs*-sih-may gu-behr-*nah*-tuh ehst.
Rome has been governed for too long by weak men.

Octavianus: **Cui Roma gubernanda est?**
                  ku-ih *ro*-muh gu-behr-*nuhn*-duh ehst?
                  By whom should Rome be governed?

Caesar: **Viris fortibus, ut urbs ad gloriam reducatur.**
                  wih-rees *fohr*-tih-bus, ut urps uhd *glo*-rih-uhm
                  reh-du-*kah*-tur.
                  By brave men, so that the city may be led back to glory.

Octavianus: **Ubi tales viri invenientur?**
                  u-bee *tah*-lays *wih*-ree ihn-weh-nih-*ehn*-tur?
                  Where will such men be found?

Caesar: **Ubicumque augustus ad iuste agendum non dubitat.**
                  u-bee-*koom*-kweh ow-*gus*-tus uhd *yoos*-tay uh-*gehn*-
                  dum non *du*-bih-tuht.
                  Wherever a venerable man does not hesitate to act
                  justly.

Words to Know

dubito, dubitare, dubitavi, dubitatus	*du*-bih-to, du-bih-*tah*-reh, du-bih-*tah*-wee, du-bih-*tah*-tus	to doubt
guberno, gubernare, gubernavi, gubernatus	gu-*behr*-no, gu-behr-*nah*-reh, gu-behr-*nah*-wee, gu-behr-*nah*-tus	to govern
omnis, omne	*ohm*-nihs, *ohm*-neh	all
pauci, paucae, pauca	*pow*-kee, *pow*-kigh, *pow*-kuh	few
rego, regere, rexi, rectus	*reh*-go, *reh*-geh-reh, *rayk*-see, *rayk*-tus	to rule
urbs, urbis, f	urps, *ur*-bihs	city

Fun & Games

See if you know your Roman history! Everyone has a purpose in life, so see if you can match the correct ruler or official with the purpose construction that best describes him.

1. ad vetandum

   A. consul   B. Romulus   C. rex   D. tribunus

2. gratia deorum laudandorum

   A. quaestor   B. Numa Pompilius   C. princeps   D. censor

3. ad carmina cantanda

   A. Caesar   B. aedilis   C. Nero   D. senator

Turn the following sentences from active to passive.

4. Romulus Romam regit.

5. Rex exercitum ducebat.

6. Princeps urbem gubernaverat.

See Appendix C for the answers.

Chapter 10

More Lasting Than Bronze: Latin Literature

A man once said that the pen is mightier than the sword, and despite the power of Rome's armies, this statement has proved true for her cultural influence across the world. Roman soldiers in red-crested helmets no longer go forth to conquer new lands, and the Colosseum is just a shattered ruin, a tourist attraction where you can pose for a picture with a man costumed as a gladiator. Latin literature, however, continues to be read, explored for new meanings, and tapped for its wealth of style and ideas.

The poet Horace once wrote about his compositions,

> **Exegi monumentum aere perennius.** (*Carmina* III.30.1)
>
> ehks-*ay*-gee moh-nu-*mehn*-tum *igh*-reh peh-*rehn*-nih-us.
>
> I have created a monument more lasting than bronze.

In this chapter, you meet some of the famous authors of Roman antiquity, writers whose works have stood the test of time. You can also investigate two important grammatical constructions, the indirect statement and the conditional sentence. Without these, much of Latin literature would not exist.

The Written Word

In ancient times, as in modern times, literature fell into two camps: poetry (verse) and prose (paragraphs). Between then and now, though, the importance and role of poetry has gone through a major shift. Today, poetry seems confined to literary journals and song lyrics. The primary form of written communication in the modern world, both for instruction and entertainment, is prose. The novel, not the sonnet, reigns supreme.

The situation was reversed, however, in the ancient world. Writers used prose for general communication in history books and speeches, for example. (That's not to say the prose wasn't elegant. The speeches of Cicero, for example, have provided countless generations with models of eloquence.) The Romans didn't really have novels per se. For sheer entertainment, the Romans liked poetry, and Roman poets complied with poems about love and hate, life and death, and all the other themes of human life. Roman plays (the comedies and the tragedies) were also written in verse as were their epics.

Before the days of copyrights

The Latin word for "publish" is **edere** (*ay*-deh-reh), which literally means "to give forth." An author published a work by giving a copy to someone, whose slaves made a copy. At that point, the work was out of the author's hands, making any corrections extremely difficult to put into a later edition. For this reason, Horace cautioned poets to keep their work nine years before considering publication, adding **[N]escit vox missa reverti** (*Ars Poetica* 388) (*nehs*-kiht woks *mihs*-suh reh-*wehr*-tee) — "The voice sent forth does not know how to return."

Another way to get books (if you didn't have slaves who could make personal copies for you) was to visit the local **librarius** (lih-*brah*-rih-us; bookseller). You could rummage through the bookseller's boxes or baskets (in those days, books were in the form of scrolls) looking for what you wanted. The **librarii** also had a staff of copyists who could produce whatever you wanted (similar to e-publishing and publish-on-demand books today). A famous bookstore in Rome was that of the Sosii brothers. It was so well known, in fact, that today the Web site Sosii Booksellers at the Atrium (http://web.idirect.com/~atrium/sosii.html) uses the name to help sell antiquarian books.

The novelty of Latin novels

The closest thing to the modern novel appeared twice in Latin literature. In the first century A.D., Petronius wrote a work called *Satyricon,* which described the comic misadventures of a trio of young men. Unfortunately, this work hasn't survived intact. The most famous part of what remains describes the dinner party of Trimalchio, a wealthy man with few manners.

The only complete Latin novel to survive was written in the second century A.D. by Apuleius. Known by two different titles, *Metamorphoses* (*Changes*) or *Asineus Aureus* (*The Golden Ass*), it describes the life of a man who gets turned into a donkey. Many adventures follow, providing the framework to tell the most well-known part of the story, the tale of Cupid and Psyche.

Who's who of Latin authors

The Latin word for author, **auctor, auctoris,** m (*owk*-tohr, owk-*to*-rihs), literally means "one who brings about increase." So in this section, you can find out about the Roman writers who increased the world of knowledge and art in their own time and for ages to come. The following list introduces you to only a few of Rome's leading literary lights, some you've undoubtedly heard of; some you probably haven't:

- **Caesar** (100–44 B.C.): Yes, the great general was also a great writer. One of his well-known works describes his own war against the Gauls and contains the famous opening line, **Gallia est omnis divisa in partes tres.** (*De Bello Gallico* I.1) (*guhl*-lih-uh ehst *ohm*-nihs dee-*wee*-suh ihn *puhr*-tays trays) — "Gaul is, on the whole, divided into three parts."

- **Cicero** (106–43 B.C.): A statesman and philosopher, Cicero is perhaps best known as the unequalled master of Latin oratory. His philosophical works included topics like old age, friendship, and the nature of the gods.

- **Vergil** (70–19 B.C.): English poet Alfred, Lord Tennyson described Vergil as "wielder of the stateliest measure ever molded by the lips of man." Vergil (also spelled Virgil) was a success in his own day, and his fame has never diminished. His *Aeneid* — a story about the fall of Troy and the adventures of the Trojan hero Aeneas — was the work that earned Vergil his place in literary history. Vergil is also the one who gave us the line **Quidquid id est, timeo Danaos et dona ferentes.** (*Aeneid* II.48) (*kwihd*-kwihd ihd ehst, *tih*-meh-o *duh*-nuh-os eht *do*-nuh feh-*rehn*-tays) — "Whatever it is, I fear the Greeks, even bearing gifts."

- **Ovid** (43 B.C.–A.D. 17): Ovid is best known for his epic poem the *Metamorphoses,* which deals with mythology and themes of shape changing. Many famous stories come from this work, including the tales of Daedalus and Icarus (the father-and-son flying team), *Pygmalion* (the statue who game to life), and *Pyramus and Thisbe* (the star-crossed lovers). He wrote other works on love, including **Ars Amatoria** (uhrs uh-mah-*to*-rih-uh; *The Art of Love*), which gives advice on how to seduce members of the opposite sex. Its companion volume, *Remedia Amoris* (reh-*meh*-dih-uh uh-*mo*-rihs; *The Cures for Love*), tells how to get out of a relationship.

- **Plautus** (c. 254–184 B.C.): One of the earliest Latin authors, Plautus wrote plays full of slapstick and crude humor. Folks still perform his plays, which have helped shape other works, such as Shakespeare's *Comedy of Errors* and the comic film *A Funny Thing Happened on the Way to the Forum.*

- **Lucretius** (98–55 B.C.): Lucretius was a philosophical poet. In his work, he describes the gods and the underworld, and spends much time discussing atoms, how they combine to produce objects, and the nature of human vision.

✔ **Catullus** (84–54 B.C.): Catullus was one of a group of innovative poets known as **poetae novi** (po-*ay*-tigh *noh*-wee; new poets). He explored more personal themes of love, friendship, death, and betrayal in a variety of poetic meters.

✔ **Horace** (65–8 B.C.): A friend of Vergil, Horace was a prolific writer who composed poetic epistles, satires, and odes. He's the author of one of the most popular Latin expressions in modern times: **carpe diem** (*kuhr*-peh *dih*-ehm; seize the day).

✔ **Livy** (59 B.C.–A.D. 17): Livy is the author of the monumental work of Roman history, *Ab Urbe Condita, — From the Foundation of the City*. This work contained 142 books (35 still exist today) detailing Rome's history from its founding to the age of Augustus. From the title of his work came the A.U.C. dating system, which you can read more about in Chapter 6.

Measuring Latin poetry

The Romans enjoyed many styles of poetry, from elegies (poems that praised the dead) to lyric poems (poems about feelings and emotions) to epic poems (really *long* poems of heroes). Roman poets had a range of poetic meters to choose from, and they tried to make the meter they used match the action or emotion of the poem.

The scoop on dactylic hexameter

The most common meter in English poetry is iambic pentameter (which is what Shakespeare wrote in). The most common meter in Latin poetry is *dactylic hexameter.* Where English poetic meter is based on stressed and unstressed syllables, Latin meter relies on long and short syllables.

A hexameter line, as the name suggests, contains six poetic feet. In the case of dactylic hexameter, the basic foot is the *dactyl,* which in Latin is made up of one long and two short syllables. To scan a line of poetry means to identify the various feet, and the symbols for the dactylic foot are –ʊʊ.

Thus, a dactylic hexameter line looks like this:

–ʊʊ|–ʊʊ|–ʊʊ|–ʊʊ|–ʊʊ|– –

The reason that the foot looks different is that the dactylic hexameter line always ended with two long syllables, which make a poetic foot called a *spondee.* And just to make things more interesting, Latin poets could substitute spondees in place of dactyls in any of the first four feet. In fact, the only foot that had to be a dactyl was the fifth foot.

The term *meter* in English poetry generally refers to the pattern of stressed and unstressed syllables. In Latin poetry, it refers to the pattern of long and short vowels. Latin poetry was first and foremost to be heard. It wasn't enough that a poet tell a good story. The meter of the poetry needed to match the plot line, sort of like the soundtrack in a movie or the musical score of a play. Consider the importance of sound in the following line from the *Aeneid* I.53:

> **luctantis ventos tempestatesque sonoras**
>
> luk-*tahn*-tees *wehn*-tos tehm-pehs-tah-*tays*-kweh soh-*no*-rahs
>
> wrestling winds and thunderous storms

In these lines, the pounding repetition of long syllables creates a sound like that of a brewing storm, which is exactly what the line is describing.

To enjoy Latin poetry, you really don't need to know anything about meter. If you're really curious though, hop to the sidebar "The scoop on dactylic hexameter" in this chapter for a basic discussion of meters and feet and how the Roman writers used them.

Getting Grammar into Proper Condition

Cicero once said,

> **[I]acerent in tenebris omnia, nisi litterarum lumen accederet.**
> (*Pro Archia*, 14)
>
> yuh-*kay*-rehnt ihn *teh*-neh-brees ohm-nih-uh, *nih*-sih liht-teh-*rah*-rum *loo*-mehn uhk-*kay*-deh-reht.
>
> All things would lie in the shadows, if the light of literature were not falling on them.

The implication of that statement, of course, is that things don't lie in shadows because literature is shining its light. Cicero's statement describes something that is contrary to fact, and the construction that he uses to express this is a *conditional sentence.*

Conditional sentences are "if . . . then" sentences. For example, *if* (or on the condition that) you write a book, *then* the Sosii will publish it. Latin has all kinds of conditions, but four, covered in the following sections, deserve special notice.

Before you launch into the following sections, keep the following in mind:

- Latin conditions always involve the word **si** (see; if) or **nisi** (*nih*-sih; if . . . not).
- The word *then* is never expressed in a Latin condition; it's implied.
- The "if" part of a condition is the *protasis,* and the "then" part is the *apodosis.*

Future, less vivid

In the future, less vivid type of conditional sentence, the verbs in both the protasis and apodosis part of the sentence are present subjunctive. You translate this conditional sentence as "should . . . would." (If you need to review the difference between indicative and subjunctive mood, head over to Chapter 6.)

Consider this example:

> **Si librum scribas, librarii eum edant.**
>
> see *lih*-brum *skree*-bahs, lih-*brah*-rih-ee *eh*-um *ay*-duhnt.
>
> If you should write a book, the booksellers would sell it.

In this sentence, you have no guarantee that the action will happen. This is a vague, "less vivid" statement about what *could* happen in the future.

Future, more vivid

In the future, more vivid conditional sentence, the verb in the protasis can be in the future tense or the future-perfect tense. The verb in the apodosis is in the future indicative. You translate this conditional as "will/will have . . . "

Take a look at this sentence:

> **Si librum scribes, librarii eum edent.**
>
> see *lih*-brum *skree*-bays, lih-*brah*-rih-ee *eh*-um ay-dehnt.
>
> If you will write a book, the booksellers will sell it.

This sentence makes a more vivid claim about the future. It states boldly every author's dream, that all you have to do is write the book, and you will definitely get published.

Present, contrary to fact

In the present, contrary-to-fact conditional sentence, the verbs in both the protasis and apodosis are imperfect subjunctives. You translate these sentences with "were . . . would."

Si librum scriberes, librarii eum ederent.

see *lih*-brum *skree*-beh-rays, lih-*brah*-rih-ee *eh*-um *ay*-deh-rehnt.

If you were writing a book, the booksellers would sell it.

Like the quotation from Cicero at the beginning of the section, this sentence describes something that's not true. It says that you have the potential to be a best-selling author, but because you're not actually writing anything at the moment, don't quit your day job.

Past, contrary to fact

In the past, contrary-to-fact conditional sentence, the verbs in both the protasis and apodosis are pluperfect subjunctive. You translate these sentences by using "had . . . would have."

Si librum scripsisses, librarii eum edidissent.

see *lih*-brum skreep-*sihs*-says, lih-*brah*-rih-ee *eh*-um ay-dih-*dihs*-sehnt.

If you had written a book, the booksellers would have sold it.

This sentence describes something contrary to fact in a past setting. Obviously, you didn't write a book, and this sentence teases you with the thought of what might have been.

Telling It Secondhand — Indirect Statements

Using indirect statements, authors can report what someone said or heard without quoting a person directly. In the majority of narratives, indirect statements are more common than direct statements (the kind you'd put quotes around).

Imagine this. Someone tells you, "Bob got fired." Wanting to show your concern (and some tact), you go up to Bob and say, "Bob, I hear you're out of work." In addition to showing Bob that you care, you just used an indirect statement. You know that you've got an indirect statement in English if you can put the word *that* into the sentence: "Bob, I hear that you're out of work."

Latin indirect statements involve two basic elements, a noun in the accusative case and an infinitive. You can spot an indirect statement a mile away when you recognize an accusative-case noun and infinitive relatively close to each other in a sentence. For example:

> **Audio Catullum carmen novum scribere.**
>
> *ow*-dih-o kuh-*tul*-lum *kuhr*-mehn *noh*-wum *skree*-beh-reh.

Catullum is accusative, and **scribere** is a present-active infinitive, so you've got yourself an indirect statement. Throw in the word *that,* and the translation comes out "I hear that Catullus is writing a new poem."

Chapter 2 tells you about the accusative case and introduces you to the infinitive, but you need to know a bit more about infinitives before jumping into the deep end with indirect statements.

Understanding Latin infinitives

The second dictionary entry for a Latin verb is an infinitive, but it's not the only one. In fact, most Latin verbs have six infinitive forms:

- ✔ **Present active:** This is the second dictionary form of the verb and can be translated "to . . . "

- ✔ **Present passive:** This looks much like the active form except that it uses the letter **–i.** Translated "to be . . .," its exact form depends on the conjugation:

  - • In first conjugation, the present-passive-infinitive ending is **–ari.**

  - • In second conjugation, the ending is **–eri.**

  - • In third conjugation, the ending is **–i.**

  - • In fourth conjugation, the ending is **–iri.**

- ✔ **Perfect active:** Take the third dictionary entry for a verb, add the suffix **–sse,** and you've got the perfect-active infinitive. Translate with the words "to have . . . "

- ✔ **Perfect passive:** This form uses the perfect-passive participle, or fourth dictionary form. (For more on participles, see Chapter 9.) Make it a compound form by adding the word **esse** (*ehs*-seh), then translate with "to have been . . ."

- ✔ **Future active:** This form uses the future-active participle. Like the perfect passive, you add the word **esse.** The basic translation is "to be about to . . . "

- ✔ **Future passive:** Use the perfect-passive participle with **–um** ending, plus **iri** (ee-ree). The translation is "to be about to be . . . "

Table 10-1 shows the infinitives for the verb **scribo, scribere, scripsi, scriptus** (*skree*-bo, *skree*-beh-reh, *skreep*-see, *skreep*-tus; to write):

Table 10-1		Infinitives		
	Active	*Translation*	*Passive*	*Translation*
Present	scribere	to write	scribi	to be written
Perfect	scripsisse	to have written	scriptus, –a, –um esse	to have been written
Future	scripturus, –a, –um esse	to be about to write	scriptum iri	to be about to be written

"To be about to be written" sounds rather silly, doesn't it? The translations in Table 10-1 are the literal renderings for those infinitives. If you ever need to know what an infinitive really means, there you go. Most of the time, infinitives appear in indirect statements, and their translation changes according to the tense of the main verb. The section "Handling indirect statements" explains how this works.

Handling indirect statements

If you use the literal translation of an infinitive when you come up against one in a sentence, you're likely to end up with something that, although it makes sense, sounds a little odd. So when you translate infinitives in indirect statements, pay attention to the tense of the main verb. It affects how you actually translate the sentence.

For the translation of infinitives in indirect statements, Table 10-2 puts everything in order.

Table 10-2	Infinitive Translation in Indirect Statement	
Tense of Main Verb	*Infinitive*	*Infinitive Translation*
Present, Future, Future Perfect	Present	am, is, are
Present, Future, Future Perfect	Perfect	has, have, "past"
Present, Future, Future Perfect	Future	shall, will
Imperfect, Perfect, Pluperfect	Present	has, have, "past"
Imperfect, Perfect, Pluperfect	Perfect	had
Imperfect, Perfect, Pluperfect	Future	should, would

The next two sentences differ only in the tense of the main verb, but notice how the translations change:

Dicunt Plautum fabulam scribere.

dee-kunt *plow*-tum *fah*-bu-luhm *skree*-beh-reh.

Dixerunt Plautum fabulam scribere.

deeks-*ay*-runt plow-tum *fah*-bu-luhm *skree*-beh-reh.

The infinitive in both sentences, **scribere,** is present tense. The main verb of the first sentence, **dicunt,** is also present tense, so the sentence reads "They say that Plautus is writing a play." In the second sentence, the main verb changes to **dixerunt,** which is perfect tense. This gives the translation "They said that Plautus has written a play."

The tense of an infinitive is always relative to the main verb. Present tense infinitives describe action at the same time as the main verb, perfect infinitives show action prior to the main verb, and future infinitives describe action in the future of the main verb.

Talkin' the Talk

Cicero and Vergil discuss Latin literature. (Notice the different conditions and indirect statements used.)

Cicero: **Cogito poetas patriae magis quam aliquem servire.**
ko-gih-to poh-*ay*-tahs *puh*-trih-igh *muh*-gihs kwuhm *uh*-lih-kwehm sehr-*wee*-reh.
I think that poets serve their country more than anyone.

Vergilius: **Ita vero. Nisi poetae facta patrum nostrum conservavissent . . .**
ih-tuh *way*-ro. *nih*-sih poh-*ay*-tigh *fuhk*-tuh *puh*-trum *nohs*-trum kon-sehr-wah-*wihs*-sehnt . . .
Yes, indeed. Unless poets had preserved the deeds of our fathers . . .

Cicero: **. . . eosdem errores fecissemus.**
. . . eh-*os*-dehm ehr-*ro*-rays fay-kihs-*say*-mus.
. . . we would have made the same mistakes.

Vergilius: **Nisine orator esses, carmina scriberes?**
nih-sih-neh o-*rah*-tohr *ehs*-says, *kuhr*-mih-nuh *skree*-beh-rays?
If you were not an orator, would you write poems?

Cicero: **Scribo, ergo omnes litterae sunt tabula mea.**
           skree-bo, *ehr*-go *ohm*-nays *liht*-teh-righ sunt
           tuh-bu-luh *meh*-uh.
           I write, therefore all literature is my writing tablet.

Although he excelled at all other genres of writing, Cicero wasn't a poet. Unfortunately, he never understood this. A line from his poem *De Consulatu Suo*, (*On His Own Consulship*), that received much ridicule was **o fortunatam natam me consule Romam** (o for-too-*nah*-tuhm *nah*-tuhm may *kon*-su-leh *ro*-muhm), which means "O lucky Rome, born when I was consul." Not only did this poem fail the humility test, but it sounded sour to the Roman ear. Romans didn't like rhymes (which this line is full of) in their poetry.

Words to Know

carmen, carminis, n	kuhr-mehn, kuhr-mih-nihs	song, poem
cogito, cogitare, cogitavi, cogitatus	ko-gih-to, ko-gih-tah-reh, ko-gih-tah-wee, koh-gih-tah-tus	to think
litterae, litterarum, f	liht-teh-righ, liht-teh-rah-rum	literature
lumen, luminis, n	loo-meh, loo-mih-nihs	light
tempestas, tempestatis, f	tehm-pehs-tahs, tehm-pehs-tah-tihs	storm
tenebrae, tenebrarum, f	teh-neh-brigh, teh-neh-brah-rum	shadows, darkness
vox, vocis, f	woks, wo-kihs	voice

Writing for the Rest of Us

Just as not all English writing is of a quality equivalent to Shakespeare, not all Latin writing meets the high mark set by the Ciceros and Vergils of the ancient world. Romans produced other types of writing as well. Although not of the same literary quality as the works mentioned earlier in this chapter, these writings give us information about daily life in ancient Rome. Consider this the bumper-sticker-poster-board-greeting-card genre of Latin literature.

Letter writing

Mr. Formal Latin Writer himself, Cicero, is one source for a more mundane type of writing, the personal letter. Fortunately for the modern world, many of Cicero's letters were published after his death, providing a unique window into the daily life of first century B.C. Rome. From these letters, you can discover such personal events as his concern for his son's education and his grief over his daughter's death.

You can also find out how to write a letter, Latin style. It turns out that the Romans had abbreviations and set phrases just as people in the modern world do. Have you ever passed a note in school with the cryptic message CUL8R, indicating that you would see your friend later? Abbreviations are a key way of communicating in e-mails today with expressions such as LOL, BRB, and K dotting the e-landscape. (Those abbreviations mean "laugh out loud," "be right back," and "okay," for those who aren't computer savvy.)

A letter from Cicero to his friend Atticus, for example, might have begun:

> Cicero Attico s.p.d. S.v.b.e.v.

Spelled out, this is

> **Cicero Attico salutem plurimam dicit. Si vales, bene est, valeo.**
>
> *kih*-keh-ro *uht*-tih-ko suh-*loo*-tehm *ploo*-rih-muhm *dee*-kiht. see *wah*-lays, *beh*-neh ehst, *wah*-leh-o.
>
> Cicero sends the heartiest greeting to Atticus. If you are well, it is well, I am well.

A writer often dictated letters and other works to a secretary. It was Cicero's freedman secretary, Tiro, who is credited with the invention of Latin shorthand.

Another letter writer who earned some fame was Pliny the Younger (not to be confused with his uncle, Pliny the Elder, who wrote about the natural sciences, or Whiny Pliny, Tiny Pliny, and Spiny Pliny, three of the original seven dwarves). Pliny the Younger's letters are famous in the modern world for a couple of reasons:

- ✔ He was an eyewitness to the eruption of Mt. Vesuvius in A.D. 79, which claimed the life of his uncle and buried the city of Pompeii. In a letter to his friend, the historian Tacitus, he describes the destruction, including the cloud from the volcano that looked like an umbrella pine.

- ✔ One of his letters provides the earliest Latin evidence of how the Roman government viewed a new religion called Christianity. In a letter to the Emperor Trajan from around A.D. 112, Pliny asks for advice on how to deal with these people who refuse to worship the Roman gods.

Etched in stone: Inscriptions

Inscriptions were any type of writing carved into a durable material, such as metal or stone. Scholars have catalogued thousands of inscriptions from all over the Roman Empire, and you can easily decipher many of them on monuments today. Well, *easily* may be a bit of a stretch. The letters are easy to see, but knowing what they mean isn't always so simple. Inscriptions tended to use many abbreviations as in this example from the Pantheon in Rome:

M AGRIPPA L F COS TERTIUM FECIT

If all the letters were put back in, you'd have this:

Marcus Agrippa Luci filius consul tertium fecit.

muhr-kus uh-*grihp*-puh *loo*-kee *fee*-lih-us *kon*-sul *tehr*-tih-um *fay*-kiht.

Marcus Agrippa, son of Lucius, consul for the third time, made this.

Given the amount of room the inscribers had to work with on most monuments, you can see why the Romans abbreviated. The following are just a few of the abbreviations that you can find in Roman inscriptions:

- **L:** Lucius
- **C:** Gaius (An older form of this name was Caius. Eventually the name spelling changed, but the abbreviation never did.)
- **SEX:** Sextus
- **M:** Marcus
- **COS:** Consul (chief magistrate)
- **PONT MAX** or **P·M:** Pontifex Maximus (chief priest)
- **IMP:** Imperator (victorious army general)

The writing on the wall: Graffiti

The other type of easily accessible Latin writing was graffiti. A great source for ancient graffiti is the town of Pompeii, which was buried by volcanic eruptions from Mt. Vesuvius in A.D. 79. The ash and lava that destroyed the city also preserved it for centuries by protecting it from the sun's rays and the ravages of time. When archeologists excavated the city, they found a wealth of information about daily Roman life. Take a look at a few examples:

Lucius pinxit.

loo-kih-us *peenks*-iht.

Lucius painted this.

Virgula Tertio suo: Indecens es.

vihr-gu-luh *tehr*-tih-o *su*-o: *ihn*-deh-kens ehs.

Virgula to her [boyfriend] Tertius: You are a nasty boy.

Oppi, emboliari, fur, furuncule.

ohp-pee, ehm-bo-lih-*ah*-ree, foor, foo-*run*-ku-leh.

Oppius, you're a clown, a thief, and a cheap crook.

With only a brief look at Latin graffiti, you can see that the writer of Ecclesiastes is proved correct once again:

Nihil sub sole novum. (*Ecclesiastes* I:9)

nih-hihl sub *so*-leh *noh*-wum.

There is nothing new under the sun.

Fun & Games

The Sosii brothers have just hired you as a copyist for the bookstore in Rome. It's your first day on the job, and in walks a customer who can only describe the type of books she wants but can't remember the authors' names. Can you help her?

(If you need an information sheet, the authors who you're dealing with are Apuleius, Caesar, Lucretius, Ovid, and Vergil.)

1. He wrote about shepherds, farming, and a long poem about the Trojan War.

2. This poet was famous for writing about philosophy and atoms.

3. He was a general, a great speaker, and, oh yeah, he wrote something about a war in Gaul.

4. This author wrote about a man turning into a donkey.

5. This poet also wrote about shape-changing, but he had plenty of advice on the art of seduction.

See Appendix C for the answers.

Part III
Latin in the Modern World

The 5th Wave   By Rich Tennant

"One of my students just told me he wanted to study Latin because he was going to Latin America this summer and wanted to be able to speak the language."

In this part . . .

Although they're not actually speaking Latin, people in many fields use Latin pretty extensively. They take Latin words and put them together in new ways, or they use the original Latin. Scientists, doctors, lawyers, politicians, and priests all use Latin in one way or another and not just because it makes them sound smart. You've probably used Latin, too, without knowing it.

Because you're bound to run into Latin today even if you're not a Latin student, this part covers those Latin terms that have been incorporated into modern English down through the years. This part also includes a chapter that takes you blow-by-blow through translating Latin so that you can make sense of what you see and hear.

Chapter 11

Latin in Law

· ·

In This Chapter

▶ A short explanation of the history of Roman law

▶ Looking at crime and punishment in ancient Rome

▶ Understanding legalese

· ·

Most lawyers love to throw around Latin phrases. The reason for this is that ancient Rome's legal system has had a strong influence on the legal systems of most western countries. After all, at one time, the Romans had conquered most of Europe, the Middle East, and North Africa. The Roman motto was **divide et impera** (dee-*vee*-deh eht *im*-peh-rah) — "divide and conquer." As they conquered nations, they set out to "Latinize" these "barbarians" (anyone who *wasn't* Roman). Their goal was to teach them how to think, act, and be like real Romans. As the Roman Empire slowly crumbled and disappeared, the new orders in all these lands gradually adapted the existing legal system. England (and most of its former colonies) and the United States of America use a variation of the old Roman law called "Common Law." This is why lawyers today love those Latin phrases! (Well, that and the fact that you can't get out of law school without mastering them.)

This chapter gives you the information that you need to make sense of what your lawyer, judge, or parole officer is saying. Knowing what a sentence or phrase, like "The case is now **sub judice** (sub *you*-dee-kay)" or "What you are proposing is **contra legem** (*kon*-trah *lay*-ghem)," means, can help — even when you're just watching *Court TV* or *The Practice*.

Stop, thief!

If you were caught stealing in ancient Rome, the Latin word for thief, **fur** (foor), would be branded on your forehead with a branding iron — a procedure that, in addition to messing up your hair, had to hurt. That practice is the origin of our modern-day expression "to be branded a thief." The English word *furtive* — to act like a thief — also comes from this word.

A (Very) Short History of Roman Law

Kings ruled the earliest Romans. **Romulus** (*roh*-moo-lus), the first king, founded Rome on April 21, 753 B.C. (This is not really true, but the ancient Romans liked to believe it anyway.) The king's word was final and everyone obeyed him or else. The last king of Rome, **Tarquinius Superbus** (tar-*kwee*-nee-us su-*per*-bus), was driven out in 510 B.C. With the kings gone, the new government was a republic with two consuls in charge. Consuls were elected annually for a term of one year and were helped by a senate.

Ancient law among the Romans was based on ancestral customs, and the Romans referred to this as the **mos maiorum** (mos ma-*your*-um) or the "custom of the forefathers." Knowledge of these laws was limited to patrician judges.

In 450 B.C., under pressure from the **plebeians** (pleh-*bee*-yuns; the common folk), the Romans published a written version of the existing laws for the first time. These laws were known as the Twelve Tables; the Tables outlined the most important rules of the existing customary law and explained the procedure to be followed for various crimes. They made the law open and applicable to all Roman citizens, but like today, those with wealth generally found ways to escape judgment.

The Tables were published and displayed in the Roman Forum on tablets made from bronze and fixed to the **rostra** (*ros*-trah) — the speakers' platform. The laws of the Twelve Tables were never repealed, but some fell into disuse as the centuries passed. Nothing remains of these original tablets, except for some quotations from it in ancient authors' works.

One of the most famous Roman legal experts was a man named Gaius, who lived in the second century A.D. He wrote many books on Roman law, the most famous of which is his *Institutiones* (in-sti-tu-tee-*oh*-nays; *Institutes*). Four hundred years later, Emperor Justinian reorganized Roman law. His first work was also called the *Institutiones,* which was based largely on the *Institutiones* of Gaius. Published in A.D. 533, this was a short manual of the whole Roman law, intended to serve as a textbook for students. His second work, the *Digesta seu Pandectae* (dee-*ghes*-ta se-*ooh* puhn-*deck*-tigh; the *Digest* or *Pandects*), was also published in A.D. 533. The third work, published in A.D. 534, as the *Codex* (*ko*-decks; the *Code*), was a collection of the laws of the previous emperors and their answers to legal questions submitted to them. His fourth work, the *Novellae* (no-*wel*-ligh; the *Novels*) consisted of the laws Justinian made after the publication of the *Codex*.

Crime and punishment in ancient Rome

Crime in Rome, especially violent crime, increased as the wealthy landowners forced the **vulgus** (*wool*-goose), the lower class folks, off their small farms and into the big city. Slaves brought to Rome as war booty also created mass unemployment among the common people.

The Roman emperors gave **panem et circenses** (*puh*-nem eht kir-*ken*-says) — bread and circuses (that is, food and entertainment, a very early form of welfare) — to keep the common folk happy, but idleness led to increased crime. Anyone accused of a crime could be brought in front of the **praetor urbanus** (*prigh*-tawr ur-*ba*-noose; the city judge) by his accuser.

Crimes, such as false witness, adultery, and counterfeiting, were punishable by death. If you were given the death penalty, here's how the Romans would do you in: You could be

- Buried alive
- Thrown from a cliff (in cases of treason)
- Burned
- Forced to fight gladiators to the death in the amphitheater
- Thrown to the lions or other wild animals
- Forced to learn Latin (just kidding)

Less serious crimes were punished in a policy of "an eye for an eye." If you were fined, you paid the fee to the plaintiff — not the court. Sometimes, though, you'd be sent to work in the mines or made to row in the Roman galleys. (Think of the movie *Ben-Hur,* and the scene in which Charlton Heston's character is forced to row alongside other slaves and criminals.)

Members of the upper classes, which included the senatorial class and the *equestrian class,* also known as the knights, were generally exiled for a given time (food and water forbidden within a given distance of Rome) and their property confiscated. If their crime was very serious, they were often given the opportunity to commit suicide or get out of town. (Remember, having to leave Rome or to give up the benefits of Roman citizenship was a dire punishment because the Romans considered every non-Roman a barbarian and any place other than Rome — or not subject to Roman rule — uncivilized.)

Only men need apply

Did you know that in ancient Rome only men practiced as lawyers? To become a lawyer, a boy finished his primary and secondary education and then proceeded to the schools of famous **rhetors** (*ray*-tawrs), or teachers of the art of public speaking. After a young man finished this part of his education, he was ready to practice law. Because Roman lawyers were not paid much, if anything, for their services, this remained a job for men from rich families, who were independently wealthy.

Cocktail party quotes by Cicero

One of the most famous Roman lawyers of all time was a man named Marcus Tullius Cicero, a contemporary of Julius Caesar. He wrote many books on law and famous law cases. Use some of his quotes that follow to impress your friends and colleagues:

Legum servi sumus ut liberi esse possimus.
lay-goom *ser*-wee *soo*-moose oot *lee*-be-ree *ehs*-seh pos-*see*-moose.
We are slaves of the law, so that we may be able to be free.

Salus populi est suprema lex esto.
sa-loos *po*-poo-lee est soo-*pray*-muh leks *es*-toe.

Let the safety of the people be the supreme law.

Accipere quam facere praestat injuriam.
uk-*key*-pe-re kwum *fuh*-keh-reh *prigh*-stut in-*you*-ree-um.
It is better to suffer an injustice than to do an injustice.

Silent enim leges inter arma.
see-lent *aye*-nim *le*-gays *in*-ter *ar*-ma.
Laws are silent in times of war.

Romans didn't get prison sentences. In fact, Roman prisons didn't house criminals like our prisons do today. Instead, they served only to hold people awaiting trial or execution. The wealthy were generally held in house arrest at the home of a friend who would guarantee their presence at the trial. Private prisons existed for slaves.

Looking at the law court

The ancient Romans erected elaborate buildings, **basilicae,** right next to the main forum, almost like a modern-day mall. They used these buildings mostly for their law-courts, although they did rent out parts of these buildings to money-lenders and other merchants.

These buildings consisted of a central nave with an apse at one or both ends and rows of columns that formed two side aisles. Sound familiar? Yes, the early (and even modern-day) Christian churches were built using these designs.

A judge, the **iudex** (*you*-decks), sat at the judge's bench, called the **tribunal** (*tree*-boo-null). Today, the word *tribunal* is used to indicate a committee or board appointed to judge some particular case or matter.

The **reus** (*ray*-us) — the accused — appeared before the judge and faced the prosecutor, the **accusator** (ak-koo-*sa*-tawr). An **advocatio** (ad-woe-*ka*-tee-oh), an advocate or defense attorney, helped the accused. This person didn't offer legal advice as much as suggestions on how the accused could present his case in the most eloquent way. After all, Roman lawyers were trained in the art of speaking, not the law.

In more serious cases, a jury assisted the judge. Like today, the jury helped determine the guilt and also recommended a suitable sentence, which the judge could impose.

Listening to Latin Litigation: Words Used in Roman Courts

So the Romans loved to talk and argue. Laws, rules, and statutes dictated their lives. Therefore, it's not strange to find that Latin is full of terms associated with the law court. The following sections give you terms and phrases that you're likely to encounter as you study Latin. Some of these terms are probably familiar to you because of all the English words that come from them. For example, the English words *jury, crime, justice, verdict, jurisprudence,* and *litigant* all come from Latin. For Latin words that are used in English-speaking courts today, head to the section "Latin Words Used in English Courts."

Legal beagles: The cast and crew

Just like today, the Romans had a judge, a jury, a prosecutor, and an attorney. Table 11-1 gives you the Roman names of people typically involved in a lawsuit, the pronunciation of these words, and their meanings.

Cincinnatus: Dictator farmer

Romans loved their dictators! Well, at least some of them — take Cincinnatus (kin-kin-*ah*-tus) for example.

Cincinnatus was a no-nonsense sort of guy, who was also a farmer (well, okay, a rich farmer). According to legend, when the **Aequi** (*igh*-kwee), another tribe of people in Italy, attacked and routed the Roman army, Cincinnatus was called from his farm and appointed dictator. Anxious to get back to his plowing, Cincinnatus assembled an army, fought and whipped the Aequi, and then gave up his office so that he could return to his fields — all in 15 days.

Table 11-1	Latin Words for Legal Participants	
Word	**Pronunciation**	**Person**
accusator	ak-cue-*sa*-tawr	a prosecutor
advocatus	ad-wo-*ka*-tus	a lawyer
iudex	*you*-decks	a judge
iudices	*you*-dee-kays	members of the jury
magistratus	ma-ghee-*stra*-tus	magistrate
praetor	*prigh*-tawr	a magistrate
reus	*ray*-us	the accused
scriba	*skree*-bah	a clerk
testis	*tes*-tis	a witness

Latin legal lingo

Table 11-2 lists a number of additional terms that can help you understand and learn Latin.

Table 11-2	Latin Words Used in Roman Courts	
Word	**Pronunciation**	**Meaning**
crimen	*kree*-men	accusation
iudicium	you-dee-*key*-um	verdict
ius	yous	law, right
iussu	you-*sue*	by order of
iustitia	you-stee-*tee*-ah	justice
legitimus	lay-*ghee*-tee-mus	lawful
lex	leks	law
lis	lis	lawsuit
litigator	li-tee-*gah*-tor	a party in a lawsuit
veritas	*way*-ree-tus	the truth

Talkin' the Talk

The **iudex** (*you*-decks; judge) in a trial asks the **advocatio** (ad-woe-*ka*-tee-oh; defense lawyer) when the next witness is going to show up so that the trial can proceed.

Iudex:	**Ubi est testis, advocatio?** *oo*-bi est *tes*-tis, ad-woe-*ka*-tee-oh? Where is the witness, counsel?
Advocatio:	**Venit, venit.** *weh*-nit, *weh*-nit. He's coming, he's coming.
Iudex:	**Quando?** *kwuhn*-do? When?
Advocatio:	**Nunc! Est quoque testis in alia lite!** nunk! est *kwo*-kwe *tes*-tis in ah-lee-*ah* lee-*tay*! Now! He is also a witness in another lawsuit!
Iudex:	**Testis in alia lite?** *tes*-tis in ah-lee-*ah* lee-*tay*? A witness in another lawsuit?
Advocatio:	**Ita vero. Est optimus testis. Semper dicit veritatem!** ee-tah *way*-ro. est *op*-tee-mus *tes*-tis. *sem*-per *dee*-kit way-ree-*tuh*-tem! Yes. He is an excellent witness. He always speaks the truth!
Iudex:	**Quis est?** kwis est? Who is he?
Advocatio:	**Marcus.** *mar*-kus. Marcus.
Iudex:	**Nonne est frater rei?** *non*-ne est *fra*-ter *ray*-ee? Isn't he the brother of the accused?

Advocatio:	**Ita vero! Sed ille est optimus testis!**
	ee-tah *way*-ro! sehd ee-le est *op*-tee-mus *tes*-tis!
	Yes! But he is a very good witness!
Iudex:	**Non tempus est. Duc mihi legitimum testem, sine mora!**
	non *tem*-pus est. dook *mee*-hee lay-*ghee*-tee-moom *tes*-tem, *see*-nay mo-*rah*!
	There is no time. Bring me a lawful witness without delay!
Advocatio:	**O me miserum! Omnes mei testes sunt in carcere!**
	oh may *mee*-se-room! *om*-nays *may*-ee *tes*-tays soont in *kar*-ke-ray!
	O dear me! All my witnesses are in prison!
Iudex:	**Deinde iussu iudicis, haec quaestio est prorogata sine die!**
	de-*een*-de yous-*soo* you-*dee*-kis, hike kweye-*stee*-oh est pro-ro-*gah*-ta *see*-nay dee-*ay*!
	Then by order of the judge, this trial is postponed indefinitely!

Words to Know

accusator, accusatoris, m	*uhk-koo-sah-tawr, uhk-koo-sah-taw-ris*	a prosecutor
crimen, criminis, n	*kree-men, kree-mee-nis*	accusation
iudex, iudicis, m	*you-decks, you-dee-kis*	a judge
iudicium, iudicii, n	*you-dee-key-um, you-dee-key-oom*	verdict
lex, legis, f	*leks, lay-gis*	law
litigator, litigatoris, m	*lee-tee-ga-tor, lee-tee-ga-taw-ris*	a party in a lawsuit
magistratus, magistratus, m	*ma-ghee-stra-tus, ma-ghee-stra-toos*	magistrate
scriba, scribae, m	*skree-bah, skree-bigh*	a clerk
veritas, veritatis, f	*way-ree-tus, way-ree-tuh-tis*	the truth

Latin Words Used in English Courts

English legal terms are full of Latin words and phrases. Several of these terms are so common, you use them today without any problem or confusion. Take these words for example:

- ✔ **alibi** (ah-*lee*-bee; elsewhere, at another place). If you're asked to provide an alibi for your whereabouts, you know that you need to tell where you were when a crime occurred to prove that you couldn't have been the one who did the awful deed.

- ✔ **alias** (ah-*lee*-ahs; at another time, otherwise). Today, *alias* often refers to an alternative name people generally use to conceal their identity. "John Smith alias Henry Taylor alias Clyde the Hustler" means John Smith is otherwise known as Henry Taylor who is otherwise known as Clyde the Hustler.

- ✔ **per se** (purr say; by itself). Also meaning "as such" in English usage, **per se** is used casually in English conversations: I didn't call him stupid, **per se.** I simply said he had plenty to learn.

- ✔ **versus** (*wer*-soos; turned). Often abbreviated as **vs.,** the more common English meaning is "against" or "in contrast to": In the case *Roe **versus** Wade,* privacy in cases of abortion was an issue.

Table 11-3 lists other common Latin words used in English courts and legal proceedings. (Keep in mind that the pronunciation here shows how the Romans would have pronounced these words.)

Table 11-3	**Common Latin Words Used Today**		
Word	*Pronunciation*	*Original Meaning*	*Modern Meaning*
affidavit	uhf-fee-*day*-wit	he pledged	a sworn, written statement
bona fide	*boh*-nuh *fee*-day	(in) good faith	sincere, genuine
habeas corpus	ha-*bay*-us *kor*-pus	may you have the body	bring a person before a court
per diem	pur *dee*-em	per day, by the day	daily
pro bono	pro *bo*-no	for the good	done for free for the public good

(continued)

Table 11-3 (continued)

Word	Pronunciation	Original Meaning	Modern Meaning
status quo	*stuh*-toos kwo	the existing condition or state of affairs	how things are currently
sub poena	soob *poi*-na	under the penalty	an order commanding a person to appear in court under a penalty for not appearing

The following sections offer more Latin words used in courts today. Like the preceding words, you may have heard many of these words already; you may even be using them without knowing what they really mean. Don't worry. Many of those using them don't know either.

Common courtroom Latin

Many of the terms that lawyers and other legal folk use have come down to us in their original Latin forms. Table 11-4 lists some of the more common Latin words that are still used today. The following list has even more examples:

✔ **ex officio:** This word would appear in a Latin sentence such as the following:

Imperator erat ex officio quoque dux exercitus.
eem-pe-*ra*-tawr *e*-rut eks off-*ee*-kee-oh *kwo*-kwe dooks eks-*er*-key-toos.
The emperor was by virtue of his position also the leader of the army.

Today, you see or hear this word in a sentence like this:

The headmaster of the school is ex officio also a member of the school board.

✔ **persona non grata:** This word would appear in a Latin sentence such as the following:

Post caedem Caesaris, Brutus erat habitus persona non grata Romae.
post *ki*-dem ki-*sa*-ris, *broo*-tus *e*-rut ha-*bee*-tus per-*sow*-na non *gra*-ta *rom*-igh.

After the assassination of Caesar, Brutus was regarded a persona non grata in Rome.

Today, you see or hear this word in a sentence like this:

After his conviction for embezzling funds, John was treated like a persona non grata by his former colleagues.

Words of wisdom

The Romans contributed the following sayings that are still used today.

Caveat emptor.
ka-whe-at *emp*-tawr.
Let the buyer beware.

Dura lex sed lex.
doo-rah leks *sehd* leks.
The law is hard, but it is the law.

Errare humanum est.
er-*rah*-re hoo-*ma*-noom est.
To make a mistake is human.

You can hear these words and other words (shown in Table 11-4) in many places — particularly on TV or in the movies. They're common enough that the audience can get the gist of their meaning and still follow the story line, but they're obscure enough to make the actors sound like experts in the law. (In the movie *The Silence of the Lambs,* did you know what Hannibal "The Cannibal" Lechter means when he says to agent Starling, "Quid pro quo, Clarese. Quid pro quo"? If you look at Table 11-4, you will!)

Table 11-4	Latin Words Used in English Courts		
Word	*Pronunciation*	*Original Meaning*	*Modern Meaning*
ad hoc	ad hok	to this	for a specific purpose, case, or situation
corpus delicti	*kor*-pus de-*lick*-tee	body of the crime	material evidence in a crime
de facto	day *fak*-toe	from the fact	in reality; actually; in effect
de iure	day *you*-ray	from the law	according to law; by right
ad infinitum	ad in-fee-*nee*-toom	forever	forever
in absentia	in ab-sen-tee-*ah*	in (his/her) absence	in (his/her) absence
in camera	in ka-me-*rah*	in a room	in private; no spectators allowed
in loco parentis	in *lo*-ko pa-*ren*-tis	in the place of a parent	in the place of a parent
ipso facto	*eep*-so *fak*-toe	by the fact itself	by that very fact

(continued)

Table 11-4 *(continued)*

Word	Pronunciation	Original Meaning	Modern Meaning
locus delicti	*low*-koos day-*lick*-tee	scene of the crime	scene where a crime took place
modus operandi	*moh*-dus o-per-*un*-dee	mode of working	method of operating
nolo contendere	*no*-lo kon-*ten*-de-re	I do not wish to contend	a plea by the defendant that's equivalent to an admission of guilt (and leaves him subject to punish-ment) but allows him the legal option to deny the charges later
prima facie	*pree*-mah fah-*key*-ay	at first face	at first sight
pro forma	pro *for*-ma	for the sake of form	done as formality, done for the show
quid pro quo	kwid pro kwo	this for that	something for something; tit for tat; an equal exchange

Talkin' the Talk

Cicero, a lawyer, is quizzing his client Sucus about where Sucus was the night the crime was committed.

Cicero: **Ubi fuisti? Domi?**
obi foo-*ees*-tee? dough-*me*?
Where were you? At home?

Sucus: **Ita vero. Domi**
ee-ta *way*-row. dough-*me*.
Yes. At home.

Cicero: **Quid agebas?**
kwid ah-*gay*-bus?
What were you doing?

Sucus: **Me lavabam.**
may la-*wah*-bum.
I was taking a bath.

Cicero: **Numquamne a villa discessisti?**
noom-*kwam*-ne a wee-*la* dis-kehs-*sees*-tee?
You never left the house?

Sucus: **Ita! Ivi ad tabernam et emi mihi aliquid pulli.**
ee-ta! ee-*wee* ad ta-*ber*-num eht ay-*mee* *mee*-hee
a-*lee*-kwid *pul*-lee.
Yes! I went to the shop and bought myself some
chicken.

Cicero: **Itaque de facto discessisti a villa! Ivistine ad locum
delicti?**
ee-*tah*-kwe day *fak*-to dis-kehs-*sees*-tee a wee-*la*!
ee-*wis*-tee-ne ad *low*-koom day-*lik*-tee?
And so you actually did leave the house! Did you go
to the scene of the crime?

Sucus: **Non. Statim redii domum.**
non. *stah*-tim re-*dee*-ee *do*-moom.
No. I immediately returned home.

Cicero: **Sed discessisti a villa! Ipso facto tu videris nocens!**
sed dee-ske-*sees*-tee a wee-*la*! *eep*-so *fak*-to too
wee-*day*-ris *no*-kens!
But you left the house! By that very fact, you appear
guilty!

Sucus: **Ita vero. Sed nemo vidit me!**
ee-tah *way*-ro. sehd *nay*-mow *wee*-deet may!
Yes. But nobody saw me!

Cicero: **In tua absentia, quem reliquisti in loco parentis?**
een *tu*-uh ab-sen-tee-*ah*, kwem ray-*lee*-kwihs-tee in
lo-ko pa-*ren*-tis?
In your absence, whom did you leave in the place of
the parent?

Sucus: **Nemo.**
nay-mo.
Nobody.

Cicero: **Eheu! Puto te debere implorare: "Nolo contendere"!**
eh-you! *poo*-to tay de-*bay*-re im-plo-*ra*-re: "*no*-lo
con-*ten*-de-re"!
Oh no! I think that you must plead: "Nolo contendere"!

Sucus: **Putasne?**
           poo-*tuhs*-ne?
           You think so?

Cicero: **Ita vero. Prima facie tu es innocens. Sed perdemus hanc litem!**
           ee-ta *way*-ro. *pree*-ma fa-*kee*-ay too es in-*no*-kens.
           sehd per-*day*-moos hunk *lee*-tem!
           Yes. At first sight, you are innocent. But we are going to lose this case!

Words to Know

ad hoc	ad hok	for a specific purpose, case, or situation
bona fide	boh-nuh fee-day	(in) good faith
corpus delicti	kor-puss de-lick-tee	body of the crime
de facto	day fak-toe	in reality; actually
de iure	day you-ray	according to law; by right
ex officio	eks of-fee-key-oh	by virtue of position
habeas corpus	ha-bay-us kor-puss	may you have the body
ipso facto	eep-so fak-toe	by the fact itself
modus operandi	moh-dus o-per-un-dee	method of operating
per diem	purr dee-em	per day, by the day
persona non grata	per-sow-na non gra-ta	person not pleasing
prima facie	pree-mah fa-key-ay	at first appearance
pro bono	pro bo-no	done for free for the public good
pro forma	pro for-ma	for the sake of form
quid pro quo	kwid pro kwo	this for that
sub poena	sub poi-na	under the penalty

Less common Latin phrases

If you've read the earlier sections in this chapter, you know that Latin plays a big role in English legal mumbo-jumbo. We often refer to the language that lawyers use as legalese because it has so many Latin phrases and words. Table 11-5 lists a few of the less common Latin phrases that you're likely to hear only if you — or someone you know — actually ends up in a court of law.

Table 11-5		Other Latin Legal Terms	
Word	*Pronunciation*	*Original Meaning*	*Modern Meaning*
a mensa et toro	ah men-*sa* eht to-*row*	from table and bed	legal separation
casus belli	ka-*soos* bel-*lee*	occasion of war	an event that justifies a war
cui bono	coo-*ee* bo-*no*	for whom the good	whom does it benefit?
(in) flagrante delicto	in fla-*gran*-tay day-*lick*-toe	while the crime is burning	red-handed, in the act
inter alia	*in*-ter *ah*-lee-ah	among other things	among other things
mutatis mutandis	moo-*tah*-tees moo-*tun*-dees	having changed what must be changed	after making the necessary changes
non compos mentis	non *kom*-pos *men*-tis	not of sound mind	mentally incompetent
obiter dictum	oh-*bee*-ter *deek*-toom	something said in passing	something a judge says in arguing a point, but has no bearing on the final decision
onus probandi	*oh*-nis pro-*bun*-dee	burden of proving	burden of proof
pendente lite	pen-*den*-tay *lee*-tay	while judgment is pending	a case in progress
res ipsa loquitur	rays *eep*-sa lo-*kwee*-tur	the matter itself speaks	it goes without saying
sine qua non	*see*-nay kwa non	without which not	an indispensable condition; a prerequisite

(continued)

Table 11-5 *(continued)*

Word	Pronunciation	Original Meaning	Modern Meaning
sine die	*see*-nay *dee*-ay	without a day	postponed indefinitely
sub judice	sub *you*-dee-kay	under the judge	pending judgment
ultra vires	*ool*-trah *wee*-rays	beyond strength	outside one's jurisdiction

Talkin' the Talk

A **iudex** (*you*-decks; judge) questions the **reus** (*ray*-oos; accused) about his participation in a theft. He is getting tired of his evasive answers and wants to get to the truth.

Iudex:	**Vera? Vera! Cupio vera! Dic mihi ab initio ubi fueris et cum quo!** *way*-rah? *way*-rah! coo-*pee*-oh *way*-rah! dik *mee*-hee uhb ee-*nee*-tee-oh *oo*-bee foo-*eh*-ris eht koom kwo! The Truth? The truth! I want the truth! Tell me from the beginning where you were and with whom.
Reus:	**Eram, eram . . . domi!** e-ram, e-ram . . . dough-*me*! I was, I was . . . at home!
Iudex:	**Cum quo?** koom kwo? With whom?
Reus:	**Cum matre et patre.** koom *ma*-tray eht *pa*-tray. With my mother and father.
Iudex:	**Sed vigil dixit mihi se apprehendisse te in flagrante delicto!** sed *wee*-geel *deek*-sit *mee*-hee say ap-pre-hen-*dis*-se tay in fla-*grun*-tay de-*lik*-to! But the officer told me that he caught you red-handed!

Reus: **Nescio.**
nes-*key*-oh
I don't know.

Iudex: **Iuvenis, hic veritas est sine qua non.**
you-*way*-nis, heek way-*ree*-tas est *see*-nay kwa non.
Young man, here truth is a sine qua non!

Reus: **Scio.**
skee-oh.
I know.

Iudex: **Scis? Tu es non compos mentis! Puto te debere pernoctare in carcere!**
skees? Too ehs non *kom*-pos *men*-tis! *poo*-toe tay de-*bay*-re per-knock-*tah*-re in kar-*ke*-ray!
You know? You are not of sound mind! I think that you must spend the night in prison!

Reus: **In carcere? O me miserum! Quid faciam?**
in *kar*-keh-ray? oh may *mee*-se-room! kwihd fah-*key*-am?
In prison? Oh poor me! What am I to do?

Iudex: **Habuisti onus probandi te innocentem. Concidisti.**
ha-boo-*ees*-tee *oh*-noos pro-*bun*-dee tay in-no-*ken*-tem. kon-kee-*dee*-stee.
You had the burden of proving yourself innocent. You failed.

Reus: **O me miserum. Sum innocens. Crede mihi, si tibi placet!**
oh may *mee*-se-room. soom in-*no*-kens. *cray*-day *mee*-hee, see *tee*-bee *plah*-ket!
Oh poor me. I am innocent. Believe me, please!

Iudex: **Custos, inice hunc furciferum in carcerem sub iudice!**
koos-tos, in-*yee*-ke hunk foor-key-*feh*-room in kuhr-*ker*-em soob *you*-dee-kay!
Jailer, throw this jailbird into prison pending judgment!

He works hard for his money

In ancient Rome, before a system of money was invented, soldiers were initially paid in salt. They could use this as barter and exchange it for meat and other goods they wanted. The Latin word for salt is **sal** (sul), and from this early custom of paying soldiers with lumps of salt comes our modern word **sal**ary.

Words to Know

ab initio	ab ee-knee-tee-oh	from the beginning
ad libitum	ad lee-bee-tum	freely, as desired
casus belli	ka-soos bee-lee	occasion of war / an event that justifies a war
(in) flagrante delicto	inn fla-gran-tay day-lick-toe	red-handed, in the act
non compos mentis	non kom-poss men-tis	not of sound mind
onus probandi	oh-nis pro-bun-dee	burden of proving
sine qua non	see-nay kwa non	an indispensable condition; a prerequisite
sine die	see-nay dee-ay	postponed indefinitely
sub judice	sub you-dee-kay	pending judgment

Fun & Games

Choose the correct English for the following Latin words or phrases. Write down the appropriate letter in the space provided:

_____1. sine die   A) somewhere else

_____2. crimen   B) by virtue of one's position

_____3. alibi   C) material evidence in a crime

_____4. caveat emptor   D) among others

_____5. quid pro quo   E) postponed indefinitely

_____6. ex officio   F) at first sight

_____7. in camera   G) an accusation

_____8. inter alia   H) the existing state or condition

_____9. prima facie   I) let the buyer beware

_____10. lex   K) tit for tat

_____11. corpus delicti   L) a law

_____12. status quo   M) in private, without spectators

See Appendix C for the answers.

Chapter 12

Latin in Medicine

*L*ong ago, scientists and other learned people, such as lawyers and doctors, living in different countries had something in common: knowledge of Latin. (It was the mark of an educated person to have had some training in both Latin *and* Greek. As such, Latin was originally the **lingua franca** (*lin*-gwa *fran*-kah; the common language) that earlier scientists and researchers in the Western world shared. Because of this, a large number of medical terms and names for human body parts come from Latin.

This fact, of course, is more than just a historical note: Folks in the medical profession today still use many of these terms. (And you thought they were talking Greek!) This chapter gives you the information you need to make sense of what your doctor, pharmacist, nurse, case manager, or other health-care provider is saying when you hear a sentence like "Are you experiencing any symptoms of **angina?**" or "When you expectorate, is your **sputum** green in color?" or "Stop taking this medication if you experience any **vertigo.**"

Parts Is Parts: Anatomical Lingo

The Romans were practical folk. The earliest Romans were farmers, tending cattle and living in huts on the Palatine and Capitoline Hills (two of the seven hills on which Rome was built). They were interested in the human body and believed that the liver, not the heart, was where man's passions and emotions originated. Later on, educated Romans admired the Greeks for their medical knowledge and copied or adapted the Greek ideas for their own purposes in many cases. They even added names and terms for body parts that the Greeks hadn't named yet.

Romans and medicine

What the Romans knew about medicine came largely from the Greeks and the writings of **Hippocrates** (hip-*po*-kra-tays), a Greek physician who lived in the fifth century B.C. Unlike other doctors of the time who thought that illness was a punishment handed out by the gods, Hippocrates believed that every disease had a natural cause and could therefore be diagnosed and treated. He drew up a code of behavior for doctors, known as the *Hippocratic oath.* Today, graduating medical students still take the Hippocratic oath.

In ancient Rome, doctors were usually freedmen or slaves, and their training consisted of mostly apprentice work; that is, they trained as doctors by following another doctor on his rounds. Doctors also enjoyed certain privileges: For example, they were exempt from paying taxes. On the whole, though, the Romans didn't think too highly of their doctors. In his Epigrams, Roman satirist **Martialis** (mar-tee-*ah*-lis) wrote,

Nuper erat medicus, nunc est vispillo Diaulus:

quod vispillo facit, fecerat et medicus.

noo-per *eh*-rut *meh*-dee-koos, nunk ehst wis-*pil*-low dee-*ow*-lus:

kwod wis-*pil*-low *fah*-kit, fay-*ke*-rut eht *meh*-dee-koos.

Until recently, Diaulus was a doctor; now he is an undertaker:

What he is doing as an undertaker, he also used to do as a doctor.

Of course, this sentiment may not be all that harsh if you consider the life expectancy of the ancient Romans: 25 years for women and 45 years for men.

This section gives you a quick rundown of the body parts — inside and out — named by the Romans. So when you're admiring your **abs** in the mirror, flexing your **pecs** at the gym, or complaining about your **lumbago,** you can thank them.

Naming the head, shoulders, knees, and toes

Okay, a head's a head, an ear's an ear, and arms are arms. But most body parts have Latin names, too, and those names are the ones your doctor, chiropractor, or insurance company is likely to use. (Medical jargon is, after all, chock-full of Latin words.) For example, **cor** (core) means "heart." If you're talking about a coronary artery, you're talking about the artery in your heart. **Digitus** (*dee*-ghee-tus) is Latin for "finger." Table 12-1 lists other Latin-named body parts.

Table 12-1	Latin Words for Body Parts	
Word	*Pronunciation*	*Body Part*
auris	*ow*-rus	ear
bracchium	brak-*key*-um	arm
caput	*ka*-put	head
collum	*col*-lum	neck
crus	croos	leg
manus	*ma*-nus	hand
nasus	*na*-soos	nose
oculus	*o*-koo-lus	eye
os	os	mouth
pectus	*peck*-tus	chest
pes	pes	foot

Them bones!

Many of the terms for body parts that doctors and other healthcare providers use have come down to us in their original Latin forms. Many of these may already be familiar to you. For example, you've probably heard the word **femur** (*fee*-mer), which means "thighbone" or **vertebra** (*wer*-te-bra), which means "a joint" in Latin. Today, doctors use **vertebra** to refer to the bones (or joints) that form your spinal column. Table 12-2 lists some other common Latin words for bones that are still used today.

Table 12-2	Latin Words for Bones		
Word	*Pronunciation*	*Original Meaning*	*Body Part*
fibula	*fib*-oo-lah	brooch	one of two bones of the lower leg extending from the knee to the ankle
patella	pa-*tell*-ah	a dish, small platter	the kneecap
tibia	*ti*-bi-ah	pipe	one of two bones of the lower leg; also called the shinbone

(continued)

Table 12-2 *(continued)*

Word	Pronunciation	Original Meaning	Body Part
humerus	*hoo*-mer-us	upper arm, shoulder	upper arm bone that extends from the shoulder to the elbow
radius	*ray*-dee-us	rod, staff	the shorter and thicker of the two forearm bones
maxilla	mahk-*sil*-lah	jaw, cheek	jawbone
scapula	*skah*-pu-lah	shoulder	shoulder blade
ulna	*ul*-na	elbow, arm, ell	long bone at the inner side of the forearm
sacrum	*sa*-krum	holy (bone)	five fused vertebrae that connect to the pelvis

Many of the Latin names and terms are descriptive and, as such, can help you remember which word refers to what body part. For example, the Latin word **fibula** (*fib*-oo-lah) originally meant a "brooch." A Roman brooch resembled our modern-day diaper pin or safety pin. Together, the tibia and fibula resembled this kind of pin with the fibula forming the sharp, thinner part of the combination.

Flexing those muscles

The muscles of the human body have, for the most part, Latin names. You've heard of bodybuilders working on their "abs," their "lats," their "pecs," or their "glutes." But did you know that they're really speaking in abbreviated Latin? (Chances are, they didn't know either.) Table 12-3 lists the body's major muscles.

Table 12-3 — Latin Words for Muscles

Word	Pronunciation	Original Meaning	Body Part
biceps	*bee*-keps	two-headed	two-headed muscle at the front of the upper arm that flexes the forearm
fascia	*fuss*-key-ah	band	membrane that separates and encircles muscles

Word	Pronunciation	Original Meaning	Body Part
gluteus maximus	glue-*tay*-oes mahk-*see*-mus	largest gluteus (buttock)	largest muscle of your *derrière* (that's French, by the way, for rump)
latissimus dorsi	lah-*tee*-see-mus *door*-see	widest of the back	one of two muscles running from the vertebral (spinal) column to the humerus (the bone in your upper arm)
obliquus externus abdominis (often shortened to "obliques")	oh-*blee*-kwus eks-*tern*-noos ab-*dom*-ee-nus	external oblique (muscle) of the abdomen	external muscle of the abdomen, situated in a slanting position
pectoralis maior	peck-to-*rah*-lus *mah*-your	the greater pectoral (breast)	chest muscle that rotates the arm inward
rectus abdominis (often shortened to "abs")	*wreck*-tus ab-*dom*-ee-noos	straight (muscle) of the abdomen	straight muscle of the abdomen
triceps	*try*-keps	three-headed	three-headed muscle running along the back of the upper arm that extends the forearm

Interior design

Galen (*gay*-lynn) of Pergamum (A.D. 129–199), court physician of Roman Emperor Marcus Aurelius, believed that surgery was an important part of healthcare. He was especially interested in how the human body worked, and to find out, he spent much of his time dissecting plenty of animals — mainly pigs, monkeys, goats, and sheep. From this study, he drew conclusions about the human body — many of them accurate; some of them pretty off the wall.

What's with the sword and the snakes?

Ever wonder why the medical profession has as its symbol a sword with snakes circling around it? Well, first, the sword isn't a sword; it's a magic wand. Second, those are indeed snakes, but there's a good reason for them being there. Here's the story:

Apollo (a-*pol*-low) was the Roman god of medicine. His son **Aesculapius** (aes-ku-*la*-pee-us) eventually took over the family business and became the chief Roman god of medicine and healing. According to legend, Aesculapius arrived in Rome in the form of a snake and landed on the **insula Tiberina** (*in*-su-la tee-be-*ree*-na),

where he founded a hospital. (A hospital in Rome still occupies this site today.) So the snakes represent Aescaluplus.

The magic wand represents **Mercurius** (mer-*koo*-ree-us), better known to us as Mercury, the messenger of the gods, who also accompanied the souls of the dead to the Underworld. As such, Mercury could move freely between the living and the dead.

Hence, the symbol of the medical profession: Called a **caduceus** (ka-do-*kay*-us), it's the magic wand of Mercury entwined by two snakes.

Nevertheless, his study of the body, as well as his place as one of the preeminent physicians of his time, gave Galen plenty of influence as to how doctors in ancient Rome practiced. So despite the Romans' reliance on incantations, charms, amulets, and the intercession of various gods, they also had a pretty enlightened view of surgery and how it fit into medical theory.

Table 12-4 shows the Latin words used to describe organs, systems, and structures found on the inside of the human body. You may be surprised to see how many of them that you already know — and even more surprised to think that doctors in the Bronze and Iron Ages knew about them, too.

Table 12-4	Latin Words for Internal Organs		
Word	*Pronunciation*	*Original Meaning*	*Current Meaning*
alveolus	al-we-*oh*-luhs	small hollow	small air sac, found in the lungs
atrium	*ay*-tree-uhm	chamber, room	one of the two upper chambers of the heart
cerebrum	*ker*-ay-broom	brain	large, rounded structure of the brain

Word	Pronunciation	Original Meaning	Current Meaning
cervix	_ker_-wicks	neck, neck-shaped structure	neck-shaped, narrow outer end of the uterus
fistula	_fis_-too-lah	pipe, passage	passage that connects an abscess, a cavity, or a hollow organ (like the stomach or intestine) to the body surface or to another hollow organ so that fluid can pass between the two
humor	_who_-more	a fluid, body fluid	any body fluid, such as blood, lymph, or bile
lacuna	lah-_koo_-na	a cavity, space, small hollow	any cavity or space, found especially in a bone
macula	_mah_-koo-la	a spot	small area that looks different from the surrounding tissue
medulla oblongata	meh-_dool_-la ob-lon-_ga_-ta	oblongated marrow	lowermost portion of the brain
sinus	_see_-noos	fold, cavity	any of the various air-filled cavities of the skull
vena	_way_-na	vein	vein found in the body
vena cava	_way_-na _kuh_-wa	hollow vein	either of the two veins that drain blood from the upper body and the lower body and empty into the right atrium of the heart

Talkin' the Talk

Two students, Aemilia and Clodia, are cramming for final exams. They're quizzing one another about the human heart.

Aemilia: **Quid est atrium?**
kwid est *ah*-tree-um?
What is the atrium?

Clodia: **Atrium est cubiculum quod accipit sanguinem ex venis.**
ah-tree-um est koo-*bee*-koo-loom kwod ak-*key*-pit *san*-gwi-nem eks way-*nees*.
The atrium is a chamber that receives blood from the veins.

Aemilia: **Quot atria cor habet?**
kwot *ah*-tree-ah core *ha*-bet?
How many atriums does the heart have?

Clodia: **Duo.**
du-oh
Two.

Aemilia: **Recte!**
wreck-tay!
Correct!

Clodia: **Quot cubicula cor habet?**
kwot koo-*bee*-koo-lah core *ha*-bet?
How many chambers does the heart have?

Aemila: **Quattuor?**
kwuht-tu-ohr?
Four?

Clodia: **Recte! Hoc est tam facile!**
wreck-tay! hock est tuhm *fah*-key-lay!
Correct! This is so easy!

Aemilia: **Mox fiemus medicae!**
moks fee-*ay*-moose meh-*dee*-ki!
Soon we shall be doctors!

Words to Know

atrium, atrii, n	*ah-tree-uhm, ah-tree-ee*	chamber, room
caput, capitis, n	*ka-put, ka-pee-tis*	head
cerebrum, cerebri, n	*keh-ray-broom, keh-ray-bree*	brain
cervix, cervicis, f	*ker-wiks, ker-wee-kis*	neck
cor, cordis, n	*core, core-dis*	heart
manus, manus, f	*ma-noos, ma-noos*	hand
nasus, nasi, m	*na-soos, na-see*	nose
oculus, oculi, m	*o-koo-loos, o-koo-lee*	eye
pes, pedis, m	*pes, peh-dis*	foot
vena, venae, f	*way-na, way-nigh*	vein

Understanding Common Medical Terms

So you finally summon up the courage to go the doctor, but you don't know the meaning of the terms the doctor is using. When the doctor opens his mouth, this is probably what you hear:

> The tests revealed a slight *gibberish gibberish* affecting your *gibberish gibberish.*

This is probably how you *interpret* what you hear:

> You have a horrible disease that will probably kill you before you leave the office.

So the fact that most doctors use Latin and most others — including you — don't means that there's quite a communication gap and probably plenty of unnecessary panic going on in the doctor's office. Table 12-5 offers a few Latin terms to help you keep the panic at bay.

Early hospitals

The first hospitals for the poor began in temples. For example, the temple of Aesculapius was on an island in the middle of the Tiber River and initially served as a dumping ground for sick slaves. They were sent to the island so that no one would have to take care of them. Isolating sick folks was also a good way to keep others from contracting the diseases. In time, Aesculapius' temple became one of the first Roman public hospitals.

The size of the Roman Empire increased as its armed might grew. Military hospitals accompanied the armies all over the Roman world and spread their medical knowledge and practices to the locals. Highly organized and effective, these military hospitals treated soldiers wounded in battle. Broken and dislocated bones could also be taken care of there, and amputations were common.

Anesthetics, such as opium and alcohol were administered, and a great deal of surgical equipment — including scissors, tweezers, forceps, scalpels, clamps, and probes — has been found in ancient Pompeii, Ostia, and elsewhere.

Table 12-5	Medical Terms	
Word	**Pronunciation**	**Translation**
caries	kay-*ree*-ays	decay (of a bone or tooth)
cerumen	kay-*roo*-men	wax, especially of the ear
decubitus	day-*cue*-bee-tis	lying down, bedridden
delirium tremens	day-*lee*-ree-um *tray*-mens	literally, "trembling insanity"; a condition in which a person who drinks excessive amounts of alcohol over a long period of time experiences terrifying hallucinations, confusion, and trembling
fremitus	*fray*-me-tus	a murmur or vibration that can be felt by placing the hand directly on the body
in situ	in see-*too*	in the normal (or original) place
insomnia	in-som-*nee*-ah	inability to sleep properly
in vitro	in wee-*tro*	in glass, in a test tube
libido	lee-*bee*-do	sex drive

Word	Pronunciation	Translation
lumbago	lum-*bah*-go	literally, "loin," it refers to a severe pain in the lower back
nausea	gnow-*see*-a	feeling sick
nocturia	nok-too-*ree*-ah	frequent urination at night
ovum	*oh*-woom	egg
placebo	pla-*kay*-bo	literally, "I shall please"; refers to a substance containing no medication given to a patient to reinforce his expectation to get better
rubella	roo-*bel*-lah	literally, "little red things"; is another name for German measles, characterized by a red rash
sputum	*spoo*-toom	spit
statim (frequently shortened to "stat")	*stah*-tim	at once, immediately
tinnitus	*tin*-nee-tus	ringing
varicella	wa-ree-*kel*-la	literally, "speckled" (Chickenpox is the more common name for varicella.)
vertigo	*wher*-tee-go	literally, "turn"; refers to any sensation of dizziness

At the Drugstore

Surely you've noticed the abbreviation *Rx* on your prescription? Ever wonder what it means? Actually *Rx* is the abbreviation for the Latin word **recipe** (ray-key-*peh*), which is the imperative singular form of the verb **recipio** (ray-key-*pee*-oh). It can be translated as "Take!" You can read about imperative forms in Chapter 3.

Rx isn't the only holdover from Latin that you'll find on your prescriptions. Many of the terms and notations are also in Latin. But because the labels on the canisters are so small, the pharmacist uses some abbreviations for the doctor's instructions. Table 12-6 lists the Latin words that you're likely to come across and the abbreviations that go with them.

Table 12-6	Common Abbreviations on Prescriptions		
Abbreviation	*What It Stands For*	*Pronunciation*	*Meaning*
a.c.	ante cibos	*an*-teh *key*-bos	before taking food
a.d.	auris dextra	*ow*-ris *dek*-stra	right ear
ad	ad	ad	up to
ad lib.	ad libitum	ad *lee*-bee-tum	freely, as desired
agit.	agita	*ah*-ghi-tah	shake
AQ	aqua	*uh*-kwuh	water
a.s.	auris sinistra	*ow*-ris si-*nee*-stra	left ear
b.i.d.	bis in die	bees in *dee*-ay	twice a day
c.	cum	kuhm	with
et	et	et	and
f.	fac	fak	make, prepare
NPO	nihil per os	*nee*-heel per os	nothing by mouth
o.d.	oculus dexter	*o*-koo-loos *dek*-ster	right eye
o.s.	oculus sinister	*o*-koo-loos si-*nee*-ster	left eye
p.c.	post cibos	post *key*-bos	after taking food
P.O.	per os	per os	by mouth
pulv.	pulvis	*pull*-wis	powder
q.d.	quaque die	*kwa*-kwe *dee*-ay	every day
qh	quaque hora	*kwa*-kwe hoe-*rah*	every hour
q.i.d.	quater in die	*kwa*-ter in *dee*-ay	four times a day
s.	sine	*see*-nay	without
S.A.	secundum artem	se-*koon*-doom *ar*-tem	according to your judgment
SL	sub lingua	soob leen-*gwa*	under the tongue
ss.	semis	*say*-miss	one half
tid	ter in die	ter in *dee*-ay	three times a day
ung.	unguentum	un-*gwen*-tum	ointment

Talkin' the Talk

Marcus is suffering from a hangover, and visits the local **medicus** (*meh*-dee-koos; doctor) in search of a cure.

Medicus: **Ave, Marce! Quid sentis hodie?**
ah-way, *mar*-ke! kwihd *sen*-tus ho-*dee*-ay?
Hi, Mark! How are you today?

Marcus: **O caput meum! Dolet!**
oh *ka*-put *meh*-um! *doh*-let!
Oh my head! It hurts!

Medicus: **Cur?**
kur?
Why?

Marcus: **Heri bibi nimium. Potesne me adiuvare?**
hair-ee bee-*bee nee*-mee-um. po-*tes*-ne may
ad-you-*wa*-re?
Yesterday I drank too much. Can you help me?

Medicus: **Habeo remedium tibi! Recipe hoc medicamentum cum aqua per os ante cenam.**
ha-*bay*-o ray-*meh*-dee-oom *tee*-bee! ray-key-*pay* hok
meh-dee-ka-*men*-toom koom *uh*-kwuh per os *uhn*-tay
kay-nuhm.
I have a remedy for you! Take this medicine with
water by mouth before dinner.

Marcus: **Sed . . . , sed . . . , olet. Vomitabo. Deinde venter mihi quoque dolebit.**
sehd . . . , sehd . . . *oh*-let. wo-mee-*tah*-bo. de-*een*-de
wen-ter *mee*-hee *kwo*-kwe doe-*lay*-bit.

Marcus: But . . . , but . . . , it smells. I'll vomit. Then my stomach will also hurt.

Medicus: **Non possum sanare et caput et ventrem. Recipe hoc et abi!**
non *pos*-sum suh-*nah*-re eht *ka*-put eht *wen*-trem.
ray-key-*pe* hoc eht ah-*bee*!
I can't heal both your head and stomach. Take this
and leave!

Marcus: **O me miserum. Hi medici sunt inutiles.**
oh may *mee*-se-room. hee meh-*dee*-key sunt in-*oo*-
tee-lays.
O poor me. These doctors are useless.

Words to Know

bis in die	bees in *dee*-ay	twice a day
caries, cariei, f	kay-ree-ays, kay-ree-ay-ee	decay (of a bone or tooth)
in situ	in *see*-too	in the normal (or original) place
ovum, ovi, n	*oh*-woom, *oh*-wee	egg
per os	per os	by mouth
secundum artem	se-kun-dum ar-tem	according to your judgment
semis	say-miss	one half
statim	stah-tim	at once, immediately
sub lingua	soob leen-gwa	under the tongue
tinnitus	tin-nee-tus	ringing

Fun & Games

A. Cut your teeth on the following prescriptions. See if you can decipher the pharmacist's directions, using the information found in this chapter.

1. F. sol. c. 250 ml. AQ et ss. tsp. pulv. Appl. sol. ad a.s. t.i.d.

2. R. 1 capsule c. AQ PO t.i.d. a.c.

B. Identify the following parts of the human body as indicated in the following sketch:

(continued)

1. caput _____

2. venter _____

3. crus _____

4. brachium _____

5. manus _____

6. digitus _____

7. oculus _____

8. pes _____

9. auris _____

10. capillus _____

See Appendix C for the answers.

● ●

Chapter 13

Latin in the Church

· ·

In This Chapter

▶ Understanding early Christian history in a nutshell

▶ Adapting to Latin as the official language

▶ Praying through several centuries in Latin

▶ Understanding common ecclesiastical terms

· ·

*L*atin is the official language of the Catholic Church, and most of its documents are composed in Latin to this day. Until the 1960s, all Catholic priests spoke Latin, and the Mass was offered up in Latin only, except for a smattering of Greek. (This should come as no surprise because the Catholic Church is also known as the *Roman* Catholic Church.) Then, after the early 1960s, permission was given for the use of spoken language in the Church's liturgy alongside the traditional Latin, and priests began offering the Mass in the language that their parishioners spoke. Although the use of Latin in the Mass declined dramatically in the years immediately following, Latin has recently experienced a revival in the Church. Today, especially in large cities, Catholics have the choice of going to a Mass offered in their native tongue or attending a Latin Mass. (In fact, to see the text of the Latin Mass alongside an English translation, go to www.geocities.com/Heartland/Plains/1732/The_Mass.htm.)

Because the Roman Catholic Church was the first organized Christian church, many of the Protestant denominations that broke away from it or that came later also have some familiarity with the Latin phrases used centuries ago. These phrases have since passed into popular culture and will probably ring a bell with you, whatever your religious outlook is.

For example, you may already be familiar with several Latin phrases that deal with the Bible and religion, such as **Deo Volente** (*day*-oh vo-*len*-tay; God willing). Many other Latin phrases and sayings are still used today. By reading this chapter, you'll know what they mean.

Ecclesiastical (church) Latin differs from Classical Latin in pronunciation and sometimes in nuances of meaning. For more information about the differences in pronunciations between these two forms of Latin, head to Chapter 2. Although Classical pronunciation is used elsewhere in this book, most of the pronunciation keys in this chapter reflect the Ecclesiastical pronunciation.

Being Christian in Ancient Rome

After the Romans crucified Jesus in Jerusalem during the reign of Emperor Tiberius, Christianity started to spread throughout the Roman Empire. Christianity was popular among the Roman slaves because of its emphasis on the poor and weak in this life and its promise of salvation in the next. Although the Romans were fairly tolerant of other religions, sparks began to fly. The Christian religion stood out from the other religions because the Romans considered the Christians to be cannibalistic traitors who would bring the gods' wrath down on them. Here's why:

✔ The Romans had gods for every aspect of living — for sowing, reaping, weather, volcanoes, war, birth, marriage, and death. To the Christians, however, these gods meant nothing, and the Romans saw their denial of them as unacceptable. The Romans feared that such blasphemy would make their gods angry and cause them to punish not only the offenders but also the Romans.

✔ Every Roman emperor was thought to be divine (a god). The Romans regarded the Christians' refusal to acknowledge the emperor as a god as treason and therefore punishable by death.

✔ Because of a misunderstanding about Christian communion (see the "Magical mystery tour" sidebar for details), the Romans believed that Christians sacrificed babies, ate people's flesh, and drank blood.

Magical mystery tour

Plenty of rumors were spread about the early Christians, who met in secret places. These secret meetings made the other Romans, who heard about the secret rites and ceremonies that the Christians practiced, highly suspicious. One rite in particular caused them a great deal of problems and confusion: holy communion. In this rite, still practiced in Christian churches today, bread and wine (or grape juice) represents or changes into Christ's body and blood; the parishioners then partake of the substance in remembrance of Christ's sacrifice.

These distinctions were lost on the Romans, who simply heard that the Christians ate flesh and drank blood, and while doing this, would say, **Hoc est corpus [meum]** (hok est *kor*-poos [*me*-oom]), which means "This is [my] body." Not understanding the symbolism of the rite, the Romans thought the Christians were performing witchcraft.

Through the ages, **Hoc est corpus** gradually became shortened to *hocus-pocus,* and that's why we associate this phrase today with the phrase magicians say when they perform magic tricks.

Although they may have been able to tolerate the treason thing, the alleged cannibalism was a bit much for the non-Christians in Rome, and they actually labeled Christians as **odium humani generis** (oh-*dee*-um hoo-*ma*-nee *je*-ne-ris), hatred of the human race!

Nobody knows the trouble I see . . .

The first Roman emperor to actively persecute the Christians was Nero of fiddle-playing fame. (Supposedly, he played while the city burned.) When a large part of Rome was destroyed in a fire in A.D. 64, Nero blamed the Christians for the destruction. Those who confessed to being Christians were sentenced to death, and a sport was made of their execution. Here's what these early Christians had to look forward to:

- ✔ Some, sewn in the skins of animals, were torn apart by dogs.

- ✔ Others were crucified or burned.

- ✔ Still others were thrown to the wild animals in the **Circus Maximus** (*keer*-koos *ma*-ksee-moos) as public entertainment.

- ✔ Some were dressed in the **tunica molesta** (*too*-nee-ka mo-*les*-ta), a long garment that resembled the modern T-shirt all covered with tar. The unlucky folks in these outfits were used as human candles at some of Nero's outdoor garden parties.

Over the next two centuries, the Christians were persecuted on and off until the time of Constantine.

What year is this?

You may have noticed that sometimes writers indicate a year with the abbreviations B.C. or A.D.; other times, they use the abbreviations B.C.E. or C.E. instead. You may wonder what the difference is.

Well, in the sixth century A.D. (or C.E.), a monk named Brother Dennis came up with the Christian way of writing the date. He calculated when he thought Christ was born and made that the first year A.D., which stands for **Anno Domini** (*un*-no *do*-mee-nee) — In the year of the Lord. (Contrary to what you may have heard, A.D. does *not* stand for After Death.) Therefore, the abbreviation B.C. indicates the years before Christ's birth. The year zero doesn't exist. This convention is clearly based on Christian beliefs.

Those who aren't Christians understandably don't want to use this system and have come up with an alternative. Instead of using A.D., they use C.E., which is an abbreviation for Common Era; instead of B.C., they use B.C.E., which is an abbreviation for — you got it! — Before the Common Era. And so everyone is happy. (Or are they?)

Getting a little relief at last

Constantine the Great fought Maxentius, a man who stole power in Rome, to become emperor of Rome. Before he went into battle, Constantine had a dream in which he saw the cross and the words **In hoc vinces** (in hok *vin*-chays), which means "in this you will be victorious." Although the augurs (soothsayers) predicted that he would lose, Constantine's troops, with a cross on their shields, defeated Maxentius and his men at the **pons Mulvius** (pons *mool*-wee-us), the Mulvian bridge just outside of Rome. Constantine was baptized and became the first Christian Roman emperor. He legalized the Christian church and ended the persecution of Christians in Rome.

The Vulgate: A Bible for the common folk

Saint Jerome, also known as **Eusebius Hieronymus** (ey-oo-*se*-bee-us hee-eh-*ro*-nee-mus), was trained in classical Latin. The writings and style of **Cicero** (*kee*-ke-ro), the great Roman orator, deeply impressed Saint Jerome. At the end of the fourth century A.D., St. Jerome translated the Bible from Hebrew into Latin, which is now called the Vulgate. This Bible, in a revised form, is the Bible used by the Roman Catholic Church.

The word Vulgate comes from the Latin **vulgus** (*vool*-goos), which means "the common people." The English word *vulgar* comes from this word, and it means something associated with the common people. Therefore, the Vulgate was written in a language that the common folk could easily understand.

Anyone game?

Dominoes, the game played throughout the world today, can be traced back to China and, some claim, to ancient Greece and Rome. Dominoes are small tiles traditionally carved from ivory or bone with small, round pips of inset ebony. These tiles are used to play many different games. Here are a couple of theories about how the game was named:

✔ At one time, people called a Catholic priest a **Benedicamus Domino** (be-ne-dee-*ka*-moos *do*-mee-no), Latin for "Let us praise the Lord," something the priest often said during Mass. **Benedicamus Domino** was soon shortened to **domino** and later became the French word for a Catholic priest's winter hood, which was black on the outside and white on the inside. The tiles were called dominoes because they were also black and white.

✔ Another version of the origin of dominoes says that monks, a long time ago, when throwing the dice while playing the game, would utter the sentence **Benedicamus Domino** for good luck and that the name of the game was later shortened to domino.

Which of these is the actual origin of the word, we'll probably never know. But it sure makes for a good story!

The Early Church and Its Adopted Language

Until the middle of the third century A.D., the Christian community at Rome spoke mostly Greek. The liturgy was celebrated in Greek, and the most important theologians still wrote in Greek.

In Africa, Greek was the chosen language of the priests, but Latin was the more familiar speech for the majority of the faithful. To communicate with their followers, the priests began to communicate in Latin. St. Augustine, a bishop in North Africa, whom many consider to be the father of western theology, helped this along immensely by writing exclusively in Latin. (He didn't know Greek very well.)

Church Latin, classical Latin, pig Latin — which is which?

Most people who study Latin at school, study the works of authors such as Catullus, Julius Caesar, Cicero, Vergil, Ovid, Pliny, Tacitus, and many others. The period when these authors wrote is regarded as the time when Latin was at its best. This stage of the development of Latin is known as the *Classical Period,* and therefore the refined language of its poets and writers is *Classical Latin.* The ordinary man in the street didn't use the same language, though. In fact, two forms of Latin actually existed side by side in Rome: that of the intellectual crowd, called the **sermo urbanus** (*ser*-mo oor-*ba*-noos; urban speech), also called the intellectual speech, and that of the illiterate Romans, called the **sermo vulgaris** (*ser*-mo wool-*ga*-ris), or the common man's speech.

But because these two groups weren't isolated from each other — they did, after all, live together in Rome — the folks who spoke **sermo urbanus** and folks who spoke **sermo vulgaris** had to be able to communicate. This led to a third form of Latin, called the **sermo cotidianus** (ser-mo ko-tee-dee-*ah*-noos), meaning everyday

conversation. The **sermo cotidianus** was a mixture of the the highbrow and the lowbrow Latin.

When the early church fathers came along and started writing in Latin, they used the **sermo cotidianus.** They also added their translations of Greek words and phrases that they were currently using. Sometimes they invented new words by adding prefixes or suffixes to already existing Latin words, or by combining two or more words to form a new word. They would also take a word already in use and add a new sense to it. For example, **fidelis** (fee-*day*-lis) originally meant "loyal" or "trustworthy," but in church Latin, it meant "the faithful." This hybrid language became *Church (Ecclesiatical) Latin.* It was an easy way for the early Church fathers to communicate with most members of the population.

If you want to read a great book that combines church Latin, murder, intrigue, and a monk who acts as a detective, read Umberto Eco's *The Name of the Rose,* set in the year A.D. 1327. It was also made into a movie of the same name, starring Sean Connery and Christian Slater.

Augustine and others who wrote in Latin greatly influenced later writers and theologians. As more and more Christians wrote and communicated in Latin, it was finally adopted as the official language of the Catholic Church.

Among Augustine's works that you may hear mentioned are the **Confessiones** (kon-fes-see-*oh*-nays), his confessions, and the **De Civitate Dei** (day chee-vee-*tah*-tay *day*-ee), the City of God.

If you've attended a Catholic christening, confirmation, wedding, funeral, or Mass, you've probably heard some of the Latin words or phrases covered in the following sections. (If you're Catholic and want to impress your priest, you can try rolling a few of them off your tongue.)

Help me, oh Lord! (and others, too)

All religions have ways of invoking the help of God, and Christianity is no different. In fact, if you look at the early history of Christians (refer to the section "Being Christian in Ancient Rome" earlier in this chapter), you can get a pretty good idea of why they have so many ways of calling on God for help. Table 13-1 lists a few of them for you, as well as other common phrases.

Table 13-1	Common Latin Religious Expressions	
Word	*Pronunciation*	*Meaning*
in saecula saeculorum	inn *say*-koo-lah say-koo-*lo*-room	for ever and ever
in excelsis	een eks-*chel*-sees	on high
adeste fideles	ah-*des*-te fee-*day*-lays	O come, all ye faithful
beati pacifici	bee-*ah*-tee pa-chee-*fee*-chee	blessed are the peacemakers
beati pauperes spiritu	bee-*ah*-tee *pow*-pe-rays *spee*-ree-too	blessed are the poor in spirit
magnificat anima mea Dominum	ma-*nyi*-fee-kut *ah*-nee-ma *me*-ah *do*-mee-noom	my soul does magnify the Lord
misere mei, Deus	*mee*-se-ray *may*-ee *day*-oos	have mercy on me, oh God
Deus misereatur	*day*-oos mee-se-re-*ah*-toor	may God have mercy

Word	Pronunciation	Meaning
Deus vobiscum	*day*-oos voe-*bees*-koom	God be with you
Dominus vobiscum	*do*-mee-noos voe-*bees*-koom	the Lord be with you
Deus det nobis suam pacem	*day*-oos det *no*-bees *soo*-um *pa*-chem	may God grant us his peace
Deo iuvante	*day*-o you-*vun*-tay	with God's help

Whether you're Catholic or not, these expressions may seem vaguely familiar: You've heard them before, but you didn't know what they meant. Well, now you do.

Invoking the name of God

Several of the Latin phrases refer to God. Here are a couple of them:

- **Agnus Dei** (*un*-yoos *day*-ee) means "Lamb of God" and refers to Jesus Christ.

- **corpus Christi** (*kor*-poos *krees*-tee) means "the body of Christ" and refers to the *host,* that is, the bread served during communion.

- **in nomine Patris** (een no-*mee*-nay *pa*-tris) means "in the name of the Father" and refers to God.

- **Pater Noster** (*pa*-ter *nos*-ter) means "Our Father" and is the name of the Lord's Prayer.

Mary, Jesus' mother, is also named. For example, most westerners have heard the hymn "Ave Maria" — especially around Christmastime. **Ave Maria** (*ah*-vay ma-*ree*-ah) is actually Latin for "Hail, Mary." Take a look at a few other names for Mary:

- **Mater Dei** (*ma*-ter *day*-ee) means "Mother of God."

- **Beata Virgo Maria** (bee-*ah*-ta *vir*-go ma-*ree*-ah) means "Blessed Virgin Mary."

- **Stabat mater dolorosa** (*sta*-but *ma*-ter do-lo-*ro*-sa) means "the mournful mother stood" and refers to Mary when she was present at Jesus' crucifixion.

Words to Know

Latin	Pronunciation	Meaning
Anno Domini	un-no do-mee-nee	in the year of the Lord
in saecula saeculorum	inn say-koo-lah say-koo-lo-room	for ever and ever
in excelsis	een eks-chel-sees	on high
beati pacifici	bee-ah-tee pa-chee-fee-chee	blessed are the peacemakers
beati pauperes spiritu	bee-ah-tee pow-pe-rays spee-ree-too	blessed are the poor in spirit
Agnus Dei	un-yoos day-ee	Lamb of God
corpus Christi	kor-poos krees-tee	the body of Christ
in nomine Patris	een no-mee-nay pa-tris	in the name of the Father
mater Dei	ma-ter day-ee	Mother of God
Deus misereatur	day-oos mee-se-re-ah-toor	may God have mercy
Deus vobiscum	day-oos voe-bees-koom	God be with you

Talkin' the Talk

A **sacerdos** (sa-*cher*-dos; priest) ends his sermon and then blesses the **fideles** (fee-*day*-lays; the faithful, or here, the congregation). They respond accordingly.

Sacerdos: **Beati sunt pacifici.**
bee-*ah*-tee soont pa-chee-*fee*-chee.
Blessed are the peacemakers.

Fideles: **Amen.**
ah-men.
So be it.

Sacerdos:	**Beati sunt pauperes spiritu.**
	bee-*ah*-tee soont *pow*-pe-rays *spee*-ree-too.
	Blessed are the poor in spirit.
Fideles:	**Amen.**
	ah-men.
	So be it.
Sacerdos:	**Oremus. O Pater in caelis, agimus Tibi gratias.**
	o-*ray*-moos. o *puh*-tehr in *chay*-lees, a-*jee*-moos *tee*-bee *gra*-tsee-us.
	Let us pray. O Father in heaven, we give You thanks.
Sacerdos:	**Cura fideles, Domine. Serva eos.**
	koo-ra *fee*-day-lays, *do*-mee-neh. *ser*-va *eh*-os.
	Take care of your faithful, Lord. Protect them.
Sacerdos:	**Deus misereatur vobis. Deus vobiscum. Pax vobiscum.**
	de-oos me-se-re-*ah*-toor *voe*-bees. *day*-oos voe-*bees*-koom. pucks voe-*bees*-koom.
	May God have mercy on you. May God be with you. May peace be with you.
Fideles:	**Quoque tecum.**
	kwo-kwe *tay*-koom.
	And also with you.
Sacerdos:	**In nomine Patris, Filii et Spiritus Sancti.**
	in no-*mee*-nay *pa*-tris, *fee*-lee-ee eht *spee*-ree-toos *sunk*-tee.
	In the name of the Father, and of the Son, and of the Holy Spirit.
Sacerdos:	**In saecula saeculorum. Amen. Ite in pace.**
	in say-*koo*-lah say-koo-*lo*-room. *ah*-men. ee-tay in *pa*-cheh.
	For ever and ever. Amen. Go in peace.

Keeping on God's good side

In Church Latin, you'll also find phrases that express gratitude, contrition, trust in God, admissions of sin, and a willingness to leave things in God's hands. Table 13-2 lists phrases that express these things.

The pope starts here

The official title of the pope, the head of the Catholic Church, is **pontifex maximus** (pon-*tee*-feks ma-*ksee*-mus). This title was found way back in ancient Rome. Initially, the word **pontifex** meant "one skilled in the important magic of making bridges." The pontifex maximus was in charge of the **Pons Sublicius** (pons soo-*blee*-key-us), the oldest bridge and, for several centuries, the only bridge at Rome. The bridge was built entirely of wood and was considered sacred. The pontifex maximus performed certain religious rites to accompany any repairs to the bridge.

The pontifex maximus, together with the other **pontifices** (pon-tee-*fee*-kays), or priests, were responsible for the organization of the state religion. They also determined the dates of festivals and kept a record of the principal events of each year. They enjoyed certain privileges, such as exemption from taxation and military service.

In the year 46 B.C., when Julius Caesar was the **pontifex maximus,** he revised the Roman calendar, lengthening it from 10 to 12 months. This calendar, now called the Julian calendar, is named after him, and it's the one used today. In imperial times, the reigning emperor held the post of **pontifex maximus.**

So the pope today holds the official title of pontifex maximus as he's the head of the Catholic Church. This title is sometimes shortened to pontiff, another title of the pope.

Table 13-2	Words of Penance and Faith	
Word	**Pronunciation**	**Meaning**
Benedicamus Domino	be-ne dee-*ka*-moos do-*mee*-no	Let us praise the Lord
Dei gratia	*day*-ee gra-tsee-*ah*	by the grace of God
Deo Volente	*day*-oh voe-len-*tay*	God willing
Deus vult	*day*-oos voolt	God wills it
Dominus providebit	do-*mee*-noos pro-ve-*day*-bit	The Lord will provide
fiat voluntas Tua	*fee*-ut vo-*loon*-tus *too*-ah	Thy will be done
gloria Deo	glo-*ree*-ah *day*-oh	glory to God
Deo gratias	*day*-oh gra-*tsee*-us	thanks be to God
mea culpa	meh-*ah* kool-*pah*	through my fault
peccavi	pek-*ka*-vee	I have sinned

Words for the universe

In translating the Hebrew Bible into Latin, St. Jerome retold the Genesis story — the Biblical story of creation — using Latin terms. Table 13-3 lists a few of the words describing God's creation of the world as the early Christians understood it.

Table 13-3	Words Describing the World	
Word	*Pronunciation*	*Meaning*
caelum	*chay*-loom	Heaven
terra	*ter*-ra	Earth
inanis	inn-*ah*-nis	void
vacua	va-*koo*-ah	empty, barren
tenebrae	te-*ne*-bray	darkness
super	*soo*-per	above, across
faciem	fa-*chee*-em	face
regnum	*ren*-yoom	kingdom
libera	*lee*-be-ra	free
malo	*ma*-loe	evil
abyssi	ah-*bees*-see	abyss
fiat lux	*fee*-ut looks	let there be light

That's gratitude for you!

On the west coast of South Africa, about two hours' drive northwest from Cape Town, is a small fishing village with the name of Paternoster. Legend has it that, some time during the seventeenth century, several sailors on the way to or from the Far East were shipwrecked in the treacherous waters of the Atlantic Ocean. (The nearby Cape of Good Hope was also called the Cape of Storms.) After a great struggle, the sailors made it to shore. The sailors were so grateful that their lives had been spared that they all said the Lord's Prayer, which starts with the Latin words **Pater Noster** (our Father). The little town that was founded there was named "Paternoster" in gratitude.

Roman holiday

From the earliest times, people celebrated a festival at the time of the winter solstice when the days began to lengthen and the sun to return. This happened to be one of the most popular holidays among the ancient Romans. Called the **Saturnalia** (sa-toor-*na*-lee-ah), this was the week-long festival of **Saturnus** (sa-*toor*-noos). This festival ended on December 25, which was a very important day in the Roman calendar because it was the last day of the Saturnalia, and it marked the birthday of the Roman god **Mithra** (*mee*-tra) and the feast day of **Sol Invictus** (sol in-*week*-tus), the unconquered sun.

Plays, gifts, and feasting marked December 25, a truly festive day. Role reversal, such as masters serving their slaves or schoolboys teaching their teachers, often took place.

The true date of Christ's birth is unknown — no mention is made of a date in the Bible or elsewhere. December 25 came to be accepted almost everywhere as the day of Christ's birth. These celebrations, which were so familiar to and popular with the pagans, were continued even after their conversion to Christianity. The first recorded Christmas to be celebrated was in A.D. 336.

To encourage the sun's return, a log was lit in the fireplace at this time. Later, in merry old England, houses and churches were decorated with holly and ivy, and in Germany, an evergreen tree, usually a pine tree, symbol of eternal life, was placed in Christian homes. According to legend, it was Martin Luther who first decorated the Christmas tree with lights to symbolize the star-filled heavens from which Christ came down to earth.

With these words (and a few others), you can understand the following passage from the Old Testament (the book of Genesis in fact):

In principio Deus creavit caelum et terram

inn prin-*chee*-pee-o *day*-oos kray-*ah*-vit *chay*-loom eht *tehr*-ruhm

In the beginning God created heaven and earth

autem terra erat inanis et vacua

ow-tehm *ter*-ra *e*-rut in-*ah*-nis eht *va*-koo-ah

but the earth was void and barren

et erant tenebrae super faciem abyssi

eht *e*-runt te-*ne*-bray *soo*-per fa-*chee*-em ah-*bees*-see

and there was darkness above the face of the abyss

et spiritus Dei ferebatur super aquas

eht spee-*ree*-toos *day*-ee fe-ray-*bah*-toor *soo*-per *uh*-kwuhs

and the spirit of God was carried across the waters

et Deus vidit lucem quod esset bona

eht *day*-oos *vee*-dit *loo*-chem kwod *es*-set *boh*-nuh

and God saw the light, that it was good

et divisit lucem et tenebras

eht dee-*vee*-sit *loo*-chem eht te-*nay*-brus

and He separated the light and the darkness

appellavitque lucem diem et tenebras noctem.

ap-pel-*la*-vit-kwe *loo*-chem *di*-em eht te-*nay*-brus *nok*-tem.

and he called the light day and the darkness night.

Pretty neat, huh?

Words to Know

Deo Volente	day-oh voe-len-tay	God willing
fiat voluntas Tua	fee-ut vo-loon-tus	Thy will be done
Gloria Deo	glo-ree-ah day-oh	Glory to God
Gratias Deo	gra-tsee-as day-oh	Thanks be to God
mea culpa	may-ah kool-pah	through my fault
caelum, caeli, n	chay-loom, chay-lee	heaven
terra, terrae, f	ter-ra, ter-ray	earth
vacuus, vacua, vacuum	va-koo-oos, va-koo-ah, va-koo-oom	empty, barren
tenebrae, tenebrarum, f/pl	te-nay-bray, te-nay-bra-room	darkness
regnum, regni, n	ren-yoom, ren-yee	kingdom
liber, libera, liberum	lee-ber, lee-be-ra, lee-be-room	free
malum, mali, n	ma-loom, ma-lee	evil
fiat lux	fee-ut looks	let there be light

Talkin' the Talk

Some young children — Tullia, Marcia, and Quintus — are discussing the creation of earth. They're not completely sure of their facts.

Tullia: **Nonne Deus creavit hominem primum?**
non-ne *day*-oos kre-*ah*-vit ho-*mee*-nem *pree*-moom?
Didn't God create man first?

Marcia: **Non. Ille creavit hominem ultimum.**
non. *eel*-le kre-*ah*-vit ho-*mee*-nem *ool*-tee-moom.
No. He created man last.

Quintus: **Fortasse Ille creavit animalia primum?**
fohr-*tuhs*-seh *eel*-le kre-*ah*-vit a-nee-*ma*-lee-ah *pree*-moom?
Perhaps He created the animals first?

Marcia: **Non. In principio Ille creavit caelum et terram.**
non. inn prin-*chee*-pee-o *eel*-le kre-*ah*-vit *chay*-loom eht *tehr*-ruhm.
No. In the beginning He created heaven and earth.

Tullia: **Deinde hominem?**
de-*in*-de ho-*mee*-nem?
Then man?

Marcia: **Non. Terra erat vacua. Erant quoque tenebrae ubique.**
non. *ter*-ra e-rut va-koo-ah. e-rut *kwo*-kwe te-*ne*-bray oo-*bee*-kwe.
No. The earth was barren. There was also darkness everywhere.

Quintus: **Deinde animalia?**
de-*in*-de a-nee-*ma*-lee-ah?
Then the animals?

Marcia: **Non. Ille deinde creavit diem et noctem. Ille dixit: "Fiat lux!" Et erat lux!**
non. *eel*-le de-*in*-de kre-*ah*-vit *dee*-em eht *nok*-tem. *eel*-le *deek*-sit: "*fee*-ut looks!" eht e-rut looks!
No. He then created day and night. He said: "Let there be light!" And there was light!

Tullia:	**Confusa sum. Si tibi placet, lege locum nobis iterum!** kon-*foo*-sa soom. see *tee*-bee *pla*-chet, *le*-je *lo*-koom *no*-bees *i*-tay-room! I am confused. Please, read the passage to us again!
Marcia:	**Probe: In principio Deus creavit caelum et terram . . .** *pro*-bay: in prin-*chee*-pee-o *day*-oos kray-*ah*-vit *chay*-loom eht *tehr*-ruhm . . . Okay: In the beginning God created heaven and earth . . .
Quintus:	**Deo gratias!** *day*-oh gra-*tsee*-us! Thanks be to God!

Reciting the Lord's Prayer in Latin

One of the most famous of Christian prayers is the Lord's Prayer. Table 13-4 lists the words that you need to know if you want to read this prayer in its Latin form. The prayer itself with the translation follows the table.

Table 13-4	Words in the Lord's Prayer	
Word	*Pronunciation*	*Meaning*
sanctificetur	sunk-tee-fee-*chay*-toor	may it be kept holy
adveniat	ad-vay-*nee*-ut	may it come
fiat	*fee*-ut	may it be done
voluntas	voe-*loon*-tus	will
sicut	*see*-koot	just as
panem	*pa*-nem	bread
quotidianum	kwo-tee-dee-*ah*-noom	daily
hodie	ho-*dee*-ay	today
dimitte	dee-*mit*-te	forgive
debita	de-*bee*-ta	debts
debitoribus	de-bee-*tor*-ee-boos	debtors
ne inducas	nay *in*-doo-kus	do not lead

What's in a word?

Just like some city folk today look down on and make fun of people who live in the countryside, so did the ancient Romans. The Latin word for city was **urbs** (oorbs), and they had a word to describe city folk: **urbanus** (oor-*ba*-noos), which meant elegant, sophisticated, witty, or pleasant. From this comes our English word urbane, which still has the same meanings as its Latin parent.

On the other hand, the Latin word for a village or country district was **pagus** (*pa*-goos), and they described someone from the country as a **paganus** (pa-*ga*-noos) — a villager. Later, **paganus** became a synonym for a yokel or country bumpkin. Now it so happened that for the most part, the early Christians lived in the city. Those who lived in the countryside tended to worship the old gods and goddesses of Rome, and so it came about that the Christians started to refer to these people as **pagani** (pa-*ga*-nee), the plural of paganus, which was later shortened to our more familiar word "pagan."

Oratio Dominica

o-ra-*tsee*-o do-mee-*nee*-ka

The Lord's Prayer

Pater noster, qui es in caelis

puh-tehr *nos*-ter, kwee es in *chay*-lees

Our Father, who art in heaven,

sanctificetur nomen tuum.

sunk-tee-fee-*chay*-toor *no*-men *too*-oom.

may your name be kept holy.

Adveniat regnum tuum.

ad-vay-*nee*-ut *ren*-yoom *too*-oom.

Thy kingdom come.

Fiat voluntas tua

fee-ut vol-*oon*-tus *too*-ah

Thy will be done

sicut in caelo et in terra.

see-koot in chay-*loe* et in *ter*-ra.

on earth as it is in heaven.

Panem nostrum quotidianum da nobis hodie,

pa-nem *nos*-trum kwo-tee-dee-*ah*-noom da *no*-bees ho-*dee*-ay,

Give us this day our daily bread,

et dimitte nobis debita nostra

et dee-*mit*-te *no*-bees de-*bee*-ta *nos*-tra

and forgive us our debts

sicut et nos dimittimus debitoribus nostris.

see-koot eht nos dee-mit-*tee*-moos de-bee-*tor*-ee-boos *nos*-trees.

just as we forgive our debtors.

Et ne nos inducas in tentationem,

eht nay nos in-*doo*-kus in ten-*ta*-tsee-oh-nem,

And do not lead us into temptation,

sed libera nos a malo. Amen.

sed *lee*-be-ra nos ah ma-*lo*. *Ah*-men.

but deliver us from evil. Amen.

So what's with the fish?

Have you noticed that people sometimes have a fish on their car? Ever wondered why? This is a symbol that the owner of a car is a Christian. Why a fish you may wonder.

Well, during the time that the Christians were being persecuted in Rome, they had to hold their church meetings in secret. They found that the best place for these meetings was in the catacombs, an underground burial place just outside of Rome. They knew that the Romans were superstitious and weren't likely to go down there.

These catacombs consisted of several miles of passages. To make sure that no one got lost, the Christians etched fishes on the walls along the passageways. The heads pointed in the direction that the Christians had to go. To get out, one simply followed the tail's direction.

So why not an arrow instead of a fish? The reason is that most early Christians knew Greek as well, and someone discovered that the Greek word for a fish, **ichthus** (eek-thoos), is actually an acronym for **Iesus Christos Theou Uios Soter** (*ye*-soos *kris*-tos *theh*-oo *hoo*-yos *so*-ter), which means "Jesus Christ, Son of God, Savior."

That's why a fish was and still is the universal symbol for Christianity.

A final list of (and a few stories behind) Latin expressions

The problem with some Latin phrases is that they sometimes just don't make any sense. But each one of them has a story. Take a look at the following expressions that one hears regularly and then read the stories that go with them. Use them to impress your friends!

- **R.I.P.** stands for **Requiescat In Pace** (re-kwee-*es*-kut in *pa*-chay), which means "May he/she rest in peace." This is found on many old Roman tombstones and grave markers.

- **consummatum est** (kon-soo-*ma*-toom est) means "It is completed." These were Jesus' last words on the cross.

- **Quo vadis, Domine?** (kwo *va*-dis, do-*mee*-ne?) means "Where are you going, Lord?" According to legend, Peter was said to ask this question when, as he fled Rome and the persecution of the Christians, he saw a vision of Jesus at the city gates.

- **Urbi et orbi** (*oor*-bee et *oar*-bee): This phrase means "To the city [Rome] and the world." The pope pronounces these words during his blessing to make it clear that the blessing will spread not only to the city of Rome but also to the whole world.

- **Abyssus abyssum invocat** (ah-*bees*-soos ah-*bees*-soom in-*vo*-kut) means "Hell calls hell." This pithy saying means that one misstep usually leads to another.

- **I.N.R.I.: Iesus Nazarenus Rex Iudaeorum** (*yeh*-soos na-za-*ray*-noos reks you-dye-*o*-room) means "Jesus of Nazareth, King of the Jews." A Roman soldier wrote this on a small plaque and affixed it to Jesus' cross.

- **Ecce homo!** (*etch*-ay *hoe*-mo) means "Behold the man!" Pontius Pilate spoke these words when he presented Jesus, wearing a crown of thorns, to the people just before his crucifixion. *Ecce Homo* also refers to a depiction of Jesus wearing the crown of thorns.

- **Facito aliquid operis, ut te semper diabolus inveniat occupatum.** (fa-*chee*-to a-*lee*-kwid o-*pe*-ris, oot tay *sem*-per dee-*a*-bo-lus in-*vay*-nee-at ok-koo-*pa*-toom): This saying means "Always do something, so that the devil always finds you occupied." St. Jerome wrote this in his **Epistulae** (e-*pis*-tool-ay). Today we say, "Idle hands are the devil's workshop."

Words to Know

adveniat	ad-vay-nee-ut	may it come
regnum	ren-yoom	kingdom
fiat	fee-ut	may it be done
voluntas	vo-loon-tus	will
panem	pa-nem	bread
quotidianum	kwo-tee-dee-ah-noom	daily
hodie	ho-dee-ay	today
dimitte	dee-mit-te	forgive
debita	de-bee-ta	debts
debitoribus	de-bee-tor-ee-boos	debtors

Fun & Games

Here are the Ten Commandments in both English and Latin. The English is in the correct order. Can you match the Latin commandment with the correct English one? Write down the appropriate letter in the space provided:

Ten Commandments in English

1. ___You shall not have other gods before Me.

2. ___You shall not take the Name of the Lord thy God in vain.

3. ___You shall remember to keep holy the Lord's Day.

4. ___Honor your father and your mother, so that you may live long upon the land.

5. ___You shall not kill.

6. ___You shall not commit adultery.

7. ___You shall not steal.

8. ___You shall not bear false witness against your neighbor.

9. ___You shall not covet your neighbor's wife.

10. ___You shall not covet your neighbor's goods.

X Commandments in Latin

A. Non occides.

B. Honora patrem tuum et matrem tuam, ut sis longaevus super terram.

C. Non assumes nomen Domini Dei tui in vanum.

D. Non loqueris contra proximum tuum falsum testimonium.

E. Memento, ut diem Sabbati sanctifices.

F. Non concupisces omnia, quae proximi sunt.

G. Non habebis deos alienos coram me.

H. Non concupisces uxorem proximi tui.

I. Non moechaberis.

J. Non furtum facies.

See Appendix C for the answers.

Chapter 14

Latin in Zoology and Botany

· ·

· ·

Most of us call animals or plants by their common names. A tiger's a tiger. A leopard's a leopard. A mountain lion is a . . . well, a puma in certain parts of the world and a cougar in others. So therein lies the problem: People in different regions use different names for the same thing. Which can be a tad confusing. This type of confusion doesn't really impair us regular folks. After all, your neighbors aren't likely to insist that the animal they saw is really a puma or a cougar when you shriek, "I think a mountain lion just ate Fluffy!"

Now, if zoologists or botanists were as imprecise in the language they use to identify and describe animals and plants, the confusion would be the zoological/botanical equivalent of a Russian novel, with every character having upwards of a zillion names. Research would move forward at a snail's pace.

Hence, you get the *classification system,* a naming system that scientists use to tell one animal or plant from another and to make fine distinctions between similar things. As this is a Latin book, you've probably already guessed that many of the names and terms used in the classification system come from Latin.

Classifying Basics

The Greek philosopher Aristotle started a basic system of classifying plants and animals way back in the fourth century B.C. But he's not the one who gets the credit. The first person to come up with an *acceptable* system was the seventeenth century A.D. Swedish botanist, Karl von Linne. He decided to use Latin for the scientific names of plants and animals because many scientists back then already knew Latin. It was for them a universal language.

Linne divided plants and animals into seven categories, which are still used today. The following shows these categories and how the common house cat of today would be classified. (Plants are classified the same except instead of *Phylum,* plants use the category *Division.*)

Category	*Cat's Classification*	*Pronunciation*	*Translation*
Kingdom	Animalia	ah-nee-*ma*-lee-ah	animals
Phylum	Chordata	kor-*da*-ta	having a cord
Class	Mammalia	mam-*ma*-lee-ah	mammals
Order	Carnivora	kar-*nee*-wo-ra	meat-eating
Family	Felidae	fe-*lee*-digh	cats
Genus	Felis	*fay*-lis	cat
Species	domesticus	do-*mes*-tee-koos	domestic

An easy way to remember the order of the categories is to learn the following sentence: "**K**ing **D**avid (or **Ph**il) **C**omes **O**ver **F**rom **G**reece **S**undays."

If you look beyond the intimidating Latin names for plants and animals, you see a relatively simple classification system. All plants and animals are identified according to a binomial system — *bi* meaning "two," *nom* meaning name. In other words, all plants have two names: the **genus** (*ghe*-noos; kind) and the **species** (spe-*kee*-ays; appearance), both Latin words.

- ✔ **Genus:** The genus, always a noun, comes first and begins with a capital letter. The name may honor a person, describe the plant or animal, or be a character out of Greek or Roman mythology.

- ✔ **Species:** The second part of the name is the species. The species, an adjective, begins with a lowercase letter. It often refers to a place where the plant or animal is found, its characteristics or appearance, or the name of the person who gets credit for discovering it.

Here's a way to keep genus and species straight. Think of them as first and last names. Just as you have a first name and a last name, so does every plant and animal. Your last name identifies you *gen*erically as being part of a particular group — Thomsen, Marais, Millar. So your last name could be regarded as your genus. Your first name identifies you *speci*fically — Lynn, Peter, or Bernadette. This could then be your species. When writing your name to be classified, as on an official form, you put your generic name first, followed by your specific name — Thomsen, Lynn; Marais, Peter; Millar, Bernadette.

It doesn't take a genius to understand genus

The **genus** consists of a group of species that have similar characteristics. The following is a list of **genera** (ghe-*ne-ra*), the plural of **genus,** which you're likely to come across in the animal world:

- **Canis** (*ka*-nis; domestic dogs, wolves, coyotes, and dingoes)

- **Equus** (*eh*-kwoos; all kinds of horses and the zebra)

- **Falco** (*fal*-ko; falcons, kestrels, and merlins)

- **Felis** (*fay*-lis; tigers, jaguars, lynx, and other wild and domestic cats)

- **Homo** (ho-*mo*) the different species of man, such as *Homo habilis* (ho-*mo* ha-*bee*-lis; handy man), *Homo erectus* (ho-*mo* ee-*rek*-toos; erect man), and *Homo sapiens* (ho-*mo sa*-pee-ens; wise man).

- **Ursa** (*oor*-sa; the different kinds of bears, such as grizzly bears, black bears, and brown bears)

Getting specific with species

The species often describes the color of a plant or animal. Table 13-1 lists a few of these colors for you. (You may notice that many of the words refer to the same or similar colors. If you think about it, that's really not so different from what you're used to in English, in which *cerulean, azure, sapphire, cobalt* and a whole slew of other words all refer to the color blue.)

Adjectives ending in **–us** are masculine, and those ending in **–a** are feminine. In Latin, the adjective has to match the noun it modifies in case, gender, and number. So the **–us** words modify masculine nouns; the **–a** words modify feminine nouns. You can read more about adjective endings in Chapter 4.

You can call me Carol

Karl von Linne was so much into Latin that he even changed his name to Latin and used it in its new form: Carolus Linnaeus (ka-*ro*-lus leen-*nigh*-us). In 1753, this is the name he used on his species Plantarum (spe-*kee*-ays plun-*ta*-room) in which he outlined his naming system that's still used today.

See, your biology teacher isn't the one to blame.

The dog that ate the canary

You've probably heard of the Canary Islands before. This small group of islands is situated off the northwestern coast of Africa. You probably figure these islands were named after canaries, that is, the small yellow birds.

Wrong! These islands were named after dogs! Pliny the Elder, who lived in the first century A.D., named these islands the **insulae canariae**

(in-*soo-ligh ka-na*-ree-*igh*) or the Islands of the Dogs, because many packs of large, wild dogs populated the islands. (This makes sense when you think that another name for dogs is canines.)

The little yellow birds that were found on these islands were later called canaries.

Table 13-1	Common Colors among Plants and Animals	
Color	*Pronunciation*	*Meaning*
albus, alba	*ul*-boos, *ul*-ba	white
auratus, aurata	ow-*ra*-toos, ow-*ra*-ta	golden
aureus, aurea	ow-*ray*-oos, ow-*ray*-ah	golden, yellow
caeruleus, caerulea	kigh-roo-*lay*-oos kigh-roo-*lay*-ah	blue
flammeus, flammea	flum-*may*-oos, flum-*may*-ah	orange
fulvus, fulva	*fool*-woos, *fool*-wah	yellowish-brown, also red
fuscus, fusca	*foos*-koos, *foos*-ka	brown
luteus, lutea	loo-*tay*-oos, loo-*tay*-ah	yellow
niger, nigra	*nee*-gher, *nee*-ghra	black, dark
purpureus, purpurea	poo-r-poo-*ray*-oos, poo-r-poo-*ray*-ah	purple
ruber, rubra	*roo*-ber, *roo*-bruh	red
rufus, rufa	*roo*-foos, *roo*-fah	red, reddish
viridens	*we*-ree-dens	green, greenish

Talkin' the Talk

Two young Roman boys are walking to school. They discuss what they did the previous day when they had the day off:

Marcus: **Quid fecisti heri?**
kwid fay-kis-*tee* heh-*ree*?
What did you do yesterday?

Quintus: **Heri ivi ad Colosseum.**
heh-*ree* ee-*wee ad ko-los*-say-*oom*.
Yesterday I went to the Colosseum.

Marcus: **Quae vidisti?**
kwigh wee-*dees*-tee?
What did you see?

Quintus: **Animalia.**
ah-nee-*ma*-lee-ah.
Animals.

Marcus: **Qualia?**
kwa-lee-ah?
What kind?

Quintus: **Videamus. Erant magni canes, fulvi. Erant quoque equi.**
wee-de-*ah*-moos. *eh*-runt *mung*-nee *ka*-nays, *fool*-wee. *eh*-runt *kwo*-kwe *eh*-kwee.
Let's see. There were big dogs, yellowish. There were also horses.

Marcus: **Quid haec animalia fecerunt?**
kwid highk ah-nee-ma-*lee*-ah *fay*-kay-roont?
What did these animals do?

Quintus: **Canes fugabant equos et capiebant et edebant eos.**
ka-nays foo-*gha*-bunt *eh*-kwos eht ka-pee-*ay*-bunt eht e-*day*-bunt *eh*-os.
The dogs chased them and caught them and ate them.

Marcus:	**Hmmmm. Magni fulvi canes. Quem colorem equi habuerunt?**
	hmmmm. *mung*-nee *fool*-wee *ka*-nays. kwem ko-*lo*-rem *e*-kwi ha-*boo*-ay-roont?
	Hmmmm. Big yellow dogs. What color did the horses have?
Quintus:	**Colorem? Colores! Equi habuerunt nigras et albas lineas.**
	ko-*lo*-rem? ko-*lo*-rays! *eh*-kwee ha-boo-*ay*-roont *nee*-grus eht *al*-bus lee-*neh*-us.
	Color? Colors! The horses had black and white stripes.
Marcus:	**Mehercule! Es stultus! Illi canes erant leones, et equi erant zebrae!**
	may-*her*-koo-lay! es *stool*-toos! *eel*-lee *ka*-nays *eh*-runt lee-*oh*-nays, eht *eh*-kwee *eh*-runt *dse*-brae!
	By Hercules! You are stupid! Those dogs were lions, and those horses were zebras!

Words to Know

albus, alba, album	ul-*boos*, ul-*ba*, ul-*boom*	white
animal, animalis, n	ah-nee-muhl, ah-nee-muhl-*is*	animal
canis, canis, m/f	ka-*nis*, ka-*nis*	dog
equus, equi, m	eh-*kwoos*, eh-*kwee*	horse
feles, felis, m/f	fay-*les*, fay-*lis*	a cat
fulvus, fulva, fulvum	fool-*woos*, fool-*wah*, fool-*woom*	tawny, yellow
homo, hominis, m/f	ho-*mo*, ho-*mee-nis*	a man, a human being
leo, leonis, m	lee-*oh*, lee-*oh-nis*	a lion
niger, nigra, nigrum	nee-*gher*, nee-*ghra*, nee-*ghroom*	black, dark

Out of Africa

The ancient Romans viewed Africa with much awe. They had a popular saying way back then: **ex Africa semper aliquid novi** (*eks* ah-*free*-ka sem-*per* a-*lee*-kwid *no*-wee), which means "Out of Africa always something new." When the first explorers into Africa returned, they told of a wonderful creature that they had seen. When asked to describe this wonderful animal, the explorers were first at a loss, but then they said that this animal, viewed from a distance, was as large as a horse, looked like a horse, and had a huge horn on its forehead. So started the myth of the unicorn; **uni–** (ooni–) means one and **cornu** (*kor*-noo) means horn.

Of course, they hadn't really seen a unicorn. (Well, at least not a mythical one.) What they had seen was a rhinoceros.

Fauna and Flora

Fauna was the sister of Faunus, the Roman god of the forests. Both Fauna and her brother were also associated with the small animals that lived in the woods and forests. Flora, on the other hand, was the Roman goddess of flowers. She also made trees blossom (without which there'd be no fruit) and presided over everything that blooms.

Today, we use the terms *flora* and *fauna* to indicate the animals and plants found in particular places.

I'm hairy high-and-low: Common plant genus and species names

A **genus,** as mentioned earlier in the section "Classifying Basics," is the word that indicates a group of species that have similar characteristics. The following is a list of **genera** (ghe-*ne*-ra), the plural of **genus,** which you're likely to come across in the plant world:

- **Allium** (al-*lee*-oom; onions, leeks, chives, shallots, and garlic)
- **Lectuca** (lec-*too*-ka; lettuce)
- **Malus** (*ma*-loos; apples, crab apples)
- **Prunus** (*proo*-noos; plums, cherries, almonds, apricots, peaches)

▶ **Quercus** (*kwer*-koos; all kinds of oak trees, such as the white oak, red oak, black oak, pin oak and others)

▶ **Solanum** (so-*la*-noom; nightshades, eggplants, potatoes)

Just as is the case with animals, a plant species name is often an adjective. These adjectives describe the plant's appearance or other characteristic that can help people tell one plant from another.

The Latin word **flos** (flose), which means a "flower," is masculine in gender. Therefore, all the adjectives that modify or describe **flos** end in the masculine. (You can read more in Chapter 4 about adjective endings.) Table 13-2 lists some of the more common of these adjectives.

Table 13-2	Common Plant and Animal Names	
Epithet	*Pronunciation*	*Meaning*
grandiflora	grun-dee-*floor*-ah	having large flowers
maculata	ma-koo-*la*-ta	spotted
nana	*na*-na	dwarf
odorata	oh-door-*ah*-ta	scented
pendula	*pen*-doo-lah	hanging
pubescens	poo-*bes*-kens	hairy
reptans	*rep*-tuns	creeping, ground-hugging
rugosa	roo-*go*-sa	wrinkled
sanguinea	sun-gwee-*ne*-ah	bloody or red
scandens	*skan*-dens	climbing
sempervirens	sem-per-*wee*-rens	evergreen
stricta	*streek*-ta	upright
tomentosa	toe-men-*toe*-sa	wooly, downy

You all know that the plant and animal world is vast, and that we have but only scratched the surface here. Because the Latin forms of the genus and species don't decline or change their endings (refer to Chapter 2), it's not too difficult to use a good Latin dictionary to help you decipher the necessary information.

Plants and animals often use similar adjectives to indicate a species. But this shouldn't cause any confusion because the genus tells you whether you're discussing a plant or animal.

A rose is a rose is a rose, or is it?

Some plants have interesting names; their names have hidden meaning. For example, a daisy is so named because it was originally "Day's eye." A dandelion comes from the French *dent de lion* (dont de *lee*-on), which means "tooth of the lion," as its leaves resemble just that. A primrose (although not really a rose) comes from the Latin **Prima rosa** (*pree*-ma *ro*-sa), which means "first rose," as it's one of the first flowers to blossom in early spring. Following are a few more interesting names of plants:

- ✔ **Gladiolus** is a plant with leaves shaped like small swords. The Latin word for sword is **gladius** (gla-*dee*-us). The small version of a **gladius** in Latin is **gladiolus** (gla-dee-*oh*-lus), which is why they chose this name for the plant!

- ✔ **Iris** (*i*-ris) was the Greek and Roman messenger goddess. She was also the goddess of the rainbow with its seven colors. So it's no surprise that botanists named this plant with its variously colored flowers the Iris.

- ✔ **Nasturtium** (nuhs-*toor*-tee-oom) is a common garden flower whose leaves are used as a seasoning, especially in vinegar. This flower has only a mildly pungent odor but a very bitter taste, and its name comes from a combination of two Latin words: **nasus** (*na*-soos; nose) and **turt** (toort; twist). So Nasturtium means "nose twister"!

- ✔ **Narcissus** (nuhr-*kees*-soos) was a handsome young man who fell in love with his own reflection in pool of water out in the woods. He couldn't drag himself away from the reflection and pined away. The gods, feeling sorry for him, changed him into a flower, which bears his name. Not surprisingly, you can often find a narcissus near a river or pond.

Fun & Games

Here are some names that indicate the place or origin of a certain species. Can you match the Latin term with the correct English one?

1. **japonica** (ya-*po*-nee-kah)   A. North or South America

2. **canadensis** (ka-na-*den*-sis)   B. from the East (usually Asia)

3. **sylvestris** (seel-*wes*-tris)   C. from Japan

4. **americana** (ah-me-ree-*kah*-nah)   D. of the woods or forests

5. **montana** (mon-*tah*-nah)   E. of the sea

6. **africana** (ah-free-*kah*-na)   F. from Europe

7. **occidentalis** (ok-kee-den-*tah*-lis)   G. from the West

8. **europaeus** (ay-oo-ro-*pay*-us)   H. from Canada

9. **orientalis** (o-ree-en-*tah*-lis)   I. from Africa

10. **maritima** (ma-ree-*tee*-mah)   J. of the mountains

See Appendix C for the answers.

Chapter 15

Translating and Reading Latin

In This Chapter

▶ Understanding how Latin sentence structure differs from English

▶ Discovering a four-step process for translating a Latin sentence

▶ Practicing your translation skills

*O*ne mistake that people make when they translate from Latin to English is that they translate the first word they come across in the sentence, then they translate the next one, and then the third one, and so on. Because Latin doesn't use the same word order that English does, beginning translators end up with strange and sometimes nonsensical sentences — a sort of "Latinese." To avoid ending up with this kind of mess, you need a system that helps you accurately interpret what you're reading. That's what this chapter gives you — a four-step process that you can use to translate everything from simple to more complex Latin sentences.

And because you're more likely to read Latin than to speak it, this chapter includes a few excerpts from real Latin poetry that you can cut your translating teeth on.

Word Order or Where in the Heck Is the Subject?

Latin is an interesting and fun language. It's also more flexible than English. In English, the meaning of a sentence is tied to the word order: Where the words *are* has as much impact on meaning as *what* words are used. The subject comes first, the verb comes next, and then comes the object (if there is one).

For example, in the sentence "The dog bit the letter carrier," *dog* is the subject, *bit* is the verb, and *letter carrier* is the object. But if you switched *dog* and *letter carrier* around, this ordinary sentence becomes headline news: Letter carrier bit dog.

In Latin, the word's position isn't the thing that determines its function: The ending of the word is the thing that matters. These endings tell you whether the word is the subject, the object, or a possessive. The words themselves can be just about anywhere.

Every noun in a sentence must have a function; if it doesn't, it shouldn't be in the sentence. It's *not* the word's position in the sentence that determines its function; it's the word's ending. Look in Chapter 2 to see how these endings are formed and how they differ from one declension to another.

Making Sense of a Translation

When you approach a Latin sentence, understanding the meaning of the words is only half the battle. Now, you could go from first to last word, translating them in order, but you'd end up with something that doesn't make sense. Instead, plan your attack. Approach the sentence in the following way:

1. **Look for the verb and translate it.**

   Recognizing the verb gives you plenty of immediate information: You know the person of the verb (I, you, he/she/it, we, you, they), the number of the verb (singular, plural), the tense (present, imperfect, perfect, future, and so on) and the mood (indicative, subjunctive, imperative, or infinitive).

2. **Look for the subject of the sentence and translate it.**

   The subject is in the nominative (or subject) case. (See Chapter 2 for more information on cases.)

   If you don't find a subject (sometimes the subject is understood or not stated directly), don't worry. Without a stated subject, you use the person identified in the verb: *I, you* (singular or plural), *he, she, it, we,* or *they.*

3. **Look for the object of the sentence.**

   This word, which receives the action of the verb, is in the accusative case (see Chapter 2). Remember that not all sentences have objects.

4. **Translate what's left of the sentence.**

   Known as *All The Rest* (ATR), this is anything that isn't a subject, a verb, or an object.

When you follow this process, you're essentially imposing English sentence structure on a Latin sentence. (***Remember:*** In Latin sentences, subjects, verbs, and objects can be anywhere.) So what you're left with is a string of words that probably make some sense. (After all, by following the preceding steps, you translate the material in the subject-verb-object order that you're used to seeing in English sentences.) Still, the sentence needs a little finessing — particularly if it had much of the "all the rest" stuff. The following sections give you some practice.

Who's doing what?

If you're familiar with Latin verb endings, you're on your way to unraveling nearly any Latin sentence. Review the following:

When a verb ends in:	It means:	When a verb ends in:	It means:
–o or –m	I	–mus	we
–s	you (singular)	–tis	you (plural)
–t	he or she or it	–nt	they

For more on verb endings, head to Chapter 2.

An ending can tell you a noun's function and therefore its place in the sentence. Subjects appear in the nominative case, direct objects appear in the accusative case, indirect objects appear in the dative case, and so on. If all this case talk doesn't make sense to you, head to Chapter 2, which covers Latin cases. Verbs are a little trickier. To know how to translate a verb, you need to know what conjugation (first, second, third, and so on) it falls into. You can find that info in Chapter 2 as well.

Translating simple sentences

Here's a simple Latin sentence that you can use to try out your translation skills:

> **Puellas in horto puer exspectat.**
>
> pu-*ehl*-luhs in hor-*to* pu-ehr ex-*spek*-tuht.

If you were to translate this sentence from beginning to end, you'd end up with "The girls in the garden the boy waits for." This doesn't quite make sense. Instead, use the strategy outlined in the preceding section:

1. **Look for the verb and translate it.**

   The verb is **exspectat** (is waiting for). Already, you know the person of the verb (*he, she,* or *it*) and the number (singular). You can use this information to help you identify the subject, which has to agree in number.

2. **Look for the subject of the sentence and translate it.**

   You've got three nouns in this sentence, and any of them could potentially be the subject: **puer** (boy), **puellas** (girls), and **horto** (garden). Here's why **puer** ends up as the subject:

Puer is in the nominative case. (***Remember:*** The subject is always in the nominative case.) It's also singular, so it agrees with the verb.

Puer could also be vocative singular, showing that someone is addressing the boy, as in "hey, boy!" The way that you know this isn't the case is because the verb isn't in second person (you). The vocative case requires second-person verbs.

Puellas is plural (it doesn't match the verb), and it's in the accusative case — not the nominative case.

Horto is singular, but it's in the ablative case.

3. **Look for the object of the sentence.**

The only word in the sentence that's in the accusative case is **puellas,** which is accusative plural. Therefore, **puellas** is the direct object.

4. **Translate what's left of the sentence.**

What you have left is **in horto. In** is a preposition (in). Because the word **horto** follows the preposition, it's in the ablative case, describing where the girls are. (One of the functions of the ablative case is to describe where something is. For more on ablatives, head to Chapter 6.)

After you get all the piece parts, put them in standard English order: subject-verb-object, and you get this: "The boy waits for the girls in the garden."

Here's another sentence for you to cut your teeth on:

Vir equos agricolae laudat.

wir *eh*-kwos ah-*gree*-ko-ligh *low*-dut.

Use the process outlined in the preceding sections:

1. **Look for the verb and translate it.**

The verb is **laudat.** It means "he, she, or it praises" (third-person singular). ***Remember:*** You won't know *who* is actually doing the praising until you figure out the subject.

2. **Look for the subject of the sentence and translate it.**

The subject of the sentence is **vir** (man). You know this because, of the nouns in the sentence (**vir, equos,** and **agricolae**), only **vir** meets the requirements: It's in the nominative case, and it's singular.

Equos is accusative plural and therefore can't be the subject.

Ruling out **agricolae** is a littler trickier because it *could* be in the nominative case, but then it would be plural — **ae** is nominative plural for this word. As a result, **agricolae** isn't the subject.

3. **Look for the object of the sentence.**

   The only word in the sentence that's in the accusative case is **equos** (the horses). So that word is the direct object.

4. **Translate what's left of the sentence.**

   What you have left is **agricolae.** This word is in the genitive singular case, which means that it shows possession. So it translates as "of the farmer."

Put it all together, and you have "The man praises the horses of the farmer."

Translating longer sentences

Obviously, simple sentences are easier to translate than more complex sentences, but regardless of the sentence's length, you follow the same procedure outlined earlier in this chapter in the section "Making Sense of a Translation." Even if you have longer sentences and more than one clause, you treat every clause like an independent sentence. Consider the following sentence, for example:

Puer canem ex villa ducit et eum in viam fugat.
pu-ehr *kuh*-nem eks *wee*-la *doo*-kit eht *eh*-um in *wee*-uhm *foo*-guht.

One clue that the preceding is a more complicated sentence is that it has two verbs: **ducit** and **fugat.** If you look more closely, you can see that you actually have two clauses (**puer canem ex villa ducit** and **eum in viam fugat**) connected by the conjunction **et** (and). Simply tackle one clause at a time:

1. **Find the verb of the first clause: ducit.**

   Ducit is a third-person singular verb. Translated, it means "he, she, or it takes."

2. **Find the subject: puer.**

   Puer is the nominative singular noun, and it means "the boy."

3. **Find the object: canem.**

   Canem is accusative singular, and it means "the dog."

4. **Translate all the rest (of this clause, that is): ex villa.**

   Ex villa means "out of the house."

Throw in **et** (and) for good measure, and your translation so far reads, "The boy takes the dog out of the house and . . . " Now you're ready to tackle the second half of the sentence:

1. **Find the verb of the second clause: fugat.**

   Fugat is a third-person singular verb. Translated, it means "he, she, or it chases."

2. **Find the subject.**

   Now things get a little tricky. This clause doesn't have a stated subject, so you have to use the implied subject of the verb, which is *he, she,* or *it.* Because **puer** (boy) is the subject of the first clause, it's pretty likely that the boy is also the subject of the second clause.

3. **Find the object: eum.**

   eum means "it."

4. **Translate all the rest: in viam.**

   in viam means "into the road."

The translation of the second clause is "(he) chases it into the road." When you put both clauses together, you get "The boy takes the dog out of the house and chases it into the road."

Talkin' the Talk

Caesar and his wife Calpurnia are discussing their plans for the day. Today is the Ides of March (March 15) 44 B.C., and Calpurnia wants Caesar to stay home. He, however, has other plans!

Calpurnia:	**Caesar, mane domi. Noli exire hodie, oro te!** *kigh*-sahr, mah-*nay* do-*me*. *no*-lee eks-*ee*-reh *ho*-dee-ay, *o*-ro te! Caesar, stay at home. Don't go out today, I beg you!
Caesar:	**Non possum manere hic! Senatores exspectant me, praesertim Brutus et Cassius.** non *pos*-soom mah-*nay*-reh heek! se-nah-*to*-rays ex-*spek*-tuhnt may, prigh-*ser*-tim *broo*-tus eht *kas*-see-oos. I can't stay here! The senators are waiting for me, especially Brutus and Cassius.
Calpurnia:	**Non credo illo Bruto. Habet macrum et ieiunum vultum.** non *kray*-do eel-lo *broo*-to. *ha*-bet *mah*-kroom eht yay-*yoo*-noom *wool*-toom. I don't trust that Brutus. He has a lean and hungry look.
Caesar:	**Deinde da ei aliquid cibi et vini.** deh-*een*-deh da *eh*-ee a-*lee*-kwid *kee*-bee eht *wee*-nee. Then give him some food and wine.

Calpurnia:	**O Caesar. Tua stultitia erit olim mors tui!** oh *kigh*-sar. *tu*-uh stool-*tee*-tee-ah *eh*-rit *oh*-lim mors *too*-ee! O Caesar. Your stupidity will one day be the death of you!
Caesar:	**Cum amicis velut Bruto et Cassio? Mehercule, numquam!** koom uh-*mee*-kees *weh*-loot broo-*to* eht kas-see-*o*? may-*her*-koo-lay, *noom*-kwam! With friends like Brutus and Cassius? By Hercules, never!
Calpurnia:	**Eges amicis velut illis sicut eges pugione in tergo! Cura te. Vale.** *eh*-gehs uh-*mee*-kees *weh*-loot eel-lees *see*-koot *eh*-gehs poo-gee-oh-*nay* in *ter*-go! *koo*-ra tay. *wah*-lay. You need friends like those just as you need a dagger in your back. Take care of yourself. Goodbye.
Caesar:	**Vale. Para mihi gratam cenam: videbo tribus horis.** *wah*-lay. pah-*ra mee*-hee *grah*-tuhm *kay*-nuhm: wee-*day*-bo *tree*-bus ho-*rees*. Goodbye. Prepare me my favorite meal: I'll see you in three hours.
Calpurnia:	**Si non veneris domum tempore, necabo te.** see non *way*-neh-ris do-*moom* tem-po-*ray*, neh-*kah*-bo tay. If you don't come home in time, I'll kill you.

Rome sweet Rome

Rome played an important part in the development of Western civilization, so it's not strange to find many sayings, such as the following list, in which Rome features.

Rome was not built in one day!

All roads lead to Rome.

When in Rome, do as the Romans do.

Rome was built on seven hills.

When the Colosseum falls, Rome shall fall. When Rome falls, so shall the whole world.

Rome is the city of love. The Romans called their city **Roma** (Ro-mah). When you write *Roma* backwards, it spells *amor* (*ah*-more), which is Latin for "love." Roma is also where the words *romance* and *romantic* come from. And that's why languages derived from Latin, such as Italian, Spanish, Portuguese, Romanian, and French, are called Romance languages.

Words to Know

domi	do-me	at home
hodie	ho-dee-ay	today
praesertim	prigh-ser-tim	especially
deinde	deh-een-deh	then
stultitia, stultitiae, f	stool-tee-tee-ah, stool-tee-tee-igh	stupidity
olim	oh-lim	one day
numquam	noom-kwam	never
velut	weh-loot	like
sicut	see-koot	just as
cena, cenae, f	kay-nah, kay-nigh	dinner, meal

Real live Latin: Messin' with Martialis

In this section, you get to try your hand at some real Latin — that is, Latin written by an actual Roman. **Martialis** (Muhr-tee-*ah*-lis), who lived and wrote poetry in the second half of the first century A.D., wrote the following epigram. His epigrams are funny and throw plenty of light on the social life of the Romans of his time.

Here's the vocabulary that you need to translate this first excerpt, which gives you an idea of what Martialis thought of doctors.

Word	Meaning
nuper	recently, until recently
medicus	doctor
vispillo	undertaker
facio	I do, I am doing

Cover up the second column and use the four-step process outlined earlier in this chapter.

Original/Pronunciation

Nuper erat medicus, nunc est vispillo Diaulus.
(*noo*-per *eh*-rut *meh*-dee-koos, nunk eh-st
wis-*pil*-low dee-*ow*-lus.)

Translation

Until recently, Diaulus was
a doctor; now he is an
undertaker.

Quod vispillo facit, fecerat et medicus.
(kwod wis-*pil*-low *fah*-kit, *fay*-ke-rut eht
meh-dee-koos.)

What he is doing as an
undertaker, he also did as
a doctor.

Martialis, or Martial as he is known to us, had the knack of making fun of
people. In the next poem, he compares two women. Some of the words that
you need to translate the excerpt follow. **Thais** and **Laecania** are the names of
the women.

Word	*Meaning*
habeo	I have
niger	black
niveus	(snow) white
dens	tooth
ratio	reason
emptus	bought, purchased
haec	this one, the latter (feminine)
illa	that one, the former (feminine)

Original/Pronunciation

Thais habet nigros, niveos Laecania dentes.
(*tie*-is *ha*-bet *nee*-gros, nee-*weh*-os
ligh-*ka*-nee-ah *den*-tays.)

Translation

Thais has black teeth,
Laecania has snow-white
teeth.

Quae ratio est? Emptos haec habet, illa suos!
(kwigh *rah*-tee-oh est? *ehmp*-tos hike *ha*-bet,
eel-lah *soo*-os!)

What is the reason? The
latter has ones purchased,
the former has her own!

Translating complex sentences

In English, a complex sentence is one that has a *main* (or *independent*) *clause*
(one that can stand on its own) and a *dependent clause* (one that can't). An
example is the sentence "The chicken crossed the road because he wanted to
get to the other side." The main clause is "The chicken crossed the road."
The dependent clause is "because he wanted to get to the other side."

Most dependent clauses can fall just about anywhere in the sentence — beginning, middle, or end. In the sample just given, the dependent clause is at the end of the sentence. But it could just as easily fall at the beginning: "Because he wanted to get to the other side, the chicken crossed the road." Or in the middle: "The chicken, because he wanted to get to the other side, crossed the road."

Latin has these kinds of sentences, too, as the following example shows. See if you can separate the two clauses and tell which one is the main clause and which one is the dependent clause.

> **Vir, qui in horto sedet, patrem exspectat.**
> wir, kwee in hor-*to seh*-det, *pah*-trem ex-*spek*-tuht.

The main clause is **Vir patrem exspectat.** In this sentence, the dependent clause (**qui in horto sedet**) begins with the relative pronoun **qui** (kwee) and falls in the middle. In translating such a sentence, you translate each clause separately and then put them back together.

To translate the main clause, find and translate the verb, the subject, any objects, and then all the rest. You should end up with the following. (If you need help doing this, head to the section "Making Sense of a Translation" earlier in this chapter for tips on how to translate a sentence one element at a time.)

Function	*Word*	*Translation*
Subject	Vir	the man
Verb	exspectat	is waiting for
Object	patrem	father
ATR (All The Rest)	N/A	N/A

So far, the translation reads "The man is waiting for father."

Using the same technique, translate the elements of the second clause:

Function	*Word*	*Translation*
Subject	qui	who
Verb	sedet	is sitting
Object	no object	N/A
ATR	in horto	in the garden

The translation of the second clause is "who is sitting in the garden."

When you put the sentence back together, you get "The man, who is sitting in the garden, is waiting for father."

More live Latin: Catullus's catch

Catullus was a poet living in Rome during the first half of the first century B.C. He was madly in love with a young lady and wrote short poems to tell her how he felt. After a while, he realized that he wasn't the only man — other than her husband, that is — whom she was seeing. Catullus, disappointed, expressed his conflicting feelings in the following poem.

Try covering up the second column so that you can practice your translation skills. Following are the words that you need to interpret this poem:

Word	*Meaning*
odi	I hate
quare	why
fortasse	perhaps
requiro	I ask
nescio	I don't know
fieri	to happen
excrucior	I am tormented

Original/Pronunciation	*Translation*
Odi et amo. Quare id faciam, fortasse requiris. (*oh*-dee eht *ah*-mo. *kwah*-re id fa-*kee*-uhm, fohr-*tuhs*-seh re-*kwee*-ris.)	I hate and I love. Why do I do it, perhaps you ask.
Nescio, sed fieri sentio et excrucior. (*neh*-skee-oh, sehd fee-*ay*-ree sen-*tee*-oh eht ex-*kroo*-kee-or.)	I don't know, but I feel it happening and I am tormented.

Following is another poem written by Catullus. Addressed to his friend Fabullus, the poem invites Fabullus to a party. But there's a catch! Read on to find out more. See the words that follow to help you with the translation:

Word	*Meaning*
apud	at the house of, with
pauci	few
affero	I bring
inquam	I say
candida	blonde
cachinnis	laughter
sacculus	wallet
aranearum	spider-webs
plenus	full, filled with

Original/Pronunciation	*Translation*
Cenabis bene, mi Fabulle, apud me (kay-*nuh*-bis *beh*-neh, mee fuh-*bool*-leh, *ah*-pood may)	You will dine well, my Fabullus, at my house
paucis, si tibi di favent, diebus, (pow-*kees*, see *tee*-bee dee *fah*-went, dee-*ay*-boos,)	within a few days, if the gods favor you,
si tecum attuleris bonam atque magnam (see *tay*-koom uht-*too*-le-ris *boh*-num *uht*-kweh *mung*-num)	if you bring with you a nice and big
cenam, non sine candida puella (*kay*-nuhm, non *see*-nay kuhn-dee-*da* pu-*ehl*-luh)	meal, (and come) not without a blonde girl
et vino et sale et omnibus cachinnis. (eht wee-*no* eht sa-*lay* eht *om*-nee-boos *kuh*-khin-nees.)	and wine and wit and all kinds of laughter.
Haec si, inquam, attuleris venuste noster, (hike see, *in*-kwuhm, uht-*too*-le-ris we-*noos*-te *nos*-ter,)	If you bring these things, I say, our charming one,
cenabis bene: nam tui Catulli (kay-*na*-bis *beh*-neh: nuhm *too*-ee ku-*tool*-lee)	you will dine well: for your Catullus
plenus sacculus est aranearum. (*play*-noos *suk*-koo-loos est ah-ra-neh-*ah*-room.)	wallet is full of spider webs.

Poor Catullus! Hungry, thirsty, bored, no money, and no TV, but boy, can he throw a party!

Translating subjunctive mood

The sentences in this section use the subjunctive mood. Simply put, the subjunctive mood is used to convey a sense of the action not being completed or of depending on another action. (For more information on the subjunctive mood, see Chapter 6.)

Subjunctives in the main clause

When a verb in the subjunctive mood is in the main clause, it usually expresses a wish, encouragement, or a polite command/request. Consider these examples:

✔ In the following, **vivamus** and **amemus** are subjunctive verbs expressing encouragement:

Vivamus, mea Lesbia, atque amemus.

wee-*wah*-moos, *me*-uh *les*-bee-uh, *uht*-kweh uh-*may*-moos.

Let us live, my Lesbia, and let us love.

✔ In this sentence, **pugnent** is a subjunctive verb expressing a polite command:

Gladiatores in arena pugnent.

gluh-dee-ah-*to*-rays in uh-*ray*-nuh *poong*-nent.

Let the gladiators fight in the arena.

Subjunctives in dependent clauses

So what about subjunctives in dependent clauses? Well, the subjunctive mood is used for many constructions, such as purpose clauses, result clauses, indirect questions, indirect commands, conditional clauses, and many, many others. (See Chapter 6 for more information on the subjunctive mood.) Look at the following sentences:

✔ **Caesar Romam venit <u>ut gladiatores spectet</u>.**
kigh-sar *ro*-mum weh-*nit* oot gluh-dee-uh-*to*-rays *spek*-tet.
Caesar is coming to Rome to watch the gladiators.

In this sentence, the verb **spectet** is in the subjunctive mood, and clause, **ut gladiatores spectet,** is a purpose clause.

✔ **Pueri tam laeti sunt <u>ut laetitia exsultent</u>.**
pu-eh-ree tuhm *ligh*-tee soont oot ligh-*tee*-tee-ah ex-*sool*-tent.
The boys are so happy that they are jumping with joy.

The clause **ut laetitia exsultent** is a result clause. Although this looks like a purpose clause, it isn't. You can always tell that you've got a result clause because the word *so* appears in the main clause.

In English, *so* is a word by itself and is easy to recognize. In Latin, *so* is built into several words: **tot** (so many), **tantus** (so great), and **totidem** (so often), for example. In addition, several constructions themselves mean *so*: **tam, ita, sic,** and so on. If you see the word *so* in the main clause of your English translation, chances are the dependent clause is a result clause.

✔ **Pater me rogavit <u>num ad ludum irem</u>.**
pa-ter may ro-*ga*-wit noom uhd *loo*-doom *ee*-rem.
Father asked me whether I was going to school.

The clause **num ad ludum irem** is a clause showing an indirect question. (What were Father's very words? "Are you going to school?" is a direct question.)

✔ **Dux militibus imperat <u>ut fortiter pugnent</u>.**
dooks mee-*lee*-tee-boos *im*-pe-rut oot *for*-tee-ter *poong*-nent.
The general orders his soldiers to fight bravely.

The clause **ut fortiter pugnent** is an indirect command. (The general actually said to his soldiers, "Fight bravely, men!" — a direct command.)

✔ **Si hoc <u>facias</u>, stultus <u>sis</u>.**
see hok *fuh*-kee-us, *stool*-toos sees.
If you should do this, you would be foolish.

This clause is a conditional clause. In this sentence, notice that the verbs in both the main and the subordinate clauses are in the subjunctive mood.

When you see a verb in the subjunctive mood, tread carefully. Because the indicative mood is used to express facts, the subjunctive mood is used to express probability, possibility, and other things that may or may not happen.

Talkin' the Talk

Nero is trying to convince the Senate to elect his horse Incitatus to be the consul for the next year. The senators are wary, because they fear that Nero may try to kill them as he did his mother.

Nero: **Senatores, hic equus est sapiens. Ubi eum rogo "Quot sunt duo et duo?" pedem supplodit quater!**
se-na-*to*-rays, heek *eh*-kwoos est *suh*-pee-ens. oobi *eh*-um *ro*-go "kwot soont *du*-oh eht *du*-oh?" *peh*-dem *soop*-plo-dit *kwa*-ter.
Senators, this horse is intelligent. When I ask him "How much is two plus two?" he stamps his hoof four times!

Crassus: **Sed hic equus est animal. Potestne dicere?**
sehd heek *eh*-kwoos est *ah*-nee-muhl. po-*test*-ne
dee-keh-reh?
But this horse is an animal. Can it speak?

Nero: **Non potest dicere, sed scio quae putet. Incitate, quid putas?**
non *po*-test *dee*-keh-reh, sehd *skee*-oh kwigh *poo*-tet.
in-kee-*tuh*-te, kwihd *poo*-tus?
He can't speak, but I know what he's thinking.
Incitatus, what are you thinking?

Crassus: **Debeo hoc videre!**
deh-*beh*-o hok wee-*day*-re!
I've got to see this!

Nero: **Vide! Hic equus putat me debere necare aliquos senatores!**
wee-day! heek *eh*-kwoos *poo*-tuht may de-*bay*-re
ne-*ka*-reh ah-*lee*-kwos se-na-*to*-rays!
Look! This horse thinks that I should kill some senators!

Marcus: **Non me. Puto hunc equum esse sapientem. Puto te debere necare Crassum. Ille dixit te esse cerritum.**
non may. *poo*-to hoonk *eh*-kwoom *ehs*-seh suh-pee-*en*-tem. *poo*-to tay de-*bay*-re ne-*ka*-reh *kruhs*-soom. *eel*-le
deek-seet tay *ehs*-seh ker-*ree*-toom.
Not me! I think that this horse is wise. I think that you
ought to kill Crassus. He said that you are crazy.

Nero: **Crassusne dixit me esse cerritum? Milites, necate illum furciferem!**
kruhs-*soos*-ne *deek*-seet may *ehs*-seh ker-*ree*-toom?
mee-lee-tays, neh-*kuh*-te *eel*-loom foor-kee-*fe*-rem!
Crassus said that I'm crazy? Soldiers, kill that scoundrel!

Crassus: **O me miserum! Adiuvate me, amici! Servate me!**
o may *mee*-se-room! ad-you-*wa*-te may, uh-*mee*-kee!
ser-*wa*-te may!
O poor me! Help me, friends! Save me!

Nero: **Hoc docebit vos! Facite ut equus consul fiat.**
hok do-*kay*-bit wos! fuh-*kee*-te ut *eh*-kwoos *con*-sool
fee-uht.
This will teach you! See to it that the horse becomes
the consul.

Marcus:	**Senatores, eamus in curiam et deliberemus de consulatu equi. Vale, Nero!**
	se-na-*to*-rays, eh-*ah*-moos in *koo*-ree-uhm eht day-lee-beh-*ray*-moos day kon-soo-la-*too eh*-kwi. *wa*-lay, *near*-o!
	Senators, let's go into the senate-house and deliberate about the horse's consulship. Good bye, Nero!
Nero:	**Valete!**
	wah-*lay*-te!
	Goodbye!

Words to Know

sapiens, sapientis	suh-*pee*-ens, suh-*pee*-en-tis	wise
quot	kwot	how many, how much?
possum, posse, potui	pos-soom, pos-se, po-too-ee	I can, am able
scio, scire, scivi, scitus	skee-oh, skee-reh, skee-wee, skee-tus	I know
puto, putare, putavi, putatus	poo-toh, poo-tuh-re, poo-tuh-wee, poo-tuh-toos	I think
video, videre, vidi, visus	wee-day-oh, wee-day-re, wee-dee, wee-soos	I see
debeo, debere, debui, debitus	de-bay-oh, de-bay-reh, de-boo-ee, de-bee-toos	I must, ought to
neco, necare, necavi, necatus	ne-ko, ne-ka-reh, ne-ka-wee, ne-ka-toos	I kill
servo, servare, servavi, servatus	ser-wo, ser-wa-re, ser-wa-wee, ser-wa-toos	I save
eo, ire, ivi, itus	eh-oh, ee-reh, ee-wee, ee-toos	I go

Fun & Games

· ·

Choose the correct English translation for each of the following Latin sentences.
Look up words that you don't know in the Mini-Dictionary at the end of this book.

1. Ancillae urnas in urbem portant.

a. The slave-girls are carrying the water jars into the city.

b. The slave-girls were carrying the water jars into the city.

c. The slave-girls will carry the water jars into the city.

d. The slave-girls have carried the water jars into the city.

2. Cives in forum ambulabant et oratores audiebant.

a. The citizens walk into the forum and listen to the speakers.

b. The citizens walked into the forum and listened to the speakers.

c. The citizens walk into the forum to listen to the speakers.

d. The citizens walked into the forum to listen to the speakers.

3. Eamus ad circum et spectemus equos.

a. We are going to the circus and we are looking at the horses.

b. We shall go to the circus and we shall look at the horses.

c. We are going to the circus to look at the horses.

d. Let's go to the circus and look at the horses.

4. Pueri, qui in via ludunt, filii mei avunculi sunt.

a. The boys, who were playing in the road, were my uncle's sons.

b. The boys, who are playing in the road, are my uncle's sons.

c. The girls, who are playing in the road, are my uncle's daughters.

d. The girls, who are playing in the road, are my uncle's daughters.

5. Milites, pugnate ferociter et hostes superate!

a. Soldiers, let's fight bravely and conquer the enemy!

b. The soldiers fought bravely and conquered the enemy!

c. The soldiers are fighting bravely and conquering the enemy!

d. Soldiers, fight bravely and conquer the enemy!

(continued)

6. Cur fles? Quis te pulsavit?

a. Why are you crying? Who is hitting you?

b. Why are you crying? Who hit you?

c. Why were you crying? Who hit you?

d. Why were you crying? Was someone hitting you?

7. Feminae gladiatores et animalia in circo spectabant.

a. The women are coming to the circus to watch the gladiators and the animals.

b. The women will watch the gladiators and the animals in the circus.

c. The women were watching the gladiators and the animals in the circus.

d. The women are watching the gladiators and the animals in the circus.

8. Nautae, qui ad Graeciam navigabunt, naves in portu parant.

a. The sailors, who will sail to Greece, are preparing the ships in the harbor.

b. The sailors, who will sail to Greece, will prepare the ships in the harbor.

c. The sailors, who will sail to Greece, prepared the ships in the harbor.

d. The sailors, who sailed to Greece, prepared the ships in the harbor.

9. Pueri tam fessi sunt ut sub arbore sedeant.

a. The boys were so tired that they sat down under the tree.

b. The boy was so tired that he sat down under the tree.

c. The boys are so tired that they are sitting down under the tree.

d. The boy is so tired that he is sitting down under the tree.

10. Dux militibus imperavit ut fortiter pugnarent.

a. The general orders the soldiers to fight bravely.

b. The general ordered the soldier to fight bravely.

c. The general will orders the soldiers to fight bravely.

d. The general ordered the soldiers to fight bravely.

See Appendix C for the answers.

Chapter 16

Mottoes, Sayings, and Quotes: Cocktail Party Latin

- -

In This Chapter

▶ Quotes you can throw out at parties

▶ Latin words for love, war, and life

▶ Well-known Latin adages

- -

"*L*atin is a language — as dead as dead can be. First it killed the Romans, and now it's killing me!" If this saying were really true, you'd be in *big* trouble. Many words, expressions, and quotes that you use every day come directly from Latin. If you removed all the Latin words from English, you wouldn't have much left to say. Sometimes you use Latin words and expressions without even knowing they're Latin!

Still, people who can quote Latin phrases and (deliberately) pepper their sentences with Latin words give the impression of being well educated. Instead of envying those people, become one of them. (But try not to be too annoyingly condescending.) This chapter offers all sorts of Latin quotes, mottoes, and snippets of advice and wisdom, tells you who said what, and translates it all for you so that, if you decide to share a nugget or two, you'll know what you're saying. Amaze friends and impress your boss at your next party or meeting. Enjoy!

The Quotable Roman

The Romans weren't always fighting wars somewhere or conquering people and regions. They were also practical and observant. They loved to view life and comment on what they saw. Roman authors wrote on a variety of subjects: love, death, the universe, agriculture, architecture, philosophy, satire, and much, much more. Writers through the ages have quoted these ancient Roman witticisms, and many of them still pertain to our lives today.

Romans on love

"It's better to have loved and lost, than never to have loved at all!" The Romans can't take credit for that quote: It belongs to the nineteenth century English poet, Alfred, Lord Tennyson. Still, the Romans were of the same mind, and many Roman writers examined love.

The great Roman poet Vergil wrote **Amor vincit omnia et nos cedamus amori** (*uh*-mor *ween*-kit om-*nee*-a eht noss kay-*duh*-moos), which translates to "Love conquers all, and let us give in to love," one of the great seduction lines of all time."

Seneca, the Roman playwright and statesman, wrote **Si vis amari, ama** (see wees uh-*mah*-ree, *uh*-mah), which means "If you want to be loved, love," a perennial favorite of rock bands, poets, and valentine card writers.

Famous last words

The following is a list of famous last words uttered by characters from the ancient world:

Noli turbare calculos meos! (*no*-lee toor-*pa*-re *kuhl*-koo-los *meh*-os; Don't upset my calculations!) — Archimedes, the great Greek mathematician, spoke these words to a Roman soldier during the conquest of Syracuse. He had drawn some calculations in the sand outside of his house, and the soldier was standing dangerously close to what he'd written. The soldier's response? He killed him.

Paete, non dolet. (*pigh*-teh non *doh*-let; It doesn't hurt, Paetus.) — Arria was the wife of Paetus, a man who plotted against the Emperor Claudius and was sentenced to commit suicide. When Paetus hesitated, Arria plunged the dagger into her own chest and then handed the knife to him with these last words.

Acta est fabula, plaudite! (*uhk*-tuh est fuh-*boo*-luh, *plow*-dee-teh; The play is over, applaud!) — Augustus Caesar, grand-nephew and successor of Julius Caesar.

Adhuc vivo! (*uhd*-hook *wee*-wo!; I am still alive!) But not for long. Caligula, a Roman emperor known for his cruelty, once said **Oderint dum metuant.** (*oh*-deh-rint doom *meh*-too-uhnt; Let them hate me as long as they fear me.) He spoke these words after being stabbed by his own bodyguards. He died shortly thereafter.

Qualis artifex pereo! (*kwuh*-lihs *uhr*-tee-feks *per*-eh-oh!; What an artist perishes in me!) — Nero, infamous emperor of Rome.

Ego me bene habeo. (*eh*-go may *be*-neh ha-*bay*-oh; I'm feeling well.) — Sextus Afranius Burrus, a high-ranking official who served Nero.

Vae puto me deum fieri! (wigh *poo*-to may *de*-oom fee-*ay*-ree; Alas, I think I'm becoming a god!) — Vespasian, a Roman emperor.

From Catullus, another famous Roman poet, you get the following:

> ✔ **Difficile est longum subito deponere amorem.** (deef-*fee*-kee-leh est *lon*-goom *soo*-bee-to day-*pon*-ehe-re *uh*-mo-rem; It is difficult to suddenly give up a long love.)

> ✔ **Vivamus, mea Lesbia, atque amemus.** (*wee*-wah-moos, *me*-uh *les*-bee-uh, *uht*-kweh uh-*may*-moos; Let us live, my Lesbia, and let us love.)

Ovid, the Roman poet who wrote, among other things, *Metamorphoses* (*Transformations*), has the following to say about love:

> ✔ **Amor tussisque non celantur.** (*uh*-mor *toos*-sis-kwe non *kay*-luhn-toor; Love and a cough aren't concealed.) Romantic, wasn't he?

> ✔ **Militat omnis amans et habet sua castra Cupido.** (mee-*lee*-tuht *om*-nis *uh*-muns eht *ha*-bet *soo*-uh *kuhs*-truh; Every lover is a soldier and has his camp in Cupid.)

A few other lovely quotes that you can use to impress your friends are

> ✔ *On love in the future:* **Cras amet qui numquam amavit quique amavit cras amet.** (kruhs *uh*-met kwee *noom*-kwuhm uh-*ma*-weet *kwee*-kwe uh-*ma*-weet kruhs *uh*-met; Let he love tomorrow who has never loved and let he who has loved love tomorrow.) — *Pervigilium Veneris* (per-wee-*ghee*-lee-oom *way*-neh-ris), an anonymous poem that celebrates the power of Venus.

> ✔ *On love and fidelity:* **Expertus, dico, nemo est in amore fidelis.** (eks-*per*-toos, *dee*-ko, *nay*-mo est in uh-*mo*-ray; I say, as an expert, no one is faithful in love.) — Propertius, Roman poet.

> ✔ *On love and wisdom:* **Amare et sapere vix deo conceditur.** (uh-*ma*-re eht suh-*pay*-re weeks *deh*-oh kon-*kay*-dee-toor; Even a god can scarcely love and be wise at the same time.) — Publilius Syrus (poob-*lee*-lee-oos *sih*-roos), a Roman writer of farces.

> ✔ *On love and fighting:* **Amantium ira amoris integratio est.** (uh-*mun*-tee-oom *ee*-ruh est uh-*mo*-ris in-teh-*gruh*-tee-oh est; The anger of lovers is the renewal of love. Or in modern-speak: The best of a fight is making up afterwards.) — Terence, writer of Roman comedies.

> ✔ *On love and lovers:* **Amantes sunt amentes** (uh-*muhn*-tays soont uh-*men*-tays; Lovers are lunatics.) — Anonymous.

Romans on war

The Romans were famous for fighting wars all over Europe, the Middle East, and Africa. They never met a race of people that they didn't want to subdue, civilize, or annihilate. The following are some of the many references to war that you can find in the works of Roman authors:

✔ **Silent enim leges inter arma.** (*see*-lent *ay*-nim *leh*-gays *in*-ter *uhr*-muh; For laws are silent in times of war.) — Cicero, Roman statesman and philosopher.

✔ **Carthago delenda est.** (kuhr-*tuh*-go day-*len*-duh est; Carthage must be destroyed.) — Cato the Elder, who saw Carthage as a major threat to Rome, ended each and every speech to the Senate with these words.

✔ **Bella detesta matribus.** (*bel*-luh day-*tes*-tuh *muh*-tree-boos; Wars, detested by mothers.) — Horace, Roman poet.

✔ **Dulce et decorum est pro patria mori.** (*dool*-keh eht deh-*ko*-room est pro puh-tree-*ah* mo-*ree*; It's sweet and glorious to die for one's father-land.) — Horace.

✔ **Qui desiderat pacem, praeparet bellum.** (kwee day-*see*-de-ruht *puh*-kem, prigh-puh-*ret bel*-loom; Whoever desires peace, should prepare for war.) — Varro, Roman scholar and writer.

✔ **Bella, horrida bella.** (*Bel*-luh, hor-*ree*-duh *bel*-luh; Wars, terrible wars.) — Vergil.

From the mouth of Julius Caesar

Julius Caesar was one of the most famous of the Romans. Not only was he a great statesman and author, but he was also an excellent general. Julius Caesar led the Roman army to victory in many countries, including France, Britain, Spain, Africa, the Middle East, and Greece. Back in Rome, it was he who revised the old calendar, adding two months and extending it to 365¼ days. Not surprisingly, this calendar is known today as the *Julian calendar*. On the Ides of March (March 15th), 44 B.C., a group of Roman senators, who would've claimed that he got what was coming, assassinated Caesar. The following are a few of Caesar's famous sayings:

✔ **Alea iacta est.** (*uh-lee*-uh *yuk*-tuh est; The die is cast.) Caesar said this after he led an army across the Rubicon (a river in northern Italy) in 49 B.C. Roman law forbade any general from leading troops across the Rubicon. Once across the river, Caesar knew that he couldn't go back and that he had made an irreversible decision.

✔ **Et tu, Brute?** (et too, *broo*-teh?; Even you, Brutus?) Caesar said this to Brutus just after Brutus stabbed him. (To see how other ancients bowed out of life, head to the sidebar "Famous last words.")

✔ **Gallia est omnis divisa in partes tres.** (*guhl*-lee-uh est *om*-nis dee-*wee*-suh est in *puhr*-tays trays; All of Gaul is divided into three parts.) This quote makes up the first line in Caesar's commentaries on his war in Gaul.

✔ **Veni, vidi, vici.** (*way*-nee, *wee*-dee, *wee*-kee; I came, I saw, I conquered.) Caesar said this when he reported back to Rome after the battle of Zela in 47 B.C.

Give me another beer: Romans on drink

The Romans loved their wine and drank a great deal. The following quotations indicate the Romans' fondness for the fruits of Bacchus:

- **Bibere humanum est, ergo bibamus.** (*bee*-beh-reh hoo-*mah*-noom est, *er*-go bee-*bah*-moos; To drink is human, let us therefore drink.) — Anonymous.

- **In vino veritas.** (in *wee*-no *weh*-ree-tuhs; In wine is the truth.) — Anonymous.

- **Nemo enim fere saltat sobrius, nisi forte insanit.** (*nay*-mo *ay*-nim *feh*-ray *suhl*-tuht *so*-bree-oos, *nih*-sin *fohr*-teh in-*saw*-nit; For almost nobody dances sober, unless he happens to be insane.) — Cicero.

- **Nunc est bibendum.** (noonk est bee-*ben*-doom; Now we must drink.) — Horace.

- **Bibamus, moriendum est.** (bee-*bah*-moos, moh-ree-*en*-doom est; Let us drink, we all have to die.) — Seneca.

Latin quotes from other famous people

You don't find Latin quotes only in ancient texts. Inscribed on the inside of Queen Katarina Jagellonica of Sweden's wedding ring are the words **Nemo nisi mors.** (*nay*-mo *nih*-sih mors; Nobody except death [will part us].) The king of England is known as **Defensor fidei** (day-*fen*-sor fee-*day*-ee), or the "Defender of the faith." Nor will you find that all famous Latin quotes came from the Romans. Following are a few famous utterings of some non-Romans:

- **Deus vocatus atque invocatus aderit.** (*deh*-oos wo-*kah*-toos *uht*-kweh een-wo-*kah*-toos *uh*-deh-rit; God, whether summoned or not, will be there.) This epitaph appears on the tomb of Carl Jung (1875–1961), noted Swiss psychologist and psychiatrist.

- **Austriae est imperare orbi universo.** (ow-*stree*-igh est eem-peh-*ruh*-reh *or*-pee oo-nee-*wer*-so; It is Austria's destiny to rule the whole world.) — Frederick III, Holy Roman Emperor during the fifteenth century. As a bonus, you can use this quote to remember the vowels (a, e, i, o, u) in the English alphabet — or use the vowels in the English alphabet to remember this quote.

- **Ipsa scientia potestas est.** (*eep*-suh skee-*ehn*-tee-uh po-*tes*-tuhs est; Knowledge itself is power.) — Francis Bacon (1561–1626), English philosopher and statesman.

- **Vix ulla tam iniqua pax, quin bello vel aequissimo sit potior.** (weeks *ool*-luh tuhm in-*ee*-kwuh puks, kwin *bel*-loh wel igh-*kwees*-see-mo seet po-*tee*-or; Scarcely is there any peace so unjust that it is better than even the fairest war.) — Erasmus (1466?–1536), Dutch theologian and scholar.

✔ **Sic semper tyrannis!** (sik *sem*-per tee-*run*-nees!; Thus always to tyrants!) — John Wilkes Booth (1838–1852), U.S. actor and assassin of American President Abraham Lincoln.

✔ **Cogito ergo sum.** (*ko*-ghee-to *er*-go soom; I think, therefore I exist.) — Rene Descartes (1596–1650), French philosopher and mathematician.

✔ **Si monumentum requiris, circumspice!** (see mo-noo-*men*-toom ray-*kwee*-ris, keer-koom-*spee*-keh; If you're looking for a monument, look around.) — Sir Christopher Wren (1632–1723) on his epitaph in St. Paul's Cathedral, which he designed.

✔ **Ora et labora.** (*oh*-ruh eht *luh*-bo-ruh; Pray and work.) — St. Benedict (480?–543?), monk and founder of the Benedictine order.

✔ **Dum excusare credis, accusas.** (doom eks-koo-*sah*-reh *kray*-dis, uhk-*koo*-suhs; When you believe that you're excusing yourself, you're accusing yourself.) — St. Jerome (340?–420), monk, church scholar, and author of the Vulgate, the Latin Bible. (See Chapter 13 for more information on Latin and the Church.)

Talkin' the Talk

Two Romans are at a party. One is a **iurisconsultus** (you-ris-kon-*sool*-toos; lawyer), nursing a drink, and the other is a **medicus** (*may*-dee-koos; doctor). They're discussing the prospects of having a new emperor.

Medicus:	**Imperator mortuus est. Imperator novus diu vivat!** im-peh-*ruh*-tor mor-*too*-oos est. im-peh-*ruh*-tor *no*-woos *dee*-oo *wee*-wuht! The emperor is dead. Long live the new emperor!
Iurisconsultus:	**Ita vero! Sed desiderabo veterem. Caligula imperatore, habui plurimos clientes.** *ee*-tuh *way*-ro! sehd day-see-deh-*rah*-bo we-*teh*-rem. kuh-*lee*-ghoo-lah im-peh-ruh-*toh-ray*, huh-*boo*-ee *ploo*-ree-mos klee-*en*-tays. Yes, indeed! But I'll miss the old one. When Caligula was emperor, I had very many clients!
Medicus:	**Et ego habui plurimos aegros.** et *eh*-go huh-*boo*-ee *ploo*-ree-mos *igh*-gross. And I had very many patients.

Iurisconsultus: **Claudius, novus imperator, non tam crudelis est quam Caligula.**
claw-*dee*-oos, *no*-wus im-peh-*ruh*-tor, non tuhm kroo-*day*-lis est kwuhm kuh-lee-*ghoo*-luh.
Claudius, the new emperor, is not as cruel as Caligula.

Medicus: **Itaque habebo minores aegros.**
ee-*tuh*-kwe ha-*bay*-boh mee-*nor*-ays *igh*-gross.
And so I will have fewer patients.

Iurisconsultus: **Fortasse debes fieri vispillo!**
fohr-*tuhs*-seh de-*bays* fee-*ay*-ree wis-*pil*-lo!
Perhaps you should think of becoming an undertaker!

Medicus: **Vispillo? Cur?**
wis-*pil*-lo? kur?
An undertaker? Why?

Iurisconsultus: **Quod facies vispillo, facis nunc medicus.**
kwod fuh-*kee*-ays wis-*pil*-lo, *fuh*-kees noonk may-*dee*-koos.
What you will do as an undertaker, you are now doing as a doctor.

Medicus: **Et quid est illud?**
et kwihd est *eel*-lood?
And what is that?

Iurisconsultus: **Sepeliens tuos aegros.**
say-peh-*lee*-ens *too*-os *igh*-gross.
Burying your patients.

Medicus: **Certe! Dummodo omnes sint iurisconsulti!**
ker-tay! doom-*mo*-do *om*-nays sint you-ris-kon-*sool*-tee!
Sure! As long as they are all lawyers!

Iurisconsultus: **Medice, cura te ipsum. Tabernari, da alteram potionem meo amico!**
meh-dee-keh, *koo*-rah tay *eep*-soom. tuh-ber-*nah*-ree, duh uhl-*teh-ruhm* po-tee-oh-*nehm* *meh*-oh uh-*mee*-ko!
Physician, heal thyself! Bartender, give another drink to my friend!

Words to Know

certe	ker-tay	certainly
cliens, clientis, m	klee-ens, klee-en-tis	client
crudelis, crudele	kroo-day-lis, kroo-day-leh	cruel
diu	dee-oo	for a long time
dummodo	doom-mo-do	provided that
imperator, imperatoris, m	im-peh-ruh-tor, im-peh-ruh-to-ris	emperor
minor, minoris	mee-nor, mee-no-ris	fewer
morior, mori, mortuus sum	mo-ree-or, mo-ree, mor-to-oos soom	to die
plurimus, plurima, plurimum	ploo-ree-moos, ploo-ree-muh, ploo-ree-moom	very many, the most
sepelio, sepelire, sepilivi, sepultum	say-peh-lee-oh, say-peh-lee-reh, say-peh-lee-wee, say-pool-toom	to bury
vetus, veteris	weh-toos, weh-teh-ris	old, former
vivo, vivere, vixi, victum	wee-wo, wee-weh-re, week-see, week-toom	to live

Advice in Latin: Words to Live By

Right in the heart of Amsterdam is a casino. The rear entrance of this casino faces a movie theater complex. Above the entrance is a Latin inscription, written in large, capital letters that says:

Homo sapiens non in ventum urinat.

Hoh-mo *suh*-pee-ens non in *wen*-toom *oo*-ree-nut.

A wise man does not urinate into the wind.

Very sage advice, indeed. But wait. There's more. The Romans had more advice to give than that. Here's a sampling of good advice and life lessons to keep in mind (or use if you have the opportunity):

- **Caveat emptor.** (kuh-*way*-uht *emp*-tor; Let the buyer beware.) — Anonymous.

- **Cave canem.** (*kuh*-way *kuh*-nem; Beware of the dog.) — Anonymous. (Of course, if you really want to keep people out of your yard, you'd probably better use the English version instead.)

- **Promoveatur ut amoveatur.** (pro-mo-weh-*ah*-toor oot ah-mo-we-*ah*-toor; Let him be promoted to get him out of the way.) — Anonymous. (This quote applies to the The Peter Principle, which suggests that people rise to their level of incompetence.)

- **Dum spiro, spero.** (doom *spee*-ro, *speh*-ro; As long as I breathe, I have hope.) — Cicero, Roman statesman and philosopher.

- **Carpe diem!** (*kuhr*-peh *dee*-em; Seize the day!) — Horace, Roman poet.

- **Ira furor brevis est.** (*ee*-ruh *foo*-ror *breh*-wis est; Anger is a brief insanity.) — Horace.

- **Mens sana in corpore sano.** (mens *suh*-nuh in *kor*-po-ray *suh*-no; A healthy mind in a healthy body.) — Juvenal, Roman satirical poet.

- **Sed quis custodiet ipsos custodes?** (sed kwihs koos-*to*-dee-et *eep*-sos koos-*to*-days; But who will guard the guards themselves?) — Juvenal.

- **Mendacem oportet esse memorem.** (men-*duh*-kem *oh*-por-tet *ehs*-seh me-*mo*-rem; A liar must have a good memory.) — Quintilian.

- **Timendi causa est nescire.** (tee-*men*-dee *cow*-suh est nay-*skee*-reh; Ignorance is the cause of fear.) — Seneca the Younger.

- **Senectus ipsa est morbus.** (se-*nek*-toos *eep*-suh est *mor*-boos; Old age itself is a disease.) — Terence.

- **Facilis descensus Averno.** (*fuh*-kee-lis est day-*sken*-soos uh-*wer*-no; Easy is the descent to Hell.) — Vergil.

- **Labor omnia vincit.** (*luh*-bor om-*nee*-uh *win*-kit; Work conquers all.) — Vergil.

Advice to a bald man

Absolutely nothing is wrong with a bald (or balding) man! Julius Caesar was balding and was notorious for his comb-over! The Romans made fun of men who tried to cover up their baldness as the following quotes show:

Calvo turpius est nihil compto. (kuhl-*wo* toor-*pee*-oos est *nee*-heel *komp*-to; Nothing is more contemptible than a bald man with a comb-over.) — Martialis.

Etiam capillus unus habet umbram. (eh-*tee*-uhm *kuh*-pee-loos *oo*-nus *huh*-bet *oom*-pruhm; Even one hair has a shadow.) — Publilius Syrus.

Mottoes in Latin

Many universities, organizations, groups, charitable institutions — sometimes even families — have a *motto*, a short, expressive word or saying that encapsulates what that group stands for or hopes to achieve. Often, these mottoes are in Latin. This section shows you just a few.

Mottoes of famous organizations and institutions

Following are a few mottoes of well-known organizations and institutions:

- **Veritas** (*way*-ree-tuhs; Truth) Harvard University.

- **Lux et Veritas** (looks eht *way*-ree-tuhs; Light and Truth) Indiana University.

- **Veritas vos liberabit** (*way*-ree-tuhs wos lee-beh-*rah*-bit; The truth will set you free.) Johns Hopkins University.

- **Semper fidelis** (*sem*-per fee-*day*-lis; Always faithful) U.S. Marine Corps.

- **Ars gratia artis** (uhrs gruh-tee-*ah uhr*-tis; Art for the sake of art) M.G.M. Studios.

- **Dominus illuminatio mea** (*do*-mee-noos eel-loo-me-*nah*-tee-oh *meh*-uh; The Lord [is] my light) Oxford University.

Pick a motto, any motto

Looking for a good motto to use for your school, club, or organization? Look no further! Here are some handy ones. And you don't have to worry about copyright! The authors have all been dead for more than 2,000 years.

Audaces fortuna iuvat. (ow-*duh*-kays for-*too*-nuh *you*-wuht; Fortune favors the bold.)

Aut viam inveniam aut faciam. (owt *wee*-uhm in-*way*-nee-uhm owt fuh-*kee*-uhm; I'll either find a way or make one.)

Docendo discimus. (do-*ken*-do *dees*-kee-moos; We learn by teaching.)

Facta non verba. (*fuhk*-tuh non *wer*-buh; Deeds, not words.)

Finis coronat opus. (*fee*-nis *ko*-ro-nuht *o*-poos; The end crowns the work.)

Non scholae sed vitae discimus. (non *sko*-ligh sehd *wee*-tigh dis-*kee*-moos; We do not learn for school but for life.)

Nulli secundus. (*nool*-lee seh-*koon*-doos; Second to none.)

Potest ex casa magnus vir exire. (*po*-test eks *ka*-sah *muhng*-noos wir eks-*ee*-reh; A great man can come from a hut.)

Potius mori quam foedari. (*po*-tee-oos *mo*-ree kwuhm foi-*duh*-ree; Rather to die than be dishonored.)

Tongue twister

Try to say the following Latin line as quickly as you can without making an error:

O Tite tute Tati tibi tanta, tyranne, tulisti!

o *tee*-teh *too*-teh *tah*-tee *tee*-bee *tun*-tah, tee-*run*-neh, too-*lee*-stee!

Oh, you tyrant, Titus Tatius, you took such great things for yourself!

Mottoes of cities and countries

As a result of the Communist scare of the 1950s, U.S. President Dwight D. Eisenhower and the U.S. Congress changed the U.S. motto to *In God We Trust*. But before the 1950s, the U.S. Motto had been the Latin phrase **e pluribus unum** (ay *ploo*-ree-boos *oon*-oom; one, out of many). Not a bad motto. Short, to the point, and meaningful. Other countries also have Latin mottoes, which, at least until the printing of this book, they haven't felt the need to change. In fact, Latin is alive and well and living in the mottoes of many countries and cities throughout the world. Here are a few:

- **A mari usque ad mare** (uh muh-ree oos-kwe uhd muh-reh; From sea to sea) Canada

- **Urbs in horto** (oorbs in hor-*to;* A city in a garden) Chicago

- **Domine, dirige nos** (do-*mee*-neh, dee-*ree*-geh nos; Lead us, Lord) London

- **Fluctuat nec mergitur** (*flook*-too-uht nehk *mer*-ghee-toor; She is tossed by the waves and does not sink) Paris

- **Nemo me impune lacessit** (*nay*-mo may eem-*poo*-nay luh-*kes*-sit; No one wounds me with impunity) Scotland

- **Ex unitate vires** (eks oo-nee-*tuh*-tay *wee*-rays; Out of unity, strength) South Africa

- **Iustitia omnibus** (you-*stee*-tee-uh *om*-nee-boos; Justice for all) Washington, D.C.

Fun & Games

The following is an interesting Latin palindrome. You can read it up *and* down the columns and backwards *and* forwards in the rows! Try it!

S	A	T	O	R
A	R	E	P	O
T	E	N	E	T
O	P	E	R	A
R	O	T	A	S

Written as a sentence, it looks like this: **Sator Arepo tenet opera rotas** (*suh*-tor ah-*re*-po *te*-net *oh*-pe-rah *ro*-tuhs). Translated, it means "Arepo, the sower, holds the wheels with difficulty."

Match the Mottoes

Following are mottoes for some of the states of the United States of America. Can you match the Latin motto with the correct English one?

1. Arizona: **Ditat Deus** (*dee*-tuht *deh*-oos)

2. Colorado: **Nil sine numine** (nil *see*-nay *noo*-me-nay)

3. Idaho: **Esto perpetua** (*es*-to per-*peh*-too-uh)

4. Maine: **Dirigo** (dee-*ree*-go)

5. Mississippi: **Virtute et armis** (wir-*too*-te eht *uhr*-mees)

6. New York: **Excelsior** (eks-*kel*-see-or)

7. Oklahoma: **Labor omnia vincit** (*luh*-bor om-*nee*-uh *ween*-kit)

8. Virginia: **Sic semper tyrannis** (seek *sem*-per tee-*run*-nees)

9. West Virginia: **Montani semper liberi** (mon-*tuh*-nee *sem*-per *lee*-beh-ree)

10. Wyoming: **Cedant arma togae** (*kay*-duhnt *uhr*-muh *tow*-gigh)

A. Work conquers all

B. Let arms yield to the toga

C. Thus always to tyrants

D. Nothing without the divine will

E. God enriches

F. Ever upward

G. Mountaineers are always free

H. I direct

I. May she live forever

J. By valor and arms

See Appendix C for the answers.

Part IV
The Part of Tens

" Sorry, but I don't undertand your 'Ecclesiastical Latin.' Could you repeat that using 'Classical' pronunciation ?"

In this part . . .

Want interesting info in short snappy lists? This is the part to come to. In Part IV, we decode ten common Latin abbreviations, alert you to ten words that often rattle the beginning student, offer lists of common Latin prefixes and suffixes, and list ten Web sites that you can go to for more information about Latin and the Romans.

Chapter 17

Ten Loanwords from Latin

● ●

In This Chapter

▶ English words that came straight from Latin

▶ Meaning may be different from the original

● ●

*I*n English, we find many words — literally thousands — adopted directly from Latin. In most cases, these words have still retained their original meanings. Words that have been used in this way are called *loanwords*. Following are ten of the more common loanwords found in English today. See how many of them you recognize — and use.

Forum

The central square of ancient Rome, where citizens met, chatted with one another, listened to political speeches, and performed business transactions, was called a **forum** (*fo*-room). Today, this word is still used to refer to a public discussion or a place where that discussion is held.

Spectator

Someone who went to the Colosseum to watch gladiators kill one another was called a **spectator** (spek-*tah*-tor). This comes from the Latin word **spectare** (spek-*tah*-re), which means "to watch" or "to look." (Just think of the English words "spectacles" and "spectacular" that are derived from this Latin word!) Today, a person who watches a sports event, a parade, or other exhibition is still called a spectator.

Factotum

An employee or assistant who serves in a wide range of jobs is called a *factotum*. The word **factotum** (fuk-*to*-toom) comes from the words **fac–** (fuk–), which means, "to do," and **totum** (*to*-toom), which means "everything." So a factotum is someone who "does everything."

Senator

In the Roman Republic, the Senate was a council of appointed officials that managed foreign relations, supervised the state religion, regulated state expenditure and taxation, and was responsible for legislature. A member of this council was called a **senator** (seh-*na*-tor). We still have senators today, doing pretty much what their predecessors did centuries ago. Unfortunately, official interns were nonexistent back then.

Radio

The Romans didn't have radios (it took one of their descendents, Italian inventor Marconi, to invent the radio), but they did have the word **radio** (ray-*dee*-oh). In those days, the word could mean, "I gleam," "I emit rays," or "I radiate." With these definitions, you can see why they chose this word for the modern-day radio.

Opus

Today, this word is usually used to describe the creative work of some great musician or writer. The plural of **opus** (*oh*-poos), which means "work," is **opera** (*oh*-pe-rah). The word originally referred to any kind of work, including a completed work of art.

Atrium

An **atrium** (*ah*-tree-oom) was the central open courtyard in a Roman house. The bedrooms, study, and dining room were all arranged around this area. The name came from **atrum** (*ah*-troom), which means "black," because the smoke of the fires inside the house blackened its walls and ceilings. Today, an atrium refers to a usually skylighted central area or rectangular court found in public or commercial buildings. An atrium is also a chamber in the human heart.

Via

When you travel to Paris via London, it means that you must first stop over in London before proceeding with your journey to Paris. This word comes from the Latin word **via** (wee-*ah*), which means "by way of."

Veto

A **tribunus plebis** (tree-*boo*-noos *play*-bis) — tribune of the common folk — was an elected official who could stop legislature from being passed by standing up in the senate and saying **Veto!** (*we*-to), which means "I forbid." Today, a veto refers to the official rejection of any proposed act or law.

Ego

Latin for the first-person singular, I, is **ego** (*eh*-go). So your ego is obviously your opinion of yourself, even though others may not share in it. An *egoist* is someone who thinks mostly about himself or herself and is therefore egocentric.

Chapter 18

Ten False Friends: Common Mistakes in Latin

*T*he Roman philosopher Seneca, who was also Nero's tutor, wrote, **Errare est humanum** (eh-*rah*-re est-hoo-*mah*-noom), which means, "To err is human."

When you translate from Latin to English, you're bound to make mistakes. The chief reasons for these errors are not knowing what the words mean, not taking time to look them up, and speeding through the translation. Chapter 15 gives you a four-step process for translating Latin that can help you avoid some of these errors. But even if you take your time and know your vocabulary pretty well, you're still liable to stumble on Latin words that look like English words but don't have the same meanings. These words are called "false friends;" if you're not careful, they could easily confuse you.

You must be careful when you translate. If you don't know a word, look it up. Don't guess. As this chapter shows, Latin can easily lead you astray. A favorite saying of the Romans was **Festina lente** (*fes*-tee-na *len*-tay), which means, "Make haste slowly." Keep this in mind when you translate. Speed kills (the translation, that is).

Audere and audire: Audaciously audible!

The Latin words for *to dare,* **audere** (ow-*day*-reh), and *to hear,* **audire** (ow-*dee*-reh), look much the same. But not only do they have different meanings, they also fall into different conjugations. **Audere** is a second-conjugation verb, and audire is a fourth-conjugation verb. (If you don't know why a verb's conjugation is important, head to Chapter 2.)

One way to remember the difference between these two words is to think of English words that are derived from them. From **audere** come the English words *audacious* and *audacity* — both have the letter *a* and both have meanings that relate to boldness. From **audire** come the words *audible, auditorium, audience,* and *auditory.* Notice the *i*'s; all these words have meanings that relate to hearing.

Crimen: Guilty or not guilty?

If you were to guess, you'd probably say that **crimen** (*kree*-men) means "crime." And you'd be wrong. **Crimen** actually means "accusation," and as any lawyer worth his or her salt can tell you, just because you've been accused doesn't mean you did it! From **crimen** come the words *incriminate* and *criminal.*

Ad or ab: To or fro?

Although **ab** and **ad** are both prepositions and despite how similar they look, they mean the exact opposite of each other. **Ad** means "to" or "towards" and is followed by the accusative case. (See Chapter 2 for information about this and the other noun cases in Latin.) To remember what **ad** means, think of words like *adhere* (stick *to*) and *advise* (offer advice *to*).

The preposition **ab** means "from" or "away" and is followed by the ablative case. By remembering the word *abduct,* which means, "to take away unlawfully," you can remember this preposition's meaning.

Invitus (by force)

Another one of those false friends, **invitus** (in-*wee*-toos) may look like it's begging to be translated as the English word *invite.* Well, it ain't. **Invitus** actually means "unwilling" or "against one's wishes."

Semper and saepe: Do you come here often or always?

Another common mistake people make is with the words **semper** and **saepe. Semper** (*sem*-per) means "always." Think of the motto of the U.S. Marine Corps: **Semper fidelis** (*sem*-per fee-*day*-lis), which means "always faithful." **Saepe** (*sigh*-peh) means "often."

You can easily get mixed up with the Latin words for *always* and *often,* but if you remember the Marines' motto, shortened to **Semper fi,** you'll *always* get it right.

Servare and servire: Are you being served or saved?

The words **servare** (ser-*wa*-reh) and **servire** (ser-*wee*-reh) look the same and have the same function (both are verbs), but they have different meanings.

Servare is a first-conjugation verb, and **servire** is a fourth-conjugation verb. (See Chapter 2 for more on conjugations.) **Servare** means "to protect" or "to save." **Servire** means "to serve."

From **servare** come words like *conserve* and *preserve;* from **servire** come the words *subservient* and *server.*

Some police departments have the motto **Servimus et servamus** (ser-*wee*-moos eht ser-*wa*-moos), which means "We serve and protect."

Tandem and tamen: I'd like to go cycling, but . . .

Another pair of words that you can easily confuse is **tandem** (*tan*-dem), which means "at last" or "at length," and **tamen** (*ta*-men), which means "but" or "however."

To remember **tandem**'s definition, think of the tandem bicycle: It's a bicycle *at length*. With tamen, you're on your own.

Fugere and fugare: Follow me, I'm right behind you!

The Romans were good soldiers and loved to fight. They were frequently on the offensive and now and then on the defensive. The Latin word meaning "to drive away" or "to chase away" is **fugare** (foo-*ga*-reh). The word meaning "to flee" or "to run away" is **fugere** (foo-*geh*-reh). Here's one way to remember that **fugare** means "to drive away": It has an *a* in it as does the word *away.*

Fugare is a first-conjugation verb, and **fugere** is a third–io verb. (Refer to Chapter 2.) From **fugere** comes the word *fugitive,* which is a person who flees. Here's a fun word that comes from **fugare: vermifuge,** which means to drive away worms. Spring that on your biology teacher or vet the next time he or she starts talking about internal parasites.

Dicere and ducere: Do as I say . . .

Dicere and **ducere** are often confused because they look so much alike. The word **dicere** (*dee*-keh-reh) means "to speak" or "to say." The word **ducere** (*doo*-keh-reh) means "to lead" or "to bring." They're both third-conjugation verbs, so you conjugate them the same way, which makes telling them apart that much more difficult. From **ducere** come the words *duct* and *viaduct;* from **dicere** come words like *dictionary* and *dictate.*

Ludus: It's not all fun and games

The Romans didn't take their schools too seriously. Their word for *school* and *games* was the same: **ludus** (*loo*-doos). It's up to you, as you translate, to pick which word is actually meant. Use context clues. If you confuse the two when you translate from Latin to English, your translations may sound ludicrous.

Chapter 19

Ten Helpful Latin-Related Web Sites

Many Web sites offer information on the history of the Romans: their lives and families, their cities and architecture, their art and literature, their military strategies and conquests, and of course, their Latin language. This chapter offers ten Web sites that you can use to learn more about the Romans and Latin. We've arranged these sites in alpha order.

This list is only a guideline. You can find many other Web sites dealing with the Romans, their world, history, literature, and language. Surf these sites to your heart's content. You'll be astounded at what you can find out about the amazing Romans and their wonderful language.

American Classical League

www.aclclassics.org

The American Classical League's Web site lets you springboard to other sites dealing with the Romans and Latin. Although it's geared towards students with several years of Latin behind them or teachers of Latin at primary and secondary schools, the links are still valuable to those wishing to improve their study of Latin.

The Classics Page at Ad Fontes Academy

http://patriot.net/~lillard/cp

The Classics Page has a link to The Latin Library, which provides you with the works of numerous Latin authors, such as Augustus, Caesar, Cato, Catullus, Juvenal, Livy, Martial, and many more. This site also has links to Classical sites of general interest, as well as Classical associations and groups, Classical journals, special sites, images of the ancient world,

Latin resources (online dictionaries, online declension exercises, and online tutor for Latin vocabulary), and other resources.

The Classics Pages

`www.users.globalnet.co.uk/%7Eloxias/oldindex.htm`

The Classics Pages offers links to numerous pages of interest to those studying Latin, including the following:

✔ Fun with Latin, where you can find various games and entertainments based on grammar exercises.

✔ Vergil's Page, where you can find English translations to Vergil's *Aeneid* Book 2 (The Fall of Troy), Book 4 (Dido), and Book 6 (The Underworld).

✔ Varro's Page, which gives information on derivations, meanings, and the etymology of English words. It also has online Classical word games and a section on "Rude Latin."

E.L. Easton — Language Online

`http://eleaston.com/latin.html`

Language Online can help you improve your Latin. The site offers links to numerous online grammar sources, such as the Oxford Latin Course, the Cambridge Latin Course, Ecce Romani (*ek*-ke ro-*ma*-ni; Behold the Romans), and Wheelock's Latin Course, as well as links to sites where you can listen to the pronunciation of Latin, or find exercises, quizzes, and tests that can help you hone your skills. For those of you who like games, the site offers noun declension and verb-conjugation games, as well as Latin crossword puzzles to help you improve your vocabulary.

Internet Resources for Classics

`www.sms.org/mdl-indx/internet.htm`

This site is an excellent gateway to all things Classical on the Web. It has a *huge* list of links, including many Classical search engines. It has **inter alia** (*in*-ter *ah*-lee-ah; among others) links to the sites showing the following:

✔ Numismatics (coins)

✔ Mythology

✔ Online dictionaries

✔ Roman ball games

✔ Roman board games

✔ Roman emperors

✔ Walking tours of the Roman forum

The search engines on this site can help you find answers to almost any question about Latin or the Romans.

Nuntii Latini: News in Latin

www.yle.fi/fbc/latini

Nuntii Latini: News in Latin is a weekly review of world news, offered in Classical Latin, the only international broadcast of its kind in the world. Produced by YLE, the Finnish Broadcasting Company, Nuntii Latini is a five-minute weekly bulletin that offers the main international topics of the week, as well as Finnish news of international interest. Nuntii Latini is heard around the world on short- or medium-wave radio and via satellite on Radio Finland. Nuntii Latini is now also available on the Internet on RealAudio at www.yle.fi/fbc/latini/recitatio.html.

The Perseus Project

www.perseus.tufts.edu

This site is great for people interested in learning more about the ancient Romans and Greeks by reading ancient texts. Search for an author and click on the work that you want to see, and the site produces the annotated text in Latin with an English translation just one click away.

Those of you interested in sports can find information about the ancient Olympic games. You can also click on event names to see descriptions of particular sports, such as boxing, wrestling, running, the pentathlon, and others.

PBS: The Roman Empire in the First Century

www.pbs.org/empires/romans

PBS recently brought out a two-part video on the Roman Empire during the first century A.D. Used partly to advertise this video, the site also has interesting and fun pages, such as an explanation of the social structure and the different classes in ancient Rome. The site also examines marriage, religious practices, and the Roman baths and entertainment and offers the following fun activities:

- ✓ **Play the Emperor of Rome Game:** Are you politically skilled to outwit Fate as Emperor of Rome? The stakes are high in this interactive game: You may be deified, but you also run the risk of being assassinated!

- ✓ **Send a Romans e-postcard:** Share "The Romans" with a friend. Just choose among the four Roman cybergreetings, type in your message, and click the send button.

- ✓ **View the Augustan Family Tree:** Were Claudius and Caligula related? Who was Nero's father? Find out with this site's helpful Augustan Family Tree.

VROMA

www.vroma.org

Vroma is a great site. You can find almost anything that's related to ancient Rome at this site. Vroma offers a vast digitized slide collection and numerous links to other sites that can help you as you continue your studies of Latin. One site, Scribax, creates random Latin sentences for translation practice (and also translates them). Other sites test you on your knowledge of Latin verbs and noun forms as well as vocabulary.

Weather in Latin

http://latin.wunderground.com

This site gives you the daily weather in Latin. Find out the forecast for your local area (worldwide). It gives you updated information on the **calor** (*ka*-lor; temperature), the **ventus** (*wen*-toos; wind information), the **umor** (*oo*-mor; precipitation), the **nix** (niks; snow), and much more.

Chapter 20

Ten Common Latin Abbreviations

Abbreviations are such handy tools. They save time, and if you don't have enough paper, as was the case with the ancient Romans, they save space, too. The word *abbreviation* comes from the Latin prefix **ad–,** which means "to," and the word **brevis** (*breh*-wis), which means "short." Hence, abbreviation is the shortening of a word or phrase to its most obvious syllables.

vs.

This is the abbreviation for **versus** (*wer*-soos), which means "turned" or "against." You use vs. to indicate two parties matched against each other or to contrast two opposing ideas, such as the South African Springboks vs. the British Lions (for a rugby match) or the *State of Utah vs. John Doe* (for a trial).

P.S.

After you've ended a letter and you want to add another thought, you use the abbreviation P.S. This stands for **Post Scriptum** (post *skreep*-toom) which means "written after."

P.S. If you want to add another afterthought after your first afterthought, you'd use P.P.S. (for Post Post Script), not P.S.S.

i.e.

When you want to make something clear by adding explanatory text, you use this abbreviation. It stands for **id est** (id est), which means "that is." Consider this example: The old man was plagued with halitosis, i.e., bad breath.

e.g.

This abbreviation is much like i.e., but you use it when you want to give an example. It stands for **exempli gratia** (ek-*sem*-plee grah-tee-*ah*), meaning "for the sake of an example." (Nowadays, people often substitute the words *such as* for e.g.) Here's an example of e.g. in action: You can find many types of classic British cars, e.g., the Morris Minor, the Mini, the M.G., the Triumph, and so on, in other parts of the world.

etc.

You use etc. when you want to show that more examples exist than those you listed. Etc. stands for **et cetera** (eht *keh*-the-rah), which means "and the rest" or "and so forth." For example: The birdfeeder attracted many common winter birds, such as doves, sparrows, starlings, etc.

A.M./P.M.

These useful abbreviations indicate the time of day. The first one, A.M. stands for **ante meridiem** (*an*-tee meh-*ree*-dee-em), which means "before noon." The second abbreviation stands for **post meridiem** (post meh-*ree*-dee-em), which means "after noon."

m.o.

The abbreviation m.o. for **modus operandi** (*moh*-dus o-per-*un*-dee), which means, "method of operating." It describes someone's pattern of behavior. For example: The detective noted that the criminal's m.o. was the same in all three crimes.

ad lib.

Ad lib. is the abbreviation for **ad libitum** (ad *lee*-bee-toom), which roughly translates to "according to one's wishes" or "as it pleases." As it's used today, ad-lib means to improvise or to do something spontaneously without rehearsal. For example, the politician was famous for thinking on his feet. He could ad-lib an entire speech on the spur of the moment.

et al.

You can extend a list of people by using this abbreviation. It stands for **et alii** (et *ah*-lee-ee), which means "and others." For example: Cliff, Jean, Eric, et al. worked hard to make the party the success that it was.

ca.

To indicate an approximate year, you use this abbreviation. It stands for **circa** (*keer*-ka), which means "around." For example: This painting was made by Renoir ca. 1890.

Chapter 21

Ten Common Latin Prefixes

In This Chapter

▶ Easy-to-remember Latin prefixes

▶ Modifying a word's meaning

*P*refixes are convenient. Add a prefix to an existing word, and you change that word's meaning completely. Take the word *ordinary*. Nothing exciting about that. But if you add the Latin prefix **extra** (*eks*-tra), which means "outside" or "beyond," then this ordinary word becomes an *extraordinary* one, which now means "outside of the ordinary" or "beyond the ordinary."

Human beings are all terrestrials (earthlings), but when a UFO lands, you expect *extraterrestrials* (*beyond the earth*-lings) to abduct you. *Abduct* also has a prefix. *Duct* comes from the Latin word **ducere** (*doo*-keh-reh), which means "to lead," and **ab** (ub), which means "away." Therefore, *abduct* literally means "to lead away." (Of course, the dictionary will tell you it means "to take away unlawfully," but that's just a more refined way of saying essentially the same thing.)

See how easy and how much fun it is to use prefixes? This chapter lists ten of the most common Latin prefixes that you're likely to encounter and are already using — whether you know it or not.

Circum–

If you're like most people, you've probably been to a circus. Even if you haven't, you know that a circus is usually performed in a huge, round tent. A circle is also a completely round object. So you probably wouldn't be surprised to find that the Latin prefix **circum** (*keer*-koom) means "round" or "around."

Pre–

Pre– is another common prefix that you see on many words. (So many, in fact, that dictionaries don't list them all.) **Pre–** means "before."

Mal–

The prefix **mal**– means bad. So if your brother's socks are **mal**odorous, they don't smell like roses; they stink!

Sub–

A **sub**marine is a boat that can move around under the surface of the sea. To get to the **sub**way, you usually have to head underground. If service at a store is **sub**standard, it means that it's not good enough, or below expectations. The prefix **sub**– (sub), therefore, means "under" or "below." The prefix **sub**– doesn't always mean under, though. It can also mean "near."

Trans–

Did you know that, when Charles Lindbergh made his first nonstop **trans**–Atlantic flight in the *Spirit of St. Louis,* he used a radio to **trans**mit messages back home? The prefix **trans**– (trance) means "cross" or "across."

Bene–

When a rock star holds a **bene**fit concert for some charity, it means that proceeds are for the good of the charity. Any kind of **bene**fit is always a good one. The prefix **bene**– (*beh*-neh) means "good" or "well."

Semi–

A **semi**circle is half a circle. A **semi**annual event is held every six months (half a year). A **sem**ester is half a school year. To be **semi**conscious is to be half conscious. So it's fairly clear that **semi**– (*seh*-me) means "half."

Multi–

A **multi**cultural society is one that comprises of many different cultures. **Multi**– (*mool*-tee), which means "many," is a useful prefix that you can use over and over again.

Re–

The prefix **re**– (ray) is useful and has more than one meaning. From **re**do, you can see that **re**– means "again," and from **re**turn, you see that it can also mean "back." Be careful with this one!

Ab–

Ab–, another common prefix, means "away." When you **ab**duct someone, you lead him away. If something is **ab**normal, it is away from the normal or strange. If you **ab**stain from something, you keep away from it.

Chapter 22

Ten Important Latin Suffixes

In This Chapter

▶ Suffixes from Latin that you can't live without

▶ Affecting a word's purpose

In the word *excommunicate,* **ex–** (eks) is the prefix and **–ate** is the suffix. Prefixes, as explained in Chapter 21, change the meaning of a word. Suffixes have just as much impact: They change a word's function. By adding a simple suffix, you can change a word from a noun to an adjective to an adverb or even to a verb. Many suffixes come from Latin. This chapter looks at some of the most common Latin suffixes.

–tor

One of the more common and useful suffixes is **–tor.** This suffix indicates someone who does something. For example, an interroga**tor** is someone who interrogates, a prosecu**tor** is someone who prosecutes, a naviga**tor** is some-one who navigates, and a sculp**tor** is someone who sculpts.

–ndum

–ndum is a useful suffix that means "that which must be." A memora**ndum,** for example, is a short note written as a reminder. The word literally means "that which must be remembered." An adde**ndum,** therefore, must be added. A refere**ndum** must be referred to.

–cide

The Romans were rather bloodthirsty, always fighting in wars or watching gladiators fight to the death. One of several words they had for "to kill" was **caedere** (*kigh*-deh-reh); the past tense in Latin is **cecidi** (*keh*-kee-dee; I killed). The **cid** part of this word came down to English as a suffix meaning "the killing of." Pesti**cide** means the killing of pests; herbi**cide** means killing pesky weeds.

–tude

The Latin suffix **–tudo** (*to*-doh) was used to form abstract nouns, such as *death, love, envy, hatred, fear,* and so on. If you attach this suffix to a word, you create a noun out of it. For example, the Latin word **fortis** (*for*-tis) means "brave." When you add the suffix **–tudo,** the meaning changes to "bravery."

–ism

The English suffix **–ism** comes from the Latin **–ismus** (*is*-moos). **–ism** usually indicates an action (hero**ism**), a process (hypnot**ism**), or a practice (terror**ism**). It's also used to indicate belief: Catholic**ism,** Hindu**ism,** Buddh**ism,** agnostic**ism,** athe**ism,** and so on. In art, you find certain movements ending with this suffix: Cub**ism,** Dada**ism,** Impression**ism,** Real**ism,** and so on.

–ist

The suffix **–ist,** like the suffix **–tor,** indicates a person who does something. It comes from the Latin pronoun **iste** (*is*-teh), which means "he" or "that man." This suffix is often used to indicate a person who has a certain belief: a Buddh**ist,** a typ**ist,** a pessim**ist,** an optim**ist,** a dent**ist,** a Fasc**ist,** and so on.

–fic

One of the most useful words in Latin is the word **facere** (*fuh*-keh-reh), which means "to make; to do." From this word come such words as *factory, manufacture, magnify,* and *fiction.* Words ending in **–fic** also come from this word. This suffix means "causing" or "making."

–ium

The suffix **–ium** makes a noun express a state or condition. Take **equilibrium** as an example. The prefix **equi–** (*e*-kwee) means equal, and **libra** (*lee*-bra) means "a pound." Equilib**rium** therefore means "equal pound" or "where the pounds are equal." Ultimately, the word means balance.

–vorous

The suffix **–vorous** has two parts: **vor** comes from the word **devoro** (day-*woa*-ro), to devour or eat up. **–ous** on its own comes from **–osus** (*oh*-soos), meaning "characterized by." Words ending in this suffix refer to eating habits.

–duct

The word **ducere** (*doo*-keh-reh) means "to lead" or "to take." The suffix **–duct** therefore indicates something that leads. An aque**duct** is a man-made construction that leads water (**aqua;** *uh*-kwuh) from its source to its destination. Another of the many words that use this suffix is pro**duct.** The prefix **pro–** means forward, so *product* literally means "to bring forward." Today, the word *product* often means a result or a direct consequence.

Part V

Appendixes

In this part . . .

As you learn Latin, you'll want quick, easy-to-use references. This appendix has them. We include noun tables that show each of the five Latin declensions and verb tables that show you how to conjugate Latin verbs. We also include a Latin-to-English and English-to-Latin Mini-Dictionary so that you can find words at a glance.

Oh, yeah. This part also has the answers to all the Fun & Games activities in the book.

Appendix A

Verb and Noun Tables

Noun Tables

First-Declension Masculine/Feminine Nouns
Example: puella, puellae, f (girl)

Case	Singular	Plural
Nominative	puella	puellae
Genitive	puellae	puellarum
Dative	puellae	puellis
Accusative	puellam	puellas
Ablative	puella	puellis

Second-Declension Masculine Nouns
Example: amicus, amici, m (friend)

Case	Singular	Plural
Nominative	amicus	amici
Genitive	amici	amicorum
Dative	amico	amicis
Accusative	amicum	amicos
Ablative	amico	amicis

Second-Declension Neuter Nouns
Example: saxum, saxi, n (rock)

Case	Singular	Plural
Nominative	saxum	saxa
Genitive	saxi	saxorum
Dative	saxo	saxis
Accusative	saxum	saxa
Ablative	saxo	saxis

Third-Declension Masculine/Feminine Nouns
Example: mater, matris, f (mother)

Case	Singular	Plural
Nominative	mater	matres
Genitive	matris	matrum
Dative	matri	matribus
Accusative	matrem	matres
Ablative	matre	matribus

Third-Declension Neuter Nouns
Example: tempus, temporis, n (time)

Case	Singular	Plural
Nominative	tempus	tempora
Genitive	temporis	temporum
Dative	tempori	temporibus
Accusative	tempus	tempora
Ablative	tempore	temporibus

Fourth-Declension Masculine/Feminine Nouns
Example: exercitus, exercitus, m (army)

Case	Singular	Plural
Nominative	exercitus	exercitus
Genitive	exercitus	exercituum
Dative	exercitui	exercitibus
Accusative	exercitum	exercitus
Ablative	exercitu	exercitibus

Fourth-Declension Neuter Nouns
Example: cornu, cornus, n (horn)

Case	Singular	Plural
Nominative	cornu	cornua
Genitive	cornus	cornuum
Dative	cornu	cornibus
Accusative	cornu	cornua
Ablative	cornu	cornibus

Fifth-Declension Masculine/Feminine Nouns
Example: dies, diei, m (day)

Case	Singular	Plural
Nominative	dies	dies
Genitive	diei	dierum
Dative	diei	diebus
Accusative	diem	dies
Ablative	die	diebus

Verb Tables

First-Conjugation Verbs
Example: amo, amare, amavi, amatus (to love)

Indicative Tense	Active Singular	Active Plural	Passive Singular	Passive Plural
Present	amo	amamus	amor	amamur
	amas	amatis	amaris	amamini
	amat	amant	amatur	amantur
Imperfect	amabam	amabamus	amabar	amabamur
	amabas	amabatis	amabaris	amabamini
	amabat	amabant	amabatur	amabantur
Future	amabo	amabimus	amabor	amabimur
	amabis	amabitis	amaberis	amabimini
	amabit	amabunt	amabitur	amabuntur
Perfect	amavi	amavimus	amatus (–a, –um) sum	amati (–ae, –a) sumus
	amavisti	amavistis	amatus (–a, –um) es	amati (–ae, –a) estis
	amavit	amaverunt	amatus (–a, –um) est	amati (–ae, –a) sunt
Pluperfect	amaveram	amaveramus	amatus (–a, –um) eram	amati (–ae, –a) eramus
	amaveras	amaveratis	amatus (–a, –um) eras	amati (–ae, –a) eratis
	amaverat	amaverant	amatus (–a, –um) erat	amati (–ae, –a) erant

	Active Singular	Active Plural	Passive Singular	Passive Plural
Future Perfect	amavero	amaverimus	amatus (–a, –um) ero	amati (–ae, –a) erimus
	amaveris	amaveritis	amatus (–a, –um) eris	amati (–ae, –a) eritis
	amaverit	amaverint	amatus (–a, –um) erit	amati (–ae, –a) erunt

Subjunctive Tense	Active Singular	Active Plural	Passive Singular	Passive Plural
Present	amem	amemus	amer	amemur
	ames	ametis	ameris	amemini
	amet	ament	ametur	amentur
Imperfect	amarem	amaremus	amarer	amaremur
	amares	amaretis	amareris	amaremini
	amaret	amarent	amaretur	amarentur
Perfect	amaverim	amaverimus	amatus (–a, –um) sim	amati (–ae, –a) simus
	amaveris	amaveritis	amatus (–a, –um) sis	amati (–ae, –a) sitis
	amaverit	amaverint	amatus (–a, –um) sit	amati (–ae, –a) sint
Pluperfect	amavissem	amavissemus	amatus (–a, –um) essem	amati (–ae, –a) essemus
	amavisses	amavissetis	amatus (–a, –um) esses	amati (–ae, –a) essetis
	amavisset	amavissent	amatus (–a, –um) esset	amati (–ae, –a) essent

Second-Conjugation Verbs
Example: video, videre, vidi, visus (to see)

Indicative Tense	Active Singular	Active Plural	Passive Singular	Passive Plural
Present	video	videmus	videor	videmur
	vides	videtis	videris	videmini
	videt	vident	videtur	videntur
Imperfect	videbam	videbamus	videbar	videbamur
	videbas	videbatis	videbaris	videbamini
	videbat	videbant	videbatur	videbantur
Future	videbo	videbimus	videbor	videbimur
	videbis	videbitis	videberis	videbimini
	videbit	videbunt	videbitur	videbuntur
Perfect	vidi	vidimus	visus (–a, –um) sum	visi (–ae, –a) sumus
	vidisti	vidistis	visus (–a, –um) es	visi (–ae, –a) estis
	vidit	viderunt	visus (–a, –um) est	visi (–ae, –a) sunt
Pluperfect	videram	videramus	visus (–a, –um) eram	visi (–ae, –a) eramus
	videras	videratis	visus (–a, –um) eras	visi (–ae, –a) eratis
	viderat	viderant	visus (–a, –um) erat	visi (–ae, –a) erant

Indicative Tense	Active Singular	Active Plural	Passive Singular	Passive Plural
Future Perfect	videro	viderimus	visus (–a, –um) ero	visi (–ae, –a) erimus
	videris	videritis	visus (–a, –um) eris	visi (–ae, –a) eritis
	viderit	viderint	visus (–a, –um) erit	visi (–ae, –a) erunt

Subjunctive Tense	Active Singular	Active Plural	Passive Singular	Passive Plural
Present	videam	videamus	videar	videamur
	videas	videatis	videaris	videamini
	videat	videant	videatur	videantur

Imperfect				
	viderem	videremus	viderer	videremur
	videres	videretis	videreris	videremini
	videret	viderent	videretur	viderentur

Perfect				
	viderim	viderimus	visus (–a, –um) sim	visi (–ae, –a) simus
	videris	videritis	visus (–a, –um) sis	visi (–ae, –a) sitis
	viderit	viderint	visus (–a, –um) sit	visi (–ae, –a) sint

Pluperfect				
	vidissem	vidissemus	visus (–a, –um) essem	visi (–ae, –a) essemus
	vidisses	vidissetis	visus (–a, –um) esses	visi (–ae, –a) essetis
	vidisset	vidissent	visus (–a, –um) esset	visi (–ae, –a) essent

Third-Conjugation Verbs
Example: pono, ponere, posui, positus (to put)

Indicative Tense	Active Singular	Active Plural	Passive Singular	Passive Plural
Present	pono	ponimus	ponor	ponimur
	ponis	ponitis	poneris	ponimini
	ponit	ponunt	ponitur	ponuntur
Imperfect	ponebam	ponebamus	ponebar	ponebamur
	ponebas	ponebatis	ponebaris	ponebamini
	ponebat	ponebant	ponebatur	ponebantur
Future	ponam	ponemus	ponar	ponemur
	pones	ponetis	poneris	ponemini
	ponet	ponent	ponetur	ponentur
Perfect	posui	posuimus	positus (–a, –um) sum	positi (–ae, –a) sumus
	posuisti	posuistis	positus (–a, –um) es	positi (–ae, –a) estis
	posuit	posuerunt	positus (–a, –um) est	positi (–ae, –a) sunt
Pluperfect	posueram	posueramus	positus (–a, –um) eram	positi (–ae, –a) eramus
	posueras	posueratis	positus (–a, –um) eras	positi (–ae, –a) eratis
	posuerat	posuerant	positus (–a, –um) erat	positi (–ae, –a) erant

Indicative Tense	Active Singular	Active Plural	Passive Singular	Passive Plural
Future Perfect	posuero	posuerimus	positus (–a, –um) ero	positi (–ae, –a) erimus
	posueris	posueritis	positus (–a, –um) eris	positi (–ae, –a) eritis
	posuerit	posuerint	positus (–a, –um) erit	positi (–ae, –a) erunt

Subjunctive Tense	Active Singular	Active Plural	Passive Singular	Passive Plural
Present	ponam	ponamus	ponar	ponamur
	ponas	ponatis	ponaris	ponamini
	ponat	ponant	ponatur	ponantur
Imperfect	ponerem	poneremus	ponerer	poneremur
	poneres	poneretis	ponereris	poneremini
	poneret	ponerent	poneretur	ponerentur
Perfect	posuerim	posuerimus	positus (–a, –um) sim	positi (–ae, –a) simus
	posueris	posueritis	positus (–a, –um) sis	positi (–ae, –a) sitis
	posuerit	posuerint	positus (–a, –um) sit	positi (–ae, –a) sint
Pluperfect	posuissem	posuissemus	positus (–a, –um) essem	positi (–ae, –a) essemus
	posuisses	posuissetis	positus (–a, –um) esses	positi (–ae, –a) essetis
	posuisset	posuissent	positus (–a, –um) esset	positi (–ae, –a) essent

Fourth-Conjugation Verbs
Example: audio, audire, audivi, auditus (to hear)

Indicative Tense	Active Singular	Active Plural	Passive Singular	Passive Plural
Present	audio	audimus	audior	audimur
	audis	auditis	audiris	audimini
	audit	audiunt	auditur	audiuntur
Imperfect	audiebam	audiebamus	audiebar	audiebamur
	audiebas	audiebatis	audiebaris	audiebamini
	audiebat	audiebant	audiebatur	audiebantur
Future	audiam	audiemus	audiar	audiemur
	audies	audietis	audieris	audiemini
	audiet	audient	audietur	audientur
Perfect	audivi	audivimus	auditus (–a, –um) sum	auditi (–ae, –a) sumus
	audivisti	audivistis	auditus (–a, –um) es	auditi (–ae, –a) estis
	audivit	audiverunt	auditus (–a, –um) est	auditi (–ae, –a) sunt
Pluperfect	audiveram	audiveramus	auditus (–a, –um) eram	auditi (–ae, –a) eramus
	audiveras	audiveratis	auditus (–a, –um) eras	auditi (–ae, –a) eratis
	audiverat	audiverant	auditus (–a, –um) erat	auditi (–ae, –a) erant

Indicative Tense	Active Singular	Active Plural	Passive Singular	Passive Plural
Future Perfect	audivero	audiverimus	auditus (–a, –um) ero	auditi (–ae, –a) erimus
	audiveris	audiveritis	auditus (–a, –um) eris	auditi (–ae, –a) eritis
	audiverit	audiverint	auditus (–a, –um) erit	auditi (–ae, –a) erunt

Subjunctive Tense	Active Singular	Active Plural	Passive Singular	Passive Plural
Present	audiam	audiamus	audiar	audiamur
	audias	audiatis	audiaris	audiamini
	audiat	audiant	audiatur	audiantur
Imperfect	audirem	audiremus	audirer	audiremur
	audires	audiretis	audireris	audiremini
	audiret	audirent	audiretur	audirentur
Perfect	audiverim	audiverimus	auditus (–a, –um) sim	auditi (–ae, –a) simus
	audiveris	audiveritis	auditus (–a, –um) sis	auditi (–ae, –a) sitis
	audiverit	audiverint	auditus (–a, –um) sit	auditi (–ae, –a) sint
Pluperfect	audivissem	audivissemus	auditus (–a, –um) essem	auditi (–ae, –a) essemus
	audivisses	audivissetis	auditus (–a, –um) esses	auditi (–ae, –a) essetis
	audivisset	audivissent	auditus (–a, –um) esset	auditi (–ae, –a) essent

Latin-English Mini-Dictionary

A

a/ab (+ ablative case noun): by, with, from

accipio, accipere, accepi, acceptus: to receive

accusator, accusatoris (m): prosecutor

ad (+ accusative case noun): to, towards

adiuvo, adiuvare, adiuvi, adiutus: to help

advenio, advenire, adveni, adventus: to arrive, reach

aestas, aestatis (f): summer

aetas, aetatis (f): age

affero, afferre, attuli, allatus: to bring

ager, agri (m): field

ago, agere, egi, actus: do, drive, discuss

agricola, agricolae (m): farmer

albus, alba, album: white

alius, alia, aliud: other, another

ambulo, ambulare, ambulavi, ambulatus: to walk

amicus, amici (m): friend

amita, amitae (f): paternal aunt

amo, amare, amavi, amatus: to love

amor, amoris (m): love

ancilla, ancillae (f): slave-girl

animal, animalis (n): animal

ante (+ accusative case noun): before

anus, anus (f): old woman

aperio, aperire, aperui, apertus: to open

apud (+ accusative case noun): at the house of, with

aqua, aquae (f): water

arbor, arboris (f): tree

arma, armorum (n.pl.): arms, weapons

ars, artis (f): art, skill, judgment

atrium, atrii (n): chamber, room

audio, audire, audivi, auditus: to hear

aut . . . aut: either . . . or

autumnus, autumni (m): fall, autumn

avia, aviae (f): grandmother

avunculus, avunculi (m): (maternal) uncle

avus, avi (m): grandfather

B

bellum, belli (n): war

bene: well

bibo, bibere, bibi, bibitus: to drink

bis: twice

bonus, bona, bonum: good

C

cado, cadere, cecidi, casurus: to fall

caelum, caeli (n): heaven, sky

calidus, calida, calidum: hot

callidus, callida, callidum: clever, shrewd

canis, canis (m/f): dog

canto, cantare, cantavi, cantatus: to sing

capio, capere, cepi, captus: to take

caput, capitis (n): head

caries, cariei (f): decay (of a bone or tooth)

carmen, carminis (n): song, poem

casa, casae (f): house

castra, castrorum (n.pl.): camp

casus, casus (m): disaster, mishap

celer, celeris, celere: fast, quick

celeriter: quickly

cena, cenae (f): dinner, meal

ceno, cenare, cenavi, cenatus: to dine

cerebrum, cerebri (n): brain

cervix, cervicis (f): neck

ceteri, ceterae, cetera: the others, the rest

cibus, cibi (m): food

civis, civis (m/f): citizen

clamo, clamare, clamavi, clamatus: to shout

claudo, claudere, clausi, clausus: to close

cogito, cogitare, cogitavi, cogitatus: to think

comes, comitis (m/f): companion

coquus, coqui (m): cook

cor, cordis (n): heart

corpus, corporis (n): body

cras: tomorrow

crimen, criminis (n): accusation

cum (+ ablative case noun): with

cur: why

curo, curare, curavi, curatus: to care, look after

curro, currere, cucurri, cursus: to run

D

de (+ ablative case noun): down (from), about

dea, deae (f): goddess

debeo, debere, debui, debitus: to owe, must

defendo, defendere, defendi, defensus: to defend

deinde: then

delictum, delicti (n): crime

dens, dentis (m): tooth

deus, dei (m): god

dico, dicere, dixi, dictus: to speak

dies, diei (m): day

difficultas, difficultatis (f): difficulty

diligenter: carefully, hard

diu: for a long time

do, dare, dedi, datus: to give

doceo, docere, docui, doctus: to teach

domi: at home

domina, dominae (f): mistress

dominus, domini (m): master

domus, domus (f): house, home

donum, doni (n): gift

dormio, dormire, dormivi, dormitus: to sleep

dubito, dubitare, dubitavi, dubitatus: to doubt

dubium, dubii (n): doubt

duco, ducere, duxi, ductus: to lead, bring

dum: while

dux, ducis (m): military general, leader

E

e/ex (+ ablative case noun): out of, from

emo, emere, emi, emptus: to buy

emptus, empta, emptum: bought, purchased

eo, ire, ivi/ii, itus: to go

equus, equi (m): horse

et: and, even, also

et . . . et: both . . . and

etiam: even, also

exspecto, exspectare, exspectavi, exspectatus: to wait for

F

fabula, fabulae (f): story

facies, faciei (f): look, expression

facilis, facile: easy

facio, facere, feci, factus: to make

factum, facti (n): deed

familia, familiae (f): family, household

femina, feminae (f): woman

feriae, feriarum (f.pl.): holiday

fero, ferre, tuli, latus: to carry, bear

festino, festinare, festinavi, festinatus: to hurry

fides, fidei (f): faith, loyalty, trust

filia, filiae (f): daughter

filius, filii (m): son

fio, fieri, factus sum: to become, happen

flagro, flagrare, flagravi, flagratus: to be on fire

fleo, flere, flevi, fletus: to weep

forma, formae (f): beauty, shape

fortasse: perhaps

fortis, forte: brave

fortiter: bravely

frater, fratris (m): brother

frigidus, frigida, frigidum: cold

fugio, fugere, fugi, fugitus: to flee

fugo, fugare, fugavi, fugatus: to chase after

fulvus, fulva, fulvum: tawny, yellow

G

gaudium, gaudii (n): joy

gratiae, gratiarum (f.pl.): thanks

gratias ago, agere, egi, actus: to give thanks

gratus, grata, gratum: pleasing

guberno, gubernare, gubernavi, gubernatus: to govern

H

habeo, habere, habui, habitus: to have

habito, habitare, habitavi, habitatus: to live

heri: yesterday

hic, haec, hoc: this one, the latter

hiems, hiemis (f): winter

hodie: today

homo, hominis (m/f): man, a human being

hortus, horti (m): garden

hostis, hostis (m/f): enemy

I = I

ibi: there

ille, illa, illud: that one, the former

imago, imaginis (f): wax mask, image

in (+ ablative case noun): in, on

in (+ accusative case noun): into

infans, infantis (m/f): baby

initium, initii (n): beginning

insula, insulae (f): island

inter (+accusative case noun): among, between

interea: meanwhile

intro, intrare, intravi, intratus: to enter

invenio, invenire, inveni, inventus: to find

ipse, ipsa, ipsum: himself, herself, itself

ira, irae (f): anger

itaque: and so

iter, itineris (n): journey

iterum: again

I=J

iam: now, already

ianua, ianuae (f): door

iubeo, iubere, iussi, iussus: to order

iudex, iudicis (m): a judge

iudicium, iudicii (n): verdict

ius, iuris (n): law

iuvenis, iuvenis (m/f): young man

iuvo, iuvare, iuvi, iutus: to help

K

Kalendae, Kalendarum (f.pl.): the calends, 1st day of the month

Karthago, Karthaginis (f): Carthage

L

labor, laboris (m): work

laboro, laborare, laboravi, laboratus: to work

laudo, laudare, laudavi, laudatus: to praise

lego, legere, legi, lectus: to read

lente: slowly

leo, leonis (m): lion

lex, legis (f): law

liber, libri (m): book

lingua, linguae (f): tongue

litterae, litterarum (f.pl.): literature

litus, litoris (n): shore

ludus, ludi (m): game, play, school

lumen, luminis (n): light

M

magister, magistri (m): teacher

magistratus, magistratus (m): magistrate

magnus, magna, magnum: big, large

malus, mala, malum: bad, evil

manus, manus (f): hand

mare, maris (n): sea

maritus, mariti (m): husband

mater, matris (f): mother

matertera, materterae (f): maternal aunt

mens, mentis (f): mind

mensa, mensae (f): table

mereo, merere, merui, meritus: to earn

meus, mea, meum: my

miles, militis (m): soldier

miser, misera, miserum: sad, miserable

mitto, mittere, misi, missus: to send

modus, modi (m): method

moneo, monere, monui, monitus: warn

mons, montis (m): mountain

mors, mortis (f): death

mortuus, mortua, mortuum: dead

multus, multa, multum: much, many

murus, muri (m): wall

N

nam: for

narro, narrare, narravi, narratus: to tell

nasus, nasi (m): nose

nauta, nautae (m): sailor

navigo, navigare, navigavi, navigatus: to sail

navis, navis (f): ship

nec/neque: and not, nor

neco, necare, necavi, necatus: to kill

nescio, nescire, nescivi, nescitus: not to know

niger, nigra, nigrum: black, dark

niveus, nivea, niveum: (snow) white

nomen, nominis (n): name

non: not

notus, nota, notum: known

novus, nova, novum: new

nox, noctis (f): night

numquam: never

nunc: now

nuntius, nuntii (m): messenger

nuper: recently, until recently

O

obfero, obferre, obtuli, oblatus: to offer

oculus, oculi (m): eye

odi, odisse: I hate

officium, officii (n): duty, office, position

olim: one day

omnis, omne: each, all

onus, oneris (n): burden

oppugno, oppugnare, oppugnavi, oppugnatus: to attack

oro, orare, oravi, oratus: to pray

os, oris (n): mouth

os, ossis (n): bone

ovum, ovi (n): egg

P

parens, parentis (m/f): parent

pareo, parere, parui, paritus: obey

paro, parare, paravi, paratus: to prepare

parvus, parva, parvum: small

pater, patris (m): father

patruelis, patruelis (m): paternal cousin

patruus, patrui (m): paternal uncle

pauci, paucae, pauca: few

pecunia, pecuniae, (f): money

per (+ accusative case noun): through, by

persona, personae (f): person, dramatic mask

pes, pedis (m): foot

peto, petere, petivi, petitus: seek, ask, head for, attack

plenus, plena, plenum: full, filled with

poena, poenae (f): punishment, penalty

pono, ponere, posui, positus: to put, place

porta, portae (f): gate

porto, portare, portavi, portatus: to carry

portus, portus (m): harbor

possum, posse, potui: to be able

post (+ accusative case noun): after

praesertim: especially

primus, prima, primum: first

pro (+ ablative case noun): for, on behalf of

probo, probare, probavi, probatus: to approve, make good

proelium, proeli (n): battle

prope (+ accusative case noun): near

puella, puellae (f): girl

puer, pueri (m): boy

pugno, pugnare, pugnavi, pugnatus: to fight

pulchritudo, pulchritudinis (f): beauty

pulso, pulsare, pulsavi, pulsatus: to hit, strike

puto, putare, putavi, putatus: to think

Q

quaero, quaere, quaesivi, quaesitus: to ask, seek

quare: why

qui, quae, quod: who, which, that

quid: what

quod: because

quot: how many, how much?

R

ratio, rationis (f): reason

redo, reddere, reddidi, reditus: to give back, return

regina, reginae (f): queen

rego, regere, rexi, rectus: to rule

relinquo, relinquere, reliqui, relictus: to leave behind

requiro, requirere, requisivi, requisitus: to ask

rex, regis (m): king

rogo, rogare, rogavi, rogatus: to ask

S

saepe: often

saluto, salutare, salutavi, salutatus: to greet

salve: hello

sapiens, sapientis: wise

saxum, saxi (n): rock

scio, scire, scivi, scitus: to know

scriba, scribae (m): clerk

scribo, scribere, scripsi, scriptus: to write

secundum (+ accusative case noun): according to

sedeo, sedere, sedi, sessus: to sit

semel: once

semper: always

senex, senis (m): old man

sermo, sermonis (m): conversation

servio, servire, servii, servitus: to serve

servo, servare, servavi, servatus: to save

servus, servi (m): slave

si: if

sic: thus, so, in this way

sicut: just as

sine (+ ablative case noun): without

situs, situs (m): place, position

solus, sola, solum: alone

soror, sororis (f): sister

specto, spectare, spectavi, spectatus: to watch

statim: at once, immediately

sto, stare, steti, status: to stand

stultitia, stultitiae (f): stupidity

sub (+ ablative case noun): under

subito: suddenly

T

taceo, tacere, tacui, tacitus: to be silent

tacitus, tacita, tacitum: quiet, silent

tandem: at length, at last

tempestas, tempestatis (f): storm

templum, templi (n): temple

tempus, temporis (n): time

tenebrae, tenebrarum (f.pl.): shadows, darkness

teneo, tenere, tenui, tentus: to hold

ter: three times

terra, terrae (f): land

territus, territa, territum: terrified

timeo, timere, timui, timitus: to fear

tollo, tollere, sustuli, sublatus: to lift, raise

totus, tota, totum: whole

trado, tradere, tradidi, traditus: to hand over

traho, trahere, traxi, tractus: to drag

triclinium, triclinii (n): dining room

tunc: then

tuus, tua, tuum: your

U

ubi: where/when

umquam: ever

urbs, urbis (f): city

urna, urnae (f): water jar

uxor, uxoris (f): wife

V

vale: goodbye

velut: like

vena, venae (f): vein

venio, venire, veni, ventus: to come

ventus, venti (m): wind

ver, veris (n): spring

verbum, verbi (n): word

veritas, veritatis (f): the truth

verto, vertere, verti, versus: to turn around

via, viae (f): road, way

video, videre, vidi, visus: to see

vinco, vincere, vici, victus: to conquer

vinum, vini (n): wine

vir, viri (m): man

vispillo, vispillonis (m): an undertaker

vix: scarcely

voco, vocare, vocavi, vocatus: to call

vox, vocis (f): voice

English-Latin Mini-Dictionary

A

about: **de** (+ ablative case noun)

according to: **secundum** (+ accusative case noun)

accusation: **crimen, criminis** (n)

after: **post** (+ accusative case noun)

again: **iterum**

age: **aetas, aetatis** (f)

all: **omnis, omne**

alone: **solus, sola, solum**

already: **iam**

also: **et, etiam**

always: **semper**

among: **inter** (+accusative case noun)

and not: **nec/neque**

and so: **itaque**

and: **et**

anger: **ira, irae** (f)

animal: **animal, animalis** (n)

another: **alius, alia, aliud**

approve (to): **probo, probare, probavi, probatus**

arms (weapons): **arma, armorum** (n.pl.)

arrive (to): **advenio, advenire, adveni, adventus**

art: **ars, artis** (f)

ask (to): **peto, petere, petivi, petitus**
: **quaero, quaere, quaesivi, quaesitus**
: **requiro, requirere, requisivi, requisitus**
: **rogo, rogare, rogavi, rogatus**

at home: **domi**

at last: **tandem**

at length: **tandem**

at once: **statim**

attack (to): **oppugno, oppugnare, oppugnavi, oppugnatus**
: **peto, petere, petivi, petitus**

aunt (paternal): **amita, amitae** (f)

autumn: **autumnus, autumni** (m)

B

baby: **infans, infantis** (m/f)

bad: **malus, mala, malum**

battle: **proelium, proelii** (n)

be able (to): **possum, posse, potui**

be on fire (to): **flagro, flagrare, flagravi, flagratus**

be silent (to): **taceo, tacere, tacui, tacitus**

bear (to): **fero, ferre, tuli, latus**

beauty: **forma, formae** (f)
: **pulchritudo, pulchritudinis** (f)

because: **quod**

become (to): **fio, fieri, factus sum**

before: **ante** (+ accusative case noun)

beginning: **initium, initii** (n)

between: **inter** (+accusative case noun)

big: **magnus, magna, magnum**

black: **niger, nigra, nigrum**

body: **corpus, corporis** (n)

bone: **os, ossis** (n)

book: **liber, libri** (m)

both . . . and: **et . . . et**

bought: **emptus, empta, emptum**

boy: **puer, pueri** (m)

brain: **cerebrum, cerebri** (n)

brave: **fortis, forte**

bravely: **fortiter**

bring (to): **affero, afferre, attuli, allatus** : **duco, ducere, duxi, ductus**

brother: **frater, fratris** (m)

burden: **onus, oneris** (n)

buy (to): **emo, emere, emi, emptus**

by: **a/ab** (+ ablative case noun) : **per** (+ accusative case noun)

C

calends (first day of the month): **Kalendae, Kalendarum** (f.pl.)

call (to): **voco, vocare, vocavi, vocatus**

camp: **castra, castrorum** (n.pl.)

care (to): **curo, curare, curavi, curatus**

carefully: **diligenter**

carry (to): **fero, ferre, tuli, latus** : **porto, portare, portavi, portatus**

Carthage: **Karthago, Karthaginis** (f)

chamber: **atrium, atrii** (n)

chase after (to): **fugo, fugare, fugavi, fugatus**

citizen: **civis, civis** (m/f)

city: **urbs, urbis** (f)

clerk: **scriba, scribae** (m)

clever: **callidus, callida, callidum**

close (to): **claudo, claudere, clausi, clausus**

cold: **frigidus, frigida, frigidum**

come (to): **venio, venire, veni, ventus**

companion: **comes, comitis** (m/f)

conquer (to): **vinco, vincere, vici, victus**

conversation: **sermo, sermonis** (m)

cook: **coquus, coqui** (m)

cousin (paternal): **patruelis, patruelis** (m)

crime: **delictum, delicti** (n)

D

dark: **niger, nigra, nigrum**

darkness: **tenebrae, tenebrarum** (f.pl.)

daughter: **filia, filiae** (f)

day: **dies, diei** (m)

dead: **mortuus, mortua, mortuum**

death: **mors, mortis** (f)

decay (of a bone or tooth): **caries, cariei** (f)

deed: **factum, facti** (n)

defend (to): **defendo, defendere, defendi, defensus**

difficulty: **difficultas, difficultatis** (f)

dine (to): **ceno, cenare, cenavi, cenatus**

dining room: **triclinium, triclinii** (n)

dinner: **cena, cenae** (f)

disaster: **casus, casus** (m)

discuss: **ago, agere, egi, actus**

do (to): **ago, agere, egi, actus**

dog: **canis, canis** (m/f)

door: **ianua, ianuae** (f)

doubt (to): **dubito, dubitare, dubitavi, dubitatus**

doubt: **dubium, dubii** (n)

down (from): **de** (+ ablative case noun)

drag (to): **traho, trahere, traxi, tractus**

drink (to): **bibo, bibere, bibi, bibitus**

drive: **ago, agere, egi, actus**

duty: **officium, officii** (n)

E

each: **omnis, omne**

earn (to): **mereo, merere, merui, meritus**

easy: **facilis, facile**

egg: **ovum, ovi** (n)

either . . . or: **aut . . . aut**

enemy: **hostis, hostis** (m/f)

enter (to): **intro, intrare, intravi, intratus**

especially: **praesertim**

even: **et**

　　 : **etiam**

ever: **umquam**

evil: **malus, mala, malum**

expression: **facies, faciei** (f)

eye: **oculus, oculi** (m)

F

faith: **fides, fidei** (f)

fall (to): **cado, cadere, cecidi, casurus**

fall (the season): **autumnus, autumni** (m)

family: **familia, familiae** (f)

farmer: **agricola, agricolae** (m)

fast: **celer, celeris, celere**

father: **pater, patris** (m)

fear (to): **timeo, timere, timui, timitus**

few: **pauci, paucae, pauca**

field: **ager, agri** (m)

fight (to): **pugno, pugnare, pugnavi, pugnatus**

find (to): **invenio, invenire, inveni, inventus**

first: **primus, prima, primum**

flee (to): **fugio, fugere, fugi, fugitus**

food: **cibus, cibi** (m)

foot: **pes, pedis** (m)

for (on behalf of): **pro** (+ ablative case noun)

for a long time: **diu**

for: **nam**

former (the): **ille**

friend: **amicus, amici** (m)

from: **a/ab** (+ ablative case noun)

from: **e/ex** (+ ablative case noun)

full, filled with: **plenus, plena, plenum**

G

game: **ludus, ludi** (m)

garden: **hortus, horti** (m)

gate: **porta, portae** (f)

general (military): **dux, ducis** (m)

gift: **donum, doni** (n)

girl: **puella, puellae** (f)

give (to): **do, dare, dedi, datus**

give back (to): **redo, reddere, reddidi, reditus**

give thanks (to): **gratias ago, agere, egi, actus**

go (to): **eo, ire, ivi/ii, itus**

god: **deus, dei** (m)

goddess: **dea, deae** (f)

good: **bonus, bona, bonum**

goodbye: **vale**

govern (to): **guberno, gubernare, gubernavi, gubernatus**

grandfather: **avus, avi** (m)

grandmother: **avia, aviae** (f)

greet (to): **saluto, salutare, salutavi, salutatus**

H

hand over (to): **trado, tradere, tradidi, traditus**

hand: **manus, manus** (f)

happen (to): **fio, fieri, factus sum**

harbor: **portus, portus** (m)

hard: **diligenter**

have (to): **habeo, habere, habui, habitus**

head for (to): **peto, petere, petivi, petitus**

head: **caput, capitis** (n)

hear (to): **audio, audire, audivi, auditus**

heart: **cor, cordis** (n)

heaven: **caelum, caeli** (n)

hello: **salve**

help (to): **adiuvo, adiuvare, adiuvi, adiutus**

help (to): **iuvo, iuvare, iuvi, iutus**

herself: **ipse, ipsa, ipsum**

himself: **ipse, ipsa, ipsum**

hit (to): **pulso, pulsare, pulsavi, pulsatus**

hold (to): **teneo, tenere, tenui, tentus**

holiday: **feriae, feriarum** (f.pl.)

home: **domus, domus** (f)

horse: **equus, equi** (m)

hot: **calidus, calida, calidum**

house: **casa, casae** (f)
  : **domus, domus** (f)

household: **familia, familiae** (f)

how many, how much: **quot**

human being: **homo, hominis** (m/f)

hurry (to): **festino, festinare, festinavi, festinatus**

husband: **maritus, mariti** (m)

I

I hate: **odi, odisse**

if: **si**

image: **imago, imaginis** (f)

immediately: **statim**

in this way: **sic**

in: **in** (+ ablative case noun)

into: **in** (+ accusative case noun)

island: **insula, insulae** (f)

itself: **ipse, ipsa, ipsum**

journey: **iter, itineris** (n)

J

joy: **gaudium, gaudii** (n)

judge (a): **iudex, iudicis** (m)

judgment: **ars, artis** (f)

just as: **sicut**

K

kill (to): **neco, necare, necavi, necatus**

king: **rex, regis** (m)

know (not to): **nescio, nescire, nescivi, nescitus**

know (to): **scio, scire, scivi, scitus**

known: **notus, nota, notum**

L

land: **terra, terrae** (f)

large: **magnus, magna, magnum**

latter (the): **hic, haec, hoc**

law: **ius, iuris** (n)
: **lex, legis** (f)

lead (to): **duco, ducere, duxi, ductus**

leader: **dux, ducis** (m)

leave behind (to): **relinquo, relinquere, reliqui, relictus**

lift (to): **tollo, tollere, sustuli, sublatus**

light: **lumen, luminis** (n)

like: **velut**

lion: **leo, leonis** (m)

literature: **litterae, litterarum** (f.pl.)

live (to): **habito, habitare, habitavi, habitatus**

look after (to): **curo, curare, curavi, curatus**

look: **facies, faciei** (f)

love (to): **amo, amare, amavi, amatus**

love: **amor, amoris** (m)

loyalty: **fides, fidei** (f)

M

magistrate: **magistratus, magistratus** (m)

make (to): **facio, facere, feci, factus**

make good (to): **probo, probare, probavi, probatus**

man: **homo, hominis** (m/f)
: **vir, viri** (m)

many: **multus, multa, multum**

mask (used in plays): **persona, personae** (f)

master: **dominus, domini** (m)

maternal aunt: **matertera, materterae** (f)

meal: **cena, cenae** (f)

meanwhile: **interea**

messenger: **nuntius, nuntii** (m)

method: **modus, modi** (m)

mind: **mens, mentis** (f)

miserable: **miser, misera, miserum**

mishap: **casus, casus** (m)

mistress: **domina, dominae** (f)

money: **pecunia, pecuniae** (f)

mother: **mater, matris** (f)

mountain: **mons, montis** (m)

mouth: **os, oris** (n)

much: **multus, multa, multum**

my: **meus, mea, meum**

N

name: **nomen, nominis** (n)

near: **prope** (+ accusative case noun)

neck: **cervix, cervicis** (f)

never: **numquam**

new: **novus, nova, novum**

night: **nox, noctis** (f)

nor: **nec/neque**

nose: **nasus, nasi** (m)

not: **non**

now: **iam**

now: **nunc**

O

obey (to): **pareo, parere, parui, paritus**

offer (to): **obfero, obferre, obtuli, oblatus**

office: **officium, officii** (n)

often: **saepe**

old man: **senex, senis** (m)

old woman: **anus, anus** (f)

on: **in** (+ ablative case noun)

once: **semel**

one day: **olim**

open (to): **aperio, aperire, aperui, apertus**

order (to): **iubeo, iubere, iussi, iussus**

other: **alius, alia, aliud**

others (the): **ceteri, ceterae, cetera**

out of: **e/ex** (+ ablative case noun)

owe (to), must: **debeo, debere, debui, debitus**

P

parent: **parens, parentis** (m/f)

penalty: **poena, poenae** (f)

perhaps: **fortasse**

person: **persona, personae** (f)

place (to): **pono, ponere, posui, positus**

place: **situs, situs** (m)

play: **ludus, ludi** (m)

pleasing: **gratus, grata, gratum**

poem: **carmen, carminis** (n)

position: **officium, officii** (n)

position (location): **situs, situs** (m)

praise (to): **laudo, laudare, laudavi, laudatus**

pray (to): **oro, orare, oravi, oratus**

prepare (to): **paro, parare, paravi, paratus**

prosecutor: **accusator, accusatoris** (m)

punishment: **poena, poenae** (f)

purchased: **emptus, empta, emptum**

put (to): **pono, ponere, posui, positus**

Q

queen: **regina, reginae** (f)

quick: **celer, celeris, celere**

quickly: **celeriter**

quiet: **tacitus, tacita, tacitum**

R

raise (to): **tollo, tollere, sustuli, sublatus**

reach (to): **advenio, advenire, adveni, adventus**

read (to): **lego, legere, legi, lectus**

reason: **ratio, rationis** (f)

receive (to): **accipio, accipere, accepi, acceptus**

recently, until recently: **nuper**

rest (the): **ceteri, ceterae, cetera**

return (to): **redo, reddere, reddidi, reditus**

road: **via, viae** (f)

rock: **saxum, saxi** (n)

room: **atrium, atrii** (n)

rule (to): **rego, regere, rexi, rectus**

run (to): **curro, currere, cucurri, cursus**

S

sad: **miser, misera, miserum**

sail (to): **navigo, navigare, navigavi, navigatus**

sailor: **nauta, nautae** (m)

save (to): **servo, servare, servavi, servatus**

scarcely: **vix**

school: **ludus, ludi** (m)

sea: **mare, maris** (n)

see (to): **video, videre, vidi, visus**

seek (to): **peto, petere, petivi, petitus
: quaero, quaere, quaesivi, quaesitus**

send (to): **mitto, mittere, misi, missus**

serve (to): **servio, servire, servii, servitus**

shadows: **tenebrae, tenebrarum** (f.pl.)

shape: **forma, formae** (f)

ship: **navis, navis** (f)

shore: **litus, litoris** (n)

shout (to): **clamo, clamare, clamavi, clamatus**

shrewd: **callidus, callida, callidum**

silent: **tacitus, tacita, tacitum**

sing (to): **canto, cantare, cantavi, cantatus**

sister: **soror, sororis** (f)

sit (to): **sedeo, sedere, sedi, sessus**

skill: **ars, artis** (f)

sky: **caelum, caeli** (n)

slave: **servus, servi** (m)

slave-girl: **ancilla, ancillae** (f)

sleep (to): **dormio, dormire, dormivi, dormitus**

slowly: **lente**

small: **parvus, parva, parvum**

so: **sic**

soldier: **miles, militis** (m)

son: **filius, filii** (m)

song: **carmen, carminis** (n)

speak (to): **dico, dicere, dixi, dictus**

spring: **ver, veris** (n)

stand (to): **sto, stare, steti, status**

storm: **tempestas, tempestatis** (f)

story: **fabula, fabulae** (f)

strike (to): **pulso, pulsare, pulsavi, pulsatus**

stupidity: **stultitia, stultitiae** (f)

suddenly: **subito**

summer: **aestas, aestatis** (f)

T

table: **mensa, mensae** (f)

take (to): **capio, capere, cepi, captus**

tawny: **fulvus, fulva, fulvum**

teach (to): **doceo, docere, docui, doctus**

teacher: **magister, magistri** (m)

tell (to): **narro, narrare, narravi, narratus**

temple: **templum, templi** (n)

terrified: **territus, territa, territum**

thanks: **gratiae, gratiarum** (f.pl.)

that one: **ille, illa, illud**

that: **qui, quae, quod**

then: **deinde
: tunc**

there: **ibi**

think (to): **cogito, cogitare, cogitavi, cogitatus
: puto, putare, putavi, putatus**

this one: **hic, haec, hoc**

three times: **ter**

through: **per** (+ accusative case noun)

thus: **sic**

time: **tempus, temporis** (n)

to, towards: **ad** (+ accusative case noun)

today: **hodie**

tomorrow: **cras**

tongue: **lingua, linguae** (f)

tooth: **dens, dentis** (m)

tree: **arbor, arboris** (f)

trust: **fides, fidei** (f)

truth: **veritas, veritatis** (f)

turn around (to): **verto, vertere, verti, versus**

twice: **bis**

U

uncle (maternal): **avunculus, avunculi** (m)

uncle (paternal): **patruus, patrui** (m)

under: **sub** (+ ablative case noun)

undertaker: **vispillo, vispillonis** (m)

V

vein: **vena, venae** (f)

verdict: **iudicium, iudicii** (n)

voice: **vox, vocis** (f)

W

wait for (to): **exspecto, exspectare, exspectavi, exspectatus**

walk (to): **ambulo, ambulare, ambulavi, ambulatus**

wall: **murus, muri** (m)

war: **bellum, belli** (n)

warn: **moneo, monere, monui, monitus**

watch (to): **specto, spectare, spectavi, spectatus**

water jar: **urna, urnae** (f)

water: **aqua, aquae** (f)

wax mask: **imago, imaginis** (f)

way: **via, viae** (f)

weapons: **arma, armorum** (n.pl.)

weep (to): **fleo, flere, flevi, fletus**

well: **bene**

what: **quid**

when: **ubi**

where: **ubi**

which: **qui, quae, quod**

while: **dum**

white (snow): **niveus, nivea, niveum**

white: **albus, alba, album**

who: **qui, quae, quod**

whole: **totus, tota, totum**

why: **quare**

why: **cur**

wife: **uxor, uxoris** (f)

wind: **ventus, venti** (m)

wine: **vinum, vini** (n)

winter: **hiems, hiemis** (f)

wise: **sapiens, sapientis**

with: **a/ab** (+ ablative case noun)
 : **cum** (+ ablative case noun)

with, at the house of: **apud** (+ accusative case noun)

without: **sine** (+ ablative case noun)

woman: **femina, feminae** (f)

word: **verbum, verbi** (n)

work: **labor, laboris** (m)

work (to): **laboro, laborare, laboravi, laboratus**

write (to): **scribo, scribere, scripsi, scriptus**

Y

yellow: **fulvus, fulva, fulvum**
yesterday: **heri**
young man: **iuvenis, iuvenis** (m/f)
your: **tuus, tua, tuum**

Appendix C

Fun & Games Answers

● ●

Chapter 1

Classical Pronunciation

fih-dehm *meh*-uhm *oh*-blih-go
wehks-*ihl*-lo kee-wih-*tah*-tih-um uh-*meh*-rih-kigh
foi-deh-rah-*tah*-rum eht *reh*-ee *poo*-blih-kigh
pro kwah stuht
oo-nee nah-tih-*o*-nee *deh*-o doo-*kehn*-teh
non dee-wih-*dehn*-digh
koom lee-behr-*tah*-teh
yoos-tih-tih-*ah*-kweh *ohm*-nih-bus

Ecclesiastical Pronunciation

fih-dehm *meh*-uhm *oh*-blih-go
vehks-*ihl*-lo chee-vih-*tah*-tsee-um uh-*meh*-rih-chay
fay-deh-rah-*tah*-rum eht *reh*-ee *poo*-blih-chay
pro kwah stuht
oo-nee nah-tsee-*o*-nee *day*-oh doo-*chehn*-teh
non dee-vih-*dehn*-day
koom lee-behr-*tah*-teh
yoos-tsee-tsee-*ah*-kweh *ohm*-nih-bus

Chapter 2

1. direct object plural

2. subject singular

3. possession plural

4. indirect object singular

5. B. are

6. D. were

7. E. will

8. E. will

9. The farmers will find the rocks.

10. The slaves and the girls were hearing the queen.

11. We are preparing food in the dining room.

Chapter 3

1. London

2. Spain

3. France (or Gaul)

4. Switzerland

5. erant

6. sunt

7. estis

8. eris

Chapter 4

1. B. avia

2. A. avunculus

3. C. mater

4. D. coniunx

Chapter 5

1. Ientaculum: panis, fructus, caseus

2. Prandium: ova, piscis, holera, vinum

3. Cena: ova, piscis, mulsum, pullus, vinum, fructus, mala

Chapter 6

1. a.d. VI Id. Iun. 2744 A.U.C.
2. a.d. XVI Kal. Feb. 2631 A.U.C.
3. a.d. VI Non. Dec. 681 A.U.C.
4. C. Venus
5. D. Fornax
6. A. Mercury
7. B. Robigus

Chapter 7

1. A. eques
2. C. sagittarius
3. B. aquilifer
4. D. speculator

Chapter 8

1. B. in amphitheatro
2. C. in circo
3. A. ad thermas
4. E. altior
5. F. maximus
6. D. facilior
7. A. maior
8. C. altissimus
9. B. facillimus

Chapter 9

1. D. tribunus
2. B. Numa Pompilius
3. B. aedilis
4. Roma a Romulo regitur.
5. Exercitus a rege ducebatur.
6. Urbs a principe gubernata erat.

Chapter 10

1. Vergil
2. Lucretius
3. Caesar
4. Apuleius
5. Ovid

Chapter 11

1. E. postponed indefinitely
2. G. an accusation
3. A. somewhere else
4. I. let the buyer beware
5. K. tit for tat
6. B. by virtue of one's position
7. M. in private, without spectators
8. D. among others
9. F. at first sight
10. L. a law
11. C. material evidence in a crime
12. H. the existing state or condition

Chapter 12

A1. Make a solution with 250 ml water and half a teaspoon of powder. Apply the solution to the left ear three times a day.

A2. Take one capsule with water by mouth three times a day before meals.

B1. caput (head)

B2. venter (stomach)

B3. crus (leg)

B4. bracchium (arm)

B5. manus (hand)

B6. digitus (finger)

B7. oculus (eye)

B8. pes (foot)

B9. auris (ear)

B10. capillus (hair)

Chapter 13

1. G. Non habebis deos alienos coram me.

2. C. Non assumes nomen Domini Dei tui in vanum.

3. E. Memento, ut diem Sabbati sanctifices.

4. B. Honora patrem tuum et matrem tuam, ut sis longaevus super terram.

5. A. Non occides.

6. I. Non moechaberis.

7. J. Non furtum facies.

8. D. Non loqueris contra proximum tuum falsum testimonium.

9. H. Non concupisces uxorem proximi tui.

10. F. Non concupisces omnia, quae proximi sunt.

Chapter 14

1. C. from Japan
2. H. from Canada
3. D. of the woods or forests
4. A. North or South America
5. J. of the mountains
6. I. from Africa
7. G. from the West
8. F. from Europe
9. B. from the East (usually Asia)
10. E. of the sea

Chapter 15

1. A. The slave-girls are carrying the water jars into the city.
2. B. The citizens walked into the forum and listened to the speakers.
3. D. Let's go to the circus and look at the horses.
4. B. The boys, who are playing in the road, are my uncle's sons.
5. D. Soldiers, fight bravely and conquer the enemy!
6. B. Why are you crying? Who hit you?
7. C. The women were watching the gladiators and the animals in the circus.
8. A. The sailors, who will sail to Greece, are preparing the ships in the harbor.
9. C. The boys are so tired that they are sitting down under the tree.
10. D. The general ordered the soldiers to fight bravely.

Chapter 16

1. E. God enriches.
2. D. Nothing without the divine will.
3. I. May she live forever.
4. H. I direct.
5. J. By valor and arms.
6. F. Ever upward.
7. A. Work conquers all.
8. C. Thus always to tyrants.
9. G. Mountaineers are always free.
10. B. Let arms yield to the toga.

Index

• F •

• X •

• Y •

Notes

3 1901 05308 9480